Contents

Introduction

Nelson Thornes and AQA

Nelson Thornes has worked in collaboration with AQA to ensure that this book offers you the best support for your AS or A Level course and helps you to prepare for your exams. The partnership means that you can be confident that the range of learning, teaching and assessment practice materials has been checked by the senior examining team at AQA before formal approval, and is closely matched to the requirements of your specification.

How to use this book

This book covers the specification for your course and is arranged in a sequence approved by AQA.

The features in this book include:

Timeline

Key events are outlined at the beginning of the book. The events are colour-coded so you can clearly see the categories of change.

Learning objectives

At the beginning of each section you will find a list of learning objectives that contain targets linked to the requirements of the specification.

Key chronology

A short list of dates usually with a focus on a specific event or legislation.

Key profile

The profile of a key person you should be aware of to fully understand the period in question.

Key terms

A term that you will need to be able to define and understand.

Did you know?

Interesting information to bring the subject under discussion to life.

Exploring the detail

Information to put further context around the subject under discussion.

A closer look

An in-depth look at a theme, person or event to deepen your understanding. Activities around the extra information may be included.

Sources

Sources to reinforce topics or themes and may provide fact or opinion. They may be quotations from historical works, contemporaries of the period or photographs.

Cross-reference

Links to related content within the book which may offer more detail on the subject in question.

Activity

Various activity types to provide you with different challenges and opportunities to demonstrate both the content and skills you are learning. Some can be worked on individually, some as part of group work and some are designed to specifically 'stretch and challenge'.

AQA History

AS Unit 1

The Reformation in Europe, c1500–1564

Exclusively endorsed by AQA

THE BELVEDERE ACADEMY
HISTORY DEPARTMENT

Philip Stanton
Series editor
Sally Waller

Nelson Thornes

Text © Philip Stanton 2009
Original illustrations © Nelson Thornes Ltd 2009

The right of Philip Stanton to be identified as author of this work has been asserted by him in accordance with the Copyright, Designs and Patents Act 1988.

All rights reserved. No part of this publication may be reproduced or transmitted in any form or by any means, electronic or mechanical, including photocopy, recording or any information storage and retrieval system, without permission in writing from the publisher or under licence from the Copyright Licensing Agency Limited, of Saffron House, 6-10 Kirby Street, London EC1N 8TS.

Any person who commits any unauthorised act in relation to this publication may be liable to criminal prosecution and civil claims for damages.

Published in 2009 by:
Nelson Thornes Ltd
Delta Place
27 Bath Road
CHELTENHAM
GL53 7TH
United Kingdom

11 12 13 / 10 9 8 7 6 5 4 3

A catalogue record for this book is available from the British Library

ISBN 978 0 7487 8266 6

Illustrations by: David Russell Illustration, Thomson Digital

Page make-up by Thomson Digital

Printed in China by 1010 Printing International Ltd

■ **Question**

Questions to prompt further discussion on the topic under consideration and are an aid to revision.

■ **Summary questions**

Summary questions at the end of each chapter to test your knowledge and allow you to demonstrate your understanding.

AQA Examiner's tip

Hints from AQA examiners to help you with your study and to prepare for your exam.

AQA Examination-style questions

Questions at the end of each section in the style that you can expect in your exam.

Learning outcomes

Learning outcomes at the end of each section remind you what you should know having completed the chapters in that section.

■ **Web links in the book**

Because Nelson Thornes is not responsible for third party content online, there may be some changes to this material that are beyond our control. In order for us to ensure that the links referred to in the book are as up-to-date and stable as possible, the web sites provided are usually homepages with supporting instructions on how to reach the relevant pages if necessary.

Please let us know at **webadmin@nelsonthornes. com** if you find a link that doesn't work and we will do our best to correct this at reprint, or to list an alternative site.

Introduction to the History series

When Bruce Bogtrotter in Roald Dahl's *Matilda* was challenged to eat a huge chocolate cake, he just opened his mouth and ploughed in, taking bite after bite and lump after lump until the cake was gone and he was feeling decidedly sick. The picture is not dissimilar to that of some A Level history students. They are attracted to history because of its inherent appeal but, when faced with a bulging file and a forthcoming examination, their enjoyment evaporates. They try desperately to cram their brains with an assortment of random facts and subsequently prove unable to control the outpouring of their ill-digested material in the examination.

The books in this series are designed to help students and teachers avoid this feeling of overload and examination panic by breaking down the AQA history specification in such a way that it is easily absorbed. Above all, they are designed to retain and promote students' enthusiasm for history by avoiding a dreary rehash of dates and events. Each book is divided into sections, closely matched to those given in the specification, and the content is further broken down into chapters that present the historical material in a lively and attractive form, offering guidance on the key terms, events and issues, and blending thought-provoking activities and questions in a way designed to advance students' understanding. By encouraging students to think for themselves and to share their ideas with others, as well as helping them to develop the knowledge and skills they will need to pass their examination, this book should ensure that students' learning remains a pleasure rather than an endurance test.

To make the most of what this book provides, students will need to develop efficient study skills from the start and it is worth spending some time considering what these involve:

- Good organisation of material in a subject-specific file. Organised notes help develop an organised brain and sensible filing ensures time is not wasted hunting for misplaced material. This book uses cross-references to indicate where material in one chapter has relevance to material in another. Students are advised to adopt the same technique.

- A sensible approach to note-making. Students are often too ready to copy large chunks of material from printed books or to download sheaves of printouts from the internet. This series is designed to encourage students to think about the notes they collect and to undertake research with a particular purpose in mind. The activities encourage students to pick out information that is relevant to the issue being addressed and to avoid making notes on material that is not properly understood.

- Taking time to think, which is by far the most important component of study. By encouraging students to think before they write or speak, be it for a written answer, presentation or class debate, students should learn to form opinions and make judgements based on the accumulation of evidence. These are the skills that the examiner will be looking for in the final examination. The beauty of history is that there is rarely a right or wrong answer so, with sufficient evidence, one student's view will count for as much as the next.

Unit 1

The topics offered for study in Unit 1 are all based on 'change and consolidation'. They invite consideration of what changed and why, as well as posing the question of what remained the same. Through a study of a period of about 50 to 60 years, students are encouraged to analyse the interplay of long-term and short-term reasons for change and to consider not only how governments have responded to the need for change but also to evaluate the ensuing consequences. Such historical analyses are, of course, relevant to an understanding of the present and, through such historical study, students will be guided towards a greater appreciation of the world around them today, as well as developing their understanding of the past.

Unit 1 is tested by a 1 hour 15 minute paper containing three questions, from which students need to select two. Details relating to the style of questions, with additional hints, are given in Table 1 and links to the examination requirements are provided throughout this book. Students should familiarise themselves with these and the marking criteria given below before attempting any of the practice examination questions at the end of each section.

Answers will be marked according to a scheme based on 'levels of response'. This means that the answer will be assessed according to which level best matches the historical skills displayed, taking both knowledge and understanding into account. All students should have a copy of these criteria and need to use them wisely.

Marking criteria

Question 1(a), 2(a) and 3(a)

Level 1 Answers will contain either some descriptive material that is only loosely linked to the focus of

Table 1 *Unit 1: style of questions and marks available*

Unit 1	Question	Marks	Question type	Question stem	Hints for students
Question 1, 2 and 3	(a)	12	This question is focused on a narrow issue within the period studied and requires an explanation	Why did... Explain why...	Make sure you explain 'why', not 'how', and try to order your answer in a way that shows you understand the inter-linkage of factors and which were the more important. You should try to reach an overall judgement/conclusion
Question 1, 2 and 3	(b)	24	This question links the narrow issue to a wider context and requires an awareness that issues and events can have different interpretations	How far... How important was... How successful...	This answer needs to be planned as you will need to develop an argument in your answer and show balanced judgement. Try to set out your argument in the introduction and, as you develop your ideas through your paragraphs, support your opinions with detailed evidence. Your conclusion should flow naturally and provide supported judgement

the question or some explicit comment with little, if any, appropriate support. Answers are likely to be generalised and assertive. The response will be limited in development and skills of written communication will be weak. *(0–2 marks)*

Level 2 Answers will demonstrate some knowledge and understanding of the demands of the question. They will **either** be almost entirely descriptive with few explicit links to the question **or** they will provide some explanations backed by evidence that is limited in range and/or depth. Answers will be coherent but weakly expressed and/or poorly structured. *(3–6 marks)*

Level 3 Answers will demonstrate good understanding of the demands of the question providing relevant explanations backed by appropriately selected information, although this may not be full or comprehensive. Answers will, for the most part, be clearly expressed and show some organisation in the presentation of material. *(7–9 marks)*

Level 4 Answers will be well focused, identifying a range of specific explanations backed by precise evidence and demonstrating good understanding of the connections and links between events/issues. Answers will, for the most part, be well written and organised. *(10–12 marks)*

Question 1(b), 2(b) and 3(b)

Level 1 Answers may **either** contain some descriptive material which is only loosely linked to the focus of the question **or** they may address only a part of the question. Alternatively, there may be some explicit comment with little, if any, appropriate support. Answers are likely to be generalised and assertive. There will be little, if any, awareness of differing

historical interpretations. The response will be limited in development and skills of written communication will be weak. *(0–6 marks)*

Level 2 Answers will show some understanding of the focus of the question. They will **either** be almost entirely descriptive with few explicit links to the question **or** they may contain some explicit comment with relevant but limited support. They will display limited understanding of differing historical interpretations. Answers will be coherent but weakly expressed and/or poorly structured. *(7–11 marks)*

Level 3 Answers will show a developed understanding of the demands of the question. They will provide some assessment, backed by relevant and appropriately selected evidence, but they will lack depth and/or balance. There will be some understanding of varying historical interpretations. Answers will, for the most part, be clearly expressed and show some organisation in the presentation of material. *(12–16 marks)*

Level 4 Answers will show explicit understanding of the demands of the question. They will develop a balanced argument backed by a good range of appropriately selected evidence and a good understanding of historical interpretations. Answers will, for the most part, show organisation and good skills of written communication. *(17–21 marks)*

Level 5 Answers will be well focused and closely argued. The arguments will be supported by precisely selected evidence leading to a relevant conclusion/judgement, incorporating well-developed understanding of historical interpretations and debate. Answers will, for the most part, be carefully organised and fluently written, using appropriate vocabulary. *(22–24 marks)*

Introduction to this book

Key terms

Liturgy: forms of services of a church, set down in print; especially how the Communion service is to be carried out.

Canon law: a set of laws laid down by the Church, which covered a wide range of problems involving laypeople (non-churchmen) such as marriage, wills and family relationships as well as purely religious issues.

Pope: the head of the Catholic Church.

Spanish Empire: Spanish soldiers conquered Mexico and Central America in the early 16th century.

Fig. 1 *Francis I, King of France, in 1525, by his chief painter, Clouet*

Central to an understanding of the Reformation in Europe in the 16th century is an appreciation that religion was at the very heart of the reasons why people of that era – from the greatest monarchs, reformers and scholars to townspeople in centres of commerce and peasants in remote villages – acted as they did. Doctrinal beliefs and forms of **liturgy**, which might seem utterly unimportant to us in the 21st century, were issues for which many were prepared to endure horrible torture or death. To treat 16th-century religious disputes lightly or with cynicism is to fail to understand the spirit of the age.

Power and the monarchs

A number of important changes were taking place during the late 15th century. The growth of powerful and united states was significant, and monarchies such as Spain and France were taking on the form by which they are recognised today. Such monarchies extended their power over a clear geographical area and built up their power by reducing that of the nobility, controlling local councils and strengthening their finances and administration. Another obvious target for this centralising process was the Church, which was wealthy and privileged, used its own system of **canon law** and had its own structure headed by the **pope**.

In Spain, Ferdinand and Isabella (1479–1516) were determined to reduce papal influence over appointments to important posts within the Church and channel more of the Church's wealth into the royal coffers. By 1516 they had gained extensive rights to appoint bishops in Spain and in the **Spanish Empire** as well as the right to tax the Church. At the same time, they did not wait for popes to start the reform of the Church but, under the leadership of Cardinal Cisneros, Archbishop of Toledo (1436–1517) initiated reforms which tried to raise standards in monasteries and improve the education of their clergy. France was the most powerful state in Europe because of its population and resources. Its kings, notably Louis XI (1461–83) and Francis I (1515–47), strove to increase royal authority. They also targeted the papacy and the wealthy Church and in 1516 similarly gained the right to appoint bishops. In effect, the Church in France became a national Church, guarding its own rights and freedoms. As in Spain, the state encouraged reforms of the Church, especially of monastic life. However, although Spain and France were consolidating their states, Italy and the Holy Roman Empire – which comprised a number of states in the area we now know as Germany – were in a process of fragmentation.

Decline in papal authority

The growth of powerful states was mirrored by a decline in the prestige of the popes. The leadership of the Church was in crisis. In 1309, because of the insecurity of the city, Pope Clement V left Rome to live in Avignon

Key terms

Babylonish captivity: a reference back to a period in Jewish history (586–538 BC) when Jews were deported from Israel to Babylon, the capital of the ancient world. The popes, however, were not really captives and they built a magnificent palace in Avignon to house their court.

General council: a solemn assembly of bishops who decided on matters of correct Church teaching or discipline. No general council can meet without the pope's consent.

Conciliar theory: the teaching that the supreme authority in the Church was not the pope but a general council. This was popular in the period 1417–60.

in southern France and his successors remained there until 1377. This **Babylonish captivity** also placed the papacy under French influence and thus the enemies of France took their chance to strengthen their own authority. In 1377 Gregory XI returned to Rome, but the election of an unpopular Italian pope (Urban VI), who was rejected by the French cardinals, resulted in the election of a rival pope, Clement VII. For 38 years there were two squabbling popes, each claiming full powers. This was a scandal to all Christian Europe.

Fig. 2 *The palace of the popes at Avignon. A contemporary called it 'a sewer where all the filth of the universe is gathered'*

This Great Schism was a low point in papal history. As both popes claimed to have no superior, it was hard to remove either one of them. Eventually a group of cardinals called a **general council** on their own authority and, after complex negotiations, the Great Schism ended when a unity candidate, Martin V, was elected in 1417. Councils continued to meet until 1449, trying to work with the popes to carry out reforms. However, the popes were terrified that they would remain subject to a council and in 1460 Pope Pius II condemned any appeal to a council that bypassed the pope and rejected the so-called **conciliar theory**.

Economic, social and cultural change

Social and economic developments are a vital context for religious change. The great scourge of the Black Death (1347–9) had reduced the population of Europe by about one-third, but by about 1450 population recovery was well under way. Between 1450 and 1650, the population doubled to about 100 million. The population rise caused an increase in demand for food and goods and this stimulated agriculture and commerce. Europe was still mainly a rural community, but a new feature was the growth of cities. In 1500 there were five cities with populations of more than 100,000 (including Milan, Naples and Paris). By 1600 eight others reached that total. Urban life intensified disorder and social problems such as prostitution, ignorance, the spread of disease and poverty. It was against this background that the religious upheavals of the 16th century took place.

There were also social changes taking place. In Germany, which had more towns and cities than anywhere else in Europe, increasing wealth meant more leisure and the desire for more education from the commercial middle-classes, encouraging them to question religious teaching. Furthermore, within Germany, there was growing discontent caused by landlords trying to raise rents and control their labour force of peasants. Such problems provided the context for divergent protest movements of the late 15th century, which involved large numbers of rural peasants and the rootless poor of the towns. Such protests were strongly anti-clerical and whipped up religious fervour, often as an escape from economic and social problems such as the famine of 1500 and the plague epidemics of 1499–1502 within the German states. Many groups adopted the emblem of the shoe, coming together as the **Bundschuh**.

Cultural changes provided a further context to religious unrest. The Renaissance was a movement involving the arts, literature, politics and history which began in the Italian city of Florence in the early 14th century. At the end of the 15th century, the Renaissance spread to northern Europe. Although there are many arguments about precise definitions, the Renaissance in Italy rediscovered the art and literature of the classical past and began to imitate such works. This affected the visual and written arts of the time and the main feature of the Renaissance was:

> the coming together of a number of greatly talented men at the same time and in the same place so that they were able to inspire each other in their quest to understand the nature of mankind and of human society and to express that understanding in books of prose and poetry, in paintings, sculpture and architecture.

*R. Hole, **Renaissance Italy**, 1998*

Artists needed people to employ them, and some of the popes of the Renaissance provided a fine example of the enjoyment of paintings, sculpture and a love of lavish displays of power and authority. However, although the Renaissance encouraged a love of show, it also encouraged a questioning spirit that led scholars to seek the truth about previously accepted beliefs. Certainly, Renaissance thinking was a powerful impetus behind religious change in the 16th century.

Key terms

Bundschuh: peasant groups mostly in south and west Germany who wanted to overthrow the existing social order. Widespread rioting and pillage took place. Their emblem was the peasants' laced boot or shoe (*Schuh*).

Key

Boundary of the Holy Roman Empire	1 Netherlands 2 Swiss Conferderation 3 Habsburg lands	4 Bohemia 5 Saxony 6 Brandenburg

Fig. 3 *Europe in 1490*

■ War and diplomacy

A backdrop to the European Reformation was war and the dangers of war. The second half of the 15th century had been one of relative peace. The long war between France and England, which had lasted from 1337 to 1453, was over. The major states of Italy had worked out a peaceful co-existence. However, Italy was a tempting prize for foreign aggression because it was wealthy, militarily weak and politically divided. The French king, Charles VIII, had a family claim to Naples, and in 1494 he invaded Italy to make good his claim. Charles easily conquered Naples, but other Italian princes, including the pope, combined to drive him out in 1495. The next king, Louis XII, pushed forward his own claim to Milan in 1499 and French aggression provoked the hostility of foreign powers such as Spain and the Holy Roman Empire. Italy was fought over by foreigners hungry for military glory, while the Italian states used diplomacy to guess which would be the winning side and be on it. The Italian wars merged into a wider conflict when Charles V of the House of Habsburg became both Holy Roman Emperor and King of Spain in 1519. His struggle with the King of France, Francis I of the House of Valois, became a titanic struggle for supremacy in Europe. The Habsburg–Valois conflict only ended in 1559. A result was that Italy lost its independence. At the other end of Europe, the Ottoman Turks of Islam maintained what the rulers and Christians of Europe saw as their frightening advance by land through the Balkans and by sea in the Mediterranean.

■ Defining 'the Reformation'

The Reformation is very much a leading theme of the 16th century. However, it is a troublesome word. An easy definition would be the process by which parts of Germany, Switzerland, and all Scandinavia and minorities in areas such as France and the Netherlands, broke away from the Catholic Church to accept the teachings of the major reformers such as Luther, Calvin and Zwingli. Independent churches were set up with their own organisations and doctrines. However, this is to refer only to the Protestant Reformation. When people at the time used the Latin word *Reformatio,* they thought only of reform within the Catholic Church, which they had always known and which was centred on Rome. They did not think of 'the Church' breaking up into separate Catholic and Protestant churches. The modern use of the term, which means just this, was only invented 200 years later. Furthermore, the word 'Reformation' was used by Protestants to suggest a change for the better – implying that the Catholic Church was beyond hope and that the reformers'changes were wholly beneficial. In studying this period of history, you should bear this in mind. On its own, the word 'Reformation' has a strong bias in favour of Martin Luther and the other Protestant reformers, and it stands apart from the term 'Catholic Reformation'. In this book you will read not only of the reforming figures such as Luther and Calvin, but also of great reformers that emerged before their 'protests' but without having the same impact. The real issue for consideration is why the 16th-century Protestant Reformation succeeded whereas previous attempts at reform, such as that of Jan Hus in the 14th century, had failed. The answer to this question is obviously linked to the political, social and economic context as well as to the people who produced the new ideas.

■ Major European rulers, *c*.1500–64

Popes

Common name	Personal name	Pontificate
Alexander VI	Rodrigo de Lanzòl-Borgia	1492–1503
Pius III	Francesco Todeschini Piccolomini	Sept–Oct 1503
Julius II	Giuliano della Rovere	1503–13
Leo X	Giovanni di Lorenzo de' Medici	1513–21
Adrian VI	Adriaan Floriszoon Boeyens	1522–3
Clement VII	Giulio di Giuliano de' Medici	1523–34
Paul III	Alessandro Farnese	1534–49
Julius III	Giovanni Maria Ciocchi del Monte	1550–5
Marcellus II	Marcello Cervini	April 1555
Paul IV	Giovanni Pietro Carafa	1555–9
Pius IV	Giovanni Angelo Medici	1559–65

Holy Roman Emperors

Name	Reign
Maximilian I	1493–1519
Charles V	1519–56
Ferdinand I	1556–64

Rulers of Spain

Name	Reign
Isabella	1474–1504 and Ferdinand 1479–1516
Charles I	1516–56 (= Holy Roman Emperor Charles V 1519–56)
Philip II	1556–98

Rulers of France

Name	Reign
Charles VIII	1483–98
Louis XII	1498–1515
Francis I	1515–47
Henry II	1547–59
Francis II	1559–60
Charles IX	1560–74

Rulers of England

Name	Reign
Henry VII	1485–1509
Henry VIII	1509–47
Edward VI	1547–53
Mary I	1553–8
Elizabeth I	1558–1603

Timeline

	1500–10	1511–20	1521–30
Germany and the Lutheran Reformation	**1505**: Luther enters monastery at Erfurt **1510**: Luther visits Rome	**1514**: Tetzel begins sale of indulgences **1517**: The 95 Theses **1518**: Meeting at Augsburg **1519**: Leipzig Debate **1520**: Luther excommunicated; the **1520** Writings	**1521**: Diet of Worms **1522**: Luther's New Testament; Melancthon compiles *Loci Communes* **1522–3**: The Knights' War **1524–5**: The Peasants' War **1525**: The Battle of Frankenhausen **1526**: Luther's German Mass: Hesse and Electoral Saxony now Lutheran **1529**: Marburg Colloquy **1530**: Confession of Augsburg; Scandinavian Reformation begins
The Catholic Church and Catholic reform	**1503**: Erasmus's *Handbook of a Christian Soldier* **1506**: New St Peter's Basilica started **1508**: Sistine Chapel started **1509**: Erasmus's *Praise of Folly* written	**1512**: Fifth Lateran Council begins; Sistine Chapel completed **1516**: Concordat of Bologna; Erasmus's New Testament first edition **1517**: Lateran Council closes; Oratory of Divine Love founded in Rome	**1522**: Ignatius of Loyola begins the Spiritual Exercises **1524**: Theatines founded **1527**: The Sack of Rome **1528**: Capuchins founded
The Swiss Reformers and Calvinism	**1505**: Birth of John Knox **1506**: Birth of Francis Xavier **1509**: Birth of John Calvin	**1511**: Birth of Servetus **1518**: Zwingli appointed a priest at the Great Minster in Zürich	**1523**: Zwingli's reformation in Zürich **1525**: Mass abolished in Zürich – persecution of the Swiss Brethren **1528**: Reformation in Berne and Basel
The Radical Reformation			**1522**: Luther denounces Carlstadt and the Zwickau prophets **1524–5**: Münzer linked to Peasants' Revolt **1527**: Schleitheim Confession **1528**: Persecutions in Moravia
Key political events	**1500**: Brazil discovered; birth of Charles V	**1519**: Cortés in Mexico; Charles V becomes Emperor	**1521**: Turks capture Belgrade **1526**: Battle of Mohacs; Diet of Speyer **1530**: Diet of Augsburg

1531–40	1541–50	1551–60	1561–70
1531: Schmalkaldic League formed **1534**: Old Testament in German; Württemberg, Ducal Saxony, Brandenburg and Pomerania become Lutheran	**1541**: Colloquy of Regensburg; bigamy of Philip of Hesse **1546**: Death of Luther **1547**: Battle of Mühlberg **1548**: Augsburg Interim	**1555**: Peace of Augsburg **1560**: Death of Melancthon	
1532: Somaschi founded **1533**: Barbabites founded **1534**: Paul III becomes pope; Ignatius founds Company of Jesus **1535**: Ursulines founded **1536**: Death of Erasmus **1537**: Consilium published **1540**: Jesuit Order founded	**1542**: Roman Inquisition founded **1545–7**: Council of Trent (First Session) **1549**: Death of Paul III; Jesuits in Brazil; Xavier in Japan; mission of Canisius to Germany	**1551–2**: Council of Trent (Second Session) **1556**: Death of Ignatius **1559**: Roman *Index of Prohibited Books*	**1562–3**: Council of Trent (Third Session) **1565**: Borromeo becomes Archbishop of Milan **1566**: Roman Catechism **1568**: Roman Breviary **1570**: Roman Missal
1531: Zwingli killed at the Battle of Kappel **1536**: First Edition of the *Institutes of the Christian Religion* **1536–8**: Calvin's first ministry in Geneva	**1541**: Calvin returns to Geneva; the Ecclesiastical Ordinances	**1555**: Defeat of the Libertines; Servetus burned at the stake; growth of Calvinism in France **1559**: Genevan Academy	**1560–2**: John Knox establishes Calvinism in Scotland **1560–3**: Palatinate becomes Calvinist **1561**: Colloquy of Poissy **1564**: Death of Calvin **1566**: Calvinist riots in the Netherlands
1533: Hoffman imprisoned in Strasbourg **1534–5**: The 'Kingdom of Münster' **1535**: The 'Amsterdam Rebellion' **1536**: Menno Simons founds north German Anabaptism	**1541–50**: Anabaptist persecutions		
1532: Pizarro conquers Peru **1534**: Day of the Placards in France	**1544**: Peace of Crépy	**1552**: Defeat of Charles V at Metz **1559**: Peace of Cateau-Cambrésis	**1562**: Religious war breaks out in France **1566**: Death of Sulieman 'the Magnificient'

Factors leading to the Reformation and the Catholic Reformation

1 Humanism and the Catholic Church c. 1500

In this chapter you will learn about:

- the main features of humanism

- the meaning of Christian humanism and the importance of the leading Christian humanist, Erasmus

- the links between the Christian humanists and the Reformation

- the 'debate' over the condition of the Catholic Church

- the problems of the Renaissance popes

- problems with the standards of the clergy.

It is indeed a golden age which has restored to light the arts that had almost been destroyed: poetry, writing, sculpture and music.

1

By Marsillio Ficino, 1492

Source 1 was written by Marsillio Ficino in 1492 and, for Renaissance scholars like him, this was a good time to be alive. Ficino was a humanist

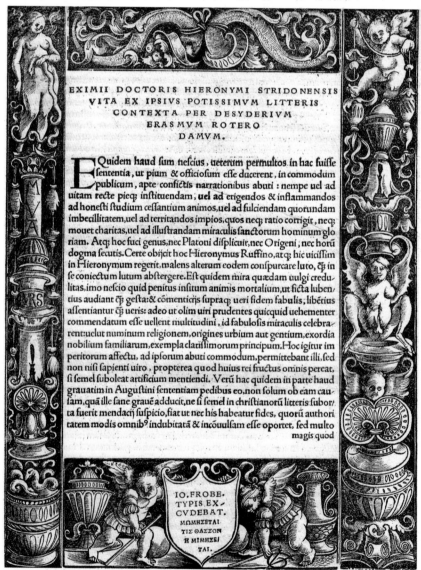

Fig. 1 *A page from the first edition of Erasmus's Greek and Latin New Testament, printed in 1516 by Froben*

and, like others described in this way, he had a huge, almost obsessive, interest in the classical world. Humanists believed the culture of Greece and Rome was a model for how people should live in society and their excitement in rediscovering and learning from the classical past permeated the scholarship of the late 15th and early 16th centuries.

Humanism had begun in Italy and then spread to northern Europe as scholars encouraged the flow of ideas across Europe by letter writing and personal contacts. The humanists tried to compare their present age with the classical past. It followed that it was essential to discover as much about the classical world as possible through finding long-lost works and bringing resources together by hunting down book collections and sales. Pope Nicholas V collected 5,000 manuscripts to begin the Vatican Library, while the **Medici** rulers of Florence and the rulers of Urbino – an independent city in north Italy whose rulers were famed for encouraging the arts – began libraries and obliged private collectors to donate to them. Manuscripts were carefully transcribed and there was frantic excitement when a new manuscript was discovered. The famous manuscript hunter Bracciolini (1380–1459), an official at the papal court, discovered the works of a lost Latin writer in a Swiss monastery 'amid a tremendous quantity of books … filthy with mould and dust in a sort of foul and gloomy dungeon at the bottom of one of the towers'.

Knowledge of classical languages was the key to unlocking the classical world, and although classical Latin and its literature had never died out, the Latin that was the working language of writing and government in the medieval period had declined far from the pure Latin style of the classical past. It was regarded as 'barbaric' by humanists, who aimed to write in a pure, refined correct Latin style. However, Greek, of which there was limited knowledge in the West, became the all-consuming 'had to have' of humanists after scholars invited from the Byzantine Empire lectured on the language in Italian cities. Many texts were discovered and translated. Greek grammars were printed in Milan in 1476 and Venice in 1484. Publication was at its peak between 1494 and 1515. The works of Greek writers, especially those on politics and philosophy, opened new horizons beyond the teaching offered by traditional universities.

Knowledge of the language led to the humanist slogan *'ad fontes!'* ('back to the sources!'). With so many new documents now available, scholars had to verify their accuracy and authority. To do this, the humanists applied a formula well known to all subsequent students of history:

> One factor must be to assess the text in every respect – its content, date, origins and why it was written, even its appearance. This meant developing ways of telling a good text from a bad text: looking at the way it was written and whether it sounded like reliable texts from the same period.

2

*D. MacCulloch, **Reformation: Europe's House Divided 1490–1700**, 2004*

This new approach was not a simple academic exercise; it had important practical results. The great humanist scholar Lorenzo Valla proved that a famous document called the 'Donation of Constantine', supposedly written in the 4th century, which claimed that the popes had been given authority over Italy by the Emperor Constantine, was in fact a fake written in the 8th century. He showed that words used in the text did not even exist when it was allegedly written.

Key terms

Medici: the Medicis were the wealthy merchant family who ruled Florence from about 1440.

Did you know?

Humanists was a word first used near the end of the 15th century to describe teachers who taught 'the good arts' or the 'human arts' (commonly referred to as 'the humanities'), as opposed to the study of religion. These terms still survive today. Those studying non-scientific subjects such as literature and history are sometimes referred to as students of 'arts subjects'.

■ Key profile

Lorenzo Valla

Lorenzo Valla (1407–57) was a humanist who both loved the Latin language and was skilled in the science of language – he could date a document from its style. His book *Notes on the New Testament* (1440) examined the dates of the Latin texts. It inspired humanists to further study. Erasmus published a version of *Notes on the New Testament*.

The most important text of all was the Bible. At the end of the 15th century, humanists applied their new approach of getting back to the sources. The results were highly significant for the Catholic Church, which was the universal Church supported by all the Christian nations of western Europe at this time.

One school of thought in the teaching of the Church was that people depended on 'the grace of God' to achieve their potential and they had limited **free will** to choose the right path. Many humanists took a different and much more positive view of human potential. Taking a lead from the classical past – before centuries of Christian teaching – humanists stressed that mankind did indeed possess free will, which could be used either for good or for bad purposes. The humanist approach to life was quite different from the Christian ideal, which was to withdraw from the world to pursue a life of prayer and contemplation in a **religious community**. Humanists believed it was an individual's choice to use his or her God-given talents to achieve their full potential in the world. They prized involvement in the political and social life of a community. The humanist approach was therefore a 'mankind-centred' rather than God-centred one. Humanist writers also set out standards of conduct that did not rely on any Christian teaching. However, not all agreed with this thinking and the problem of free will became a central debate during the Reformation.

■ Christian humanism and Erasmus

Humanism took a variety of forms, but Christian humanism was the most influential. Although most humanists accepted the essentials of the Catholic faith, they hoped to restore a simpler, purer and stronger Church that was closer to the New Testament. Consequently, Christian humanism:

- ■ was an attempt to reform the Church by calling for a return to the simplicity of the first Christians. It contrasted that time with the present Church's wealth, luxury and greed for money, which stood in the way of a personal knowledge of Christ. There was little new in this. Groups such as the Devotio Moderna, which had begun in the 14th century, had possessed similar ideas.

- ■ stressed that the Word of God, as shown in the Bible, was the only guide on to how to behave as a Christian.

- ■ looked critically at the text of the Bible to discover an accurate meaning. This meant a return to the sources.

- ■ believed that education was the way to cause change. Schools that taught humanist principles became popular for the children of leaders in society.

- ■ poured scorn on those who uncritically accepted popular superstitions such as miracle-working images and relics of the saints that were not genuine such as feathers from the wings of the Archangel Gabriel or straw from the manger of the baby Jesus.

■ Key terms

Free will: the choice to decide one's own destiny. The humanists' view contrasted with the argument that man was so inherently sinful that he could not choose the right path. If people had no free will and God had mapped a person's destiny, even before his or her birth, it followed that it was impossible for anyone to make choices.

Religious community: this usually meant living enclosed in a monastery or convent under a set of rules created by the founder, for example the rule of St Benedict. Such people were known as regulars (the Latin word for 'rule' is *regula*).

■ Exploring the detail

The Devotio Moderna

The Devotio Moderna was founded by Gerard Groote (d. 1340) as an attempt to create a monastic life without the vows. His Brethren of the Common Life joined together for prayer and concentrated on an inward, simple, personal experience of Christ. The aim of the Brethren was to 'imitate Christ' and their handbook was one of the most popular religious reads of the 15th century. The Brethren did good works and were not an exclusive group, neither did they oppose the Church.

- attacked the value of monastic life, emphasising that this did not give extra holiness and Christians should be in the world, not out of it.
- showed contempt for the prevailing teaching style in the 'schools' of the universities. Academic teachers – the 'schoolmen' – developed arguments based on the concept that the Christian faith (for example, the existence of God) could be explained by the use of reason. Humanists argued that an inner lively personal faith was more important.

Key profile

Desiderius Erasmus

Desiderius Erasmus (1467–1536) was born in Rotterdam. His real name was Gerrit Gerritzoon, but like many humanists he changed it to one that sounded more classical. He was deeply influenced by humanist teachers and the Devotio Moderna. He entered a monastery in 1486, which may have been the basis of his dislike of monks and their life, although in fact he was given great freedom to study. In 1499 he became a student at the University of Paris, but again hated the harsh life of a student. After 1500 his *Adages* gave him European fame. He was able to live the life of an independent scholar. He enjoyed the fanatical devotion of humanist groups while kings, princes and churchmen vied with each other to gain his services. Erasmus lived in England, Germany, France and Italy, which gave him the claim to be a European scholar. Challenged by Martin Luther in the 1520s, he remained a Catholic, although he was sympathetic to some of the Lutheran reformers' aims. He refused to commit to either side and so was attacked by both. His pleas for tolerance were ignored.

Erasmus had a vast knowledge of classical literature and the writings of the early Church. He spread the humanist message through his pure style and biting satire on the Church's failings. To his enemies, he was full of vanity and self-satisfaction, enjoying the good things of life, using outrageous flattery of the rich and powerful to beg favours. He had a horror of the physical, whether it was a hard bed, a draughty room, a poor meal or the filth that was common on the floors of most houses. He had a low view of women and sex.

Activity

Revision exercise

Draw a spider diagram to illustrate the main features of Christian humanism.

Fig. 2 *Erasmus by Hans Holbein, 1523*

The work of Erasmus

Northern Europe produced many great scholars, but towering above them all was Desiderius Erasmus of Rotterdam. Through his learning, writings and opinions, he reflected every aspect of Christian humanism. The major writings of Erasmus show the variety of his learning and interests.

Adages (1500)

This work reflected the aim of Erasmus to make classical learning open to a wider public. Over 800 sayings (adages) in Latin and Greek were explained, with detailed examples taken from his huge knowledge of classical literature to back them up. The book was added to until it contained over 4,000 adages. The reading public could access classical literature without reading whole books and could impress their friends with quotations.

Handbook of a Christian Soldier (1503)

The *Handbook* revealed the main purpose of Erasmus: to restore the Catholic Church to a simple imitation of the life of Christ as shown in

Key chronology

Erasmus's important writings

1500 *Adages*

1503 *Handbook of a Christian Soldier*

1511 *Praise of Folly*

1516 *The New Testament in the original Greek*

1524 *Freedom of the Will*

Did you know?

Some of the *Adages* are still common today – to die laughing; to blow one's own trumpet; to have one foot in the grave; up to the ears in; to be in the same boat; to look a gift horse in the mouth. It was Erasmus who made them popular. There was an increasing demand for entertaining literature. However, the reading public were few in number and lived mostly in towns and cites. In Germany, perhaps 400,000 out of a population of 16 million could read.

Did you know?

The Latin title of the *Praise of Folly* – *Moriae Encomium* – was a play on the name of Thomas More, an English humanist and friend of Erasmus – a typical piece of humanist showing off!

Key terms

Cardinal: the highest rank in the Catholic Church. Cardinals were members of the papal court and together elected the pope.

Activity

Source analysis

Read Sources 4, 5 and 6.

1 What would be the effect of these criticisms on Erasmus's readers?

2 Do you think it would have been possible, as Erasmus suggested, to return to the model of the lives of the Apostles?

the Gospels based on a clear knowledge of the Bible. This was the aim of Christian humanism. The aim of the *Handbook* was to educate: 'to set down a kind of summary of a guide to living, so that, equipped with it, you may gain a mind worthy of Christ'.

J. McConica in his book *Erasmus* (1991) claimed that the *Handbook* had a revolutionary impact because it went against the standards of the Catholic Church of the time. Erasmus had written that a Christian must aim for perfection in Christ. Being a priest or taking vows was not special, and the guidance of a priest was not necessary, as each person who followed the *Handbook* had his or her own guide. This 'philosophy of Christ' – Erasmus's own phrase – could result in a daring attack on the practices of the Church of his time:

> Charity does not consist in many visits to churches, bowing down in front of statues of saints, in the lighting of candles or repeating set prayers. Of these things God has no need. Charity is to love your neighbour.

3 *From Handbook of a Christian Soldier, 1503*

The *Handbook* was widely read and translated into 11 languages, including Russian. It had a huge influence on the reading public.

Praise of Folly (1511)

This book, written in Latin in 1509, is Erasmus's most famous work. It had an instant success as it brought together all the threads of Erasmus's talents and opinions. The narrator is 'Folly'. With a light touch of sarcastic humour, Folly points out the foolishness of youth, old age, men's attitude to women and marriage, then groups such as teachers, courtiers and, above all, the 'schoolmen' in the universities, are given Folly's treatment. However, then the book becomes more serious and dark, ending with a bitter, intense attack on the standards of the members of the Church.

There was Erasmus's usual contempt for monks (Source 4). He was equally disdainful of **cardinals** who were too much involved with making money and concerns of the world (Source 5). He did not spare the popes who claimed to be the representatives of Christ on earth (Source 6).

> The whole tribe is universally loathed … yet they are gloriously self-satisfied. In the first place they believe it's the highest form of piety to be so uneducated that they can't even read. Then they bray like donkeys in Church, repeating by rote the psalms they haven't understood, they imagine they are charming the ears of their heavenly audience with infinite delight. Many of them make too make a good living … bellowing for bread from door to door. This is the way these smooth individuals, in all their filth and ignorance … claim to give us a model of the lives of the Apostles.

4 *From Praise of Folly, 1511*

> They might think about the fact they are the successors of the Apostles and are expected to follow their example … they should have a boundless charity which should be at everyone's service … why do they need wealth at all if they take the place of the Apostles who were poor men.

5 *From Praise of Folly, 1511*

Practically no class of man lives so comfortably with fewer cares; for they believe they do quite enough for Christ if they play their part … by means of every kind of ceremonial and display … for them it is out of fashion to perform miracles, teaching the people is too much like hard work … and praying is a waste of time.

6	*From **Praise of Folly**, 1511*

New Testament in Greek (1516)

The publication of Erasmus's New Testament in Greek in 1516 was an event of European importance. At the time of Erasmus, the Bible used was a Latin version called the Vulgate – a 'common to all' version. However, as a humanist, Erasmus wanted to get behind the Latin to the Greek texts on which it was based. His version of the New Testament was not perfect, but it was the first time the Greek version was available to the public. More important, in a way, was his own translation of the Greek into 'pure' Latin and the explanatory notes that went with it. The notes ignored centuries of comment from the 'schoolmen'. The Latin was well written, accessible, in a pure style and differed from the Vulgate version in many places. For example, in the Vulgate Bible, John the Baptist told his listeners to 'do penance' – which backed up the Church's teaching on the subject. Erasmus's translation was to 'change your mind' – implying not *doing* something but having an inner change of heart. The effect was to weaken the Church because it undermined the authority on which it was based.

Mistakes that had developed over the centuries in the Vulgate Bible led to some slightly comical errors in places. Whereas the original had Moses's face 'shining' when he brought down the Ten Commandments, a mistranslation had him 'wearing horns' and this was duly repeated in paintings and sculpture.

The second edition of the New Testament by Erasmus produced in 1519 contained more open criticism of traditional methods of the 'schoolmen' and sold over 3,000 copies. In the preface, Erasmus expressed the hope that the Scriptures would be translated and available to all – 'even the lowliest woman'. In practice, such total availability was not likely to happen, but the Latin version of the Bible did generate excitement among scholars and the higher clergy and its new revelations based on more accurate translation would impact in time on the acceptance of the teachings of the Church.

Freedom of the Will (1524)

The humanist teaching on free will was that humankind could choose his own destiny and Erasmus wrote this work to counter the alternative view being spread by the Protestant reformer Martin Luther. Luther retaliated and tore apart Erasmus's views in *On the Bondage of the Will* (1525), suggesting that there was no place for a moderate voice like Erasmus's in the divisions that were opening up in the Church.

The links between humanism and the Reformation

Erasmus and other humanists had made educated Europe laugh at the failings of the Church. They wished to restore a simple faith based on the study of the Scriptures. Moreover, the work of humanists such as Valla and Erasmus on the New Testament had directly undermined the authority of the Church by criticising the texts on which it relied. These features of humanism had a great influence on Protestant Church reformers such as Zwingli and made the pope's representative in Germany comment in 1519 that 'Erasmus laid the egg which Luther

Fig. 3 *St Jerome (341–420). He was a brilliant linguist who produced the Latin translation of the Bible, the Vulgate. This imagined portrait is from a painting of 1625*

Cross-reference

The Church's teaching on **doing penance** is outlined on page 24.

Activity

Group activity

Put Erasmus on trial on the charge of fatally undermining the Catholic Church. One group could prepare the prosecution while another takes the role of Erasmus.

Cross-reference

The concept of **free will** is discussed on page 10.

Martin Luther's view of **free will** is discussed on pages 44–5.

Cross-reference

Valla is profiled on page 10.

Zwingli is discussed on page 54 and in more detail on pages 95–6.

Activity

Talking point

Explain why humanist teachings had a limited appeal.

Activity

Preparing a presentation

In groups, research the work of other northern humanists and prepare short presentations for the rest of your class. Particularly important are Johannes Reuchlin (1455–1522), Ulrich von Hutten (1488–1523) and Conrad Celtis (1459–1508).

hatched.' However, although Luther used some of the humanist methods of biblical criticism, he was never a humanist.

On the other hand, Erasmus had a basic obedience to the Catholic Church. He did not attack its key teachings or condemn sincere piety and his criticisms were always carefully phrased. Erasmus commented, 'I am not the stuff of which martyrs are made.' So, although Erasmus had harsh words to say about the failings of the popes, for example, he never claimed that the papacy was not in the Scriptures and should therefore be abolished, as most of the Protestant reformers were to do.

The New Testament of Erasmus was dedicated to Pope Leo X, who wrote to him in reply a flattering letter encouraging him to continue his studies. Other popes such as Julius II also took a great interest in humanist studies and Erasmus was on good terms with bishops and cardinals.

In his book *The European Reformation* (1991), Euan Cameron has pointed out that the humanists did not wish to lead a popular movement. They did not want or like to appeal to the 'great unwashed'. Classical learning and a pure Latin style meant nothing to the peasant or poor of the towns. Consequently, humanism had little impact beyond a tiny, well-educated minority and there is little evidence that humanist learning had spread widely within the Church before the Protestant challenge of the 16th century.

The condition of the Catholic Church in the early 16th century

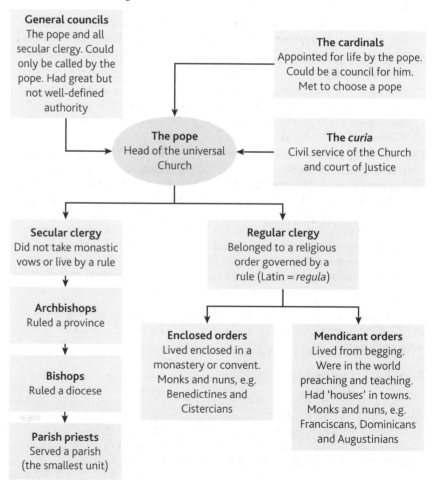

Fig. 4 *The structure of the Catholic Church*

The need for change

In 1500 the Catholic Church was the universal faith of western Europe. Its influence and canon law touched the lives of everyone; its organisation stretched from the poorest parish priest to the head of the Church the pope in Rome. The pope claimed to be the successor of the first Apostle St Peter, and Vicar (representative) of Christ on earth with absolute authority to define faith and morals. The central teachings of the Church were almost unquestioned.

There are differing views on the condition of the Catholic Church in the early 16th century. The traditional view is that corruption and spiritual decay, ignorance and financial greed were so widespread and deep that the Church was failing to carry out its functions effectively. It had failed to reform itself and drastic remedies were needed to root out its failings or 'abuses'.

The abuses theory is now part of popular history. It has the attraction of being easy to understand – something was badly wrong, it had to be fixed and this brought about the movement known as the Reformation in Europe. However, the abuses theory can be challenged:

■ The Church had always been heavily criticised for abuses, from the Apostles onwards. Over the centuries there had been cycles of decline and reform. There had been worse periods of corruption and decay (for example, the scandal of several popes at the same time in the 10th century), but the Church always proved itself able to adapt. Abuses, therefore, do not entirely explain why it was that after 1517 attacks on the Church led to a movement that broke the centuries-old power of the Catholic Church.

■ The reformers of the early 16th century were not only concerned about the abuses of the church. They condemned its fundamental teachings.

■ Although the reformers' complaints about the state of the Catholic Church won widespread support, this does not necessarily mean that they were correct about the abuses they identified. For example, one abuse was said to be the number of priests who were not practising **celibacy**, but there were no accurate statistics in the 16th century to provide evidence for this.

■ There is a more positive view of the Church in 1500. This school of thought maintains that although there were plenty of examples of ignorant priests, idle monks, sexual excesses and grasping methods to extract money – all the abuses that the reformers complained about – they were not all that widespread or particularly worse then than they had been 100 (or even 1,000) years before. The Church, in fact, was capable of reforming itself, and indeed, as Robert Scribner writes in *The German Reformation* (1986): 'There was a strong sense of devotion to the Church's teaching and a powerful revival of pious feeling in the 60 years before the Reformation.'

So, although there may have been a 'need for change', there was no need for it to cause the momentous change to the Catholic Church that actually came about.

Renaissance popes

The Church in early 16th century Europe was under the control of the pope. Popes claimed their authority from the promises Christ made to Peter, as written in Matthew's gospel, and known as the **Petrine promises**. The popes claimed to be the successors of St Peter. A central point of Catholic teaching was (and still is) to accept the authority of the pope.

However, in the 15th and early 16th centuries the leadership of the Church was in crisis. The popes' authority was in decline and there was

Key terms

Celibacy: remaining unmarried, usually as a result of a religious vow and abstaining from sexual relations. From the 11th century, the Church tried to enforce this rule strictly as a sign that priests were separate from laypeople.

Petrine promises: these are based on Matthew 16:18–19 and Christ's words to the Apostle Peter: 'You are Peter, and on this rock I will build my church … I will give you the keys of the kingdom of heaven; whatever you bind on earth will be bound in heaven.'

Cross-reference

The **revival of religious feeling** in the 60 years before the Reformation is discussed on pages 25–6.

Fig. 5 *The pope in council with his cardinals, c.1560*

Cross-reference

For the **Babylonish Captivity**, turn back to page 2.

For the **events of 1305–1460** and the **Conciliar Movement**, refer back to the Introduction to this book, page 2.

Key terms

Annates: payments made to the pope by bishops, rated at one-third of the year's income of a diocese (the area ruled by a bishop).

First Fruits: one-tenth of the year's income of every benefice payable to the pope.

Benefice: the areas from which the income of a church was obtained.

Simony: buying or selling church benefices. Named after Simon Magus, who offered money to become an Apostle. You can read the story in Acts 8:18.

Pluralism: holding more than one benefice.

Cross-reference

Another doubtful way of raising money was the **sale of indulgences**, which is discussed on pages 42–3.

Did you know?

In 1460 the discovery of alum in the lands of the pope gave a big boost to papal finances. Alum was used to fix dyes in cloth. Apart from alum, urine from public lavatories was the main way to fix dyes.

Cross-reference

For the beginning of the **Italian Wars**, see the Introduction to this book, page 4.

More detail on the **political situation in Italy** can be found on pages 20–1.

Alexander VI, Julius II and Leo X are examined in detail on pages 130–3.

growing anti-papal feeling, especially in Germany. This had first arisen as a result of the events of the period 1309–1460, including the Babylonish Captivity (1309–77), the Great Schism (1378–1417) and the rise of the Conciliar Movement that called for more general councils.

However, by the 16th century, other factors had come into play. First, there were the financial difficulties in which the popes found themselves. As well as being head of the Church, the pope was also a businessman in charge of a vast financial empire. There were fees to collect such as **Annates** and **First Fruits**, charges for permission to provide exemption from some rules of the Church, fees for permission to accept a **benefice** – a huge flow of paperwork and cash ebbed back and forth from Rome to the farthest corners of Europe. All this required administrators and was very costly. Partly because various states were beginning to reduce the flow of funds, and partly because of increased costs, the popes were in financial crisis.

More ways had to be found to raise money and these proved unpopular. There were many accusations of **simony** and **pluralism**. There were increases in the fees for taking an office in the Church; for example, the Archbishop of Salzburg was charged 10,000 guilden to be approved as archbishop.

The search for funds seemed to show that the popes were greedy for money rather than caring for the Catholic faithful. It also led them into some dubious ways of raising money.

> The Church charged its members for all its services – for marriages, baptisms, hearing someone confess their sins and burials. The cost of a case in a Church Court was excessive and appeals against its decisions were passed all the way up to Rome, again at great expense.

7

*J. A. P. Jones, **Europe 1500–1600**, 1997*

Second, the pope was also under pressure as a secular ruler – in other words, as a ruler with worldly, rather than religious, power. He was in control of the Papal States in central Italy and this involved the expense of governing and defending these areas. Papal authority was threatened in the 15th century by some of the great families of Rome itself and those living in the Romagna (in theory, subject to the popes), who refused to accept papal authority. Much worse was to follow after 1494 when the Italian Wars began and the pope became even more involved in worldly affairs.

The leadership crisis was not always helped by the Renaissance popes themselves, in particular Alexander VI (1492–1503), Julius II (1503–1513) and Leo X (1513–21). The claim of such popes to spiritual leadership was quite at odds with the reputation

Fig. 6 *Leo X by Raphael, with two cardinals: de Rossi on his right; the future Clement VII (Leo's nephew) on his left*

for scandal which attached itself to the papal court. Visitors to Rome (for example, Erasmus and Luther) were shocked by the luxury and casual attitude towards practising the Catholic faith which they saw. In Germany, there was resentment of Italian popes and a growing sense of nationalism caused ripples of protest against 'foreign' papal interference and church demands for taxation. Although the 'scandalous lives of the pope and his cardinals' were greatly exaggerated, the public lapped up the details. Lurid descriptions and crude cartoons were spread by the new printing presses and these gained even more importance after 1517 once the attack on the Catholic Church had begun.

Nevertheless, the crisis of leadership does not mean that the faith of ordinary people was weakened. Moreover, it should be remembered that some popes were interested in supporting reform of the Church. However, they were hampered by the fact that for the last 200 years the rulers of western Europe had undermined papal authority and the rights of the Church, leaving them with limited power to enforce change.

Ignorance of the clergy

There were many abuses associated with the clergy. These ranged from wanton abandonment of their spiritual duties to ignorance of the Scriptures.

Higher clergy

Bishops and archbishops tended to come from the nobility and many examples could be given of the higher clergy adopting the same lifestyle – acting as local barons, eating to excess, wearing rich garments, having large numbers of servants and building palatial houses; some were patrons of the arts. There was ignorance here of how their image would appear to ordinary Catholics expecting an example. There were problems of **absenteeism** (the Archbishop of Sens only entered his own cathedral once – for his funeral!) and pluralism (Albert, Archbishop of Mainz, bought this office along with permission to hold two other dioceses as well).

On the other hand, it is dangerous to generalise from a few worst cases. The higher clergy were unlikely to be totally 'ignorant'; most had enjoyed a reasonable level of education and we know from records that have survived that many bishops visited their parishes to correct faults and improve discipline. Absenteeism, for example, was often caused when the higher clergy were used as ministers and diplomats by their monarchs. However, in some areas there were too many bishops – in Italy 263, compared to 17 in England – and the supply of high-quality and educated bishops was limited.

Monasteries and convents

Monasteries and convents, which had traditionally been homes of learning, were in spiritual decline. Records show serious problems of lax discipline, ignorance of the daily routine of prayer, the inability to read, breaking the vows of celibacy and not living lives of poverty. Problems were caused partly because there were too many religious houses and too few monks. Many houses were no longer a community and could no longer carry out the rules of monastic life. Admission to a monastery was too easy and required no education. A wealthy convent was often seen as a convenient home for the unmarriageable daughters of the middle and noble classes who could pay for all the comforts of home but who had little interest in, and ignorance of, the meaning of the religious life.

In some areas, nevertheless, there were signs of reform. Groups of monks sometimes created stricter versions of their original rule, such as the Franciscans in Spain and the Augustinians in Germany.

Question

How successful were the popes of the period *c*.1500–22 in fulfilling their responsibilities within the Church? (You may prefer to read Chapter 11 before answering this question.)

Key terms

Absenteeism: not living in your benefice or diocese (the area ruled by a bishop).

Fig. 7 *The Ship of Fools, c.1490. Humanity is a ship travelling through time, with each character a fool in its own way; a monk and a nun are prominent 'fools'*

Lower clergy

The lower clergy are a complex group. The parish priests and clergy were often condemned for their ignorance (again, a popular target for humanists) and visitations in Italy show that there were many problems with priests who could not read the service books or say basic prayers. Ignorance was increasing because the bursaries intended for the poorer trainees for the priesthood were becoming harder to access. Entry standards were so easy that only a basic education was needed. Boys serving on the altar learned the service by heart and were made priests by bishops who knew nothing of their abilities. The lower clergy were often of the same class as their neighbours. They did not wear separate clerical clothes; they joined in all the activities of the parish, gaming and quarrelling with their neighbours. A particular problem was that the priest was entitled to the **tithe** for his upkeep. He was entitled to fees for marriages, baptisms and burials and, in some cases, free labour in his fields. These were good sources of village disputes.

The Church was producing too many priests – men who were qualified but could not get work in a pastoral role. Estimates are that there were three of these to every one employed parish priest. This group was often poor, young, resentful and under-employed with a little education – a dangerous combination that could bring disrepute to the Church.

A major problem resulted from the rule of celibacy. This rule was difficult to enforce but easy to spot when it was broken. The failings of the clergy in this were an ideal target for critics, and lustful priests and deceived husbands were stock characters of verse and plays.

Key terms

Tithe: a kind of tax, the tenth part of the produce of a person's land or livestock to be given to the priest or church for upkeep. Tithes were often replaced by a monetary payment.

Activity

Revision exercise

Use the material in this chapter and undertake some additional research in order to draw up a table giving examples of each of the following abuses in the early 16th century: simony, nepotism, pluralism and absenteeism.

Summary question

How far is it true to say that the Catholic Church was full of abuses at the beginning of the 16th century?

2 Political and religious life in Europe c.1500

In this chapter you will learn about:

- the political situation in Europe at the start of the 16th century

- the fragmentation of power and authority in political Europe

- the main beliefs of Catholics

- the extent of popular religion and the different ways in which this devotion showed itself

- the importance of heresy in undermining the Church.

Cross-reference

For more detail on the **countries of Europe** before the 16th century, see the Introduction to this book.

Exploring the detail

The Holy Roman Empire

The vast majority of the population of the Holy Roman Empire (20 million people) spoke German. By the 5th century the Roman Empire had been divided into two, with one emperor in Rome and another in Constantinople. In 476 the last Roman emperor of the West was removed and Italy was controlled by barbarian tribes. The popes needed protection from the warlike kingdoms that dominated north Italy and eventually came to rely on Charlemagne, the king of the Franks. When Charlemagne was on a visit to Rome, the pope crowned him emperor on Christmas Day 800. The Holy Roman Empire had begun.

Fig. 1 *Ottoman Janissaries and the defending Knights of St John at the Siege of Rhodes, 1522*

The political climate: the fragmentation of power in Europe

For centuries there had been some belief in the unity of Christian Europe (Christendom). Although the pope was the spiritual head of the universal church, the Holy Roman Emperor was meant to be the secular head of Christendom. Since Latin was the common language of government, scholars and the ceremonies of the Church, and as canon law crossed state boundaries, the fiction of unity remained. However, by the 16th century the reality was quite different. Europe had become fragmented into different nation-states such as France, England and Spain, while Italy, the home of the pope, remained a series of separate states and the Holy Roman Empire, over which the 'Emperor' presided, was a diverse mixture of small states and cities. Popes and emperors fought each other for supremacy and Christian states were continually at war. Therefore, although the ideal never died, in practice there was little unity in Europe.

Holy Roman Empire

The Empire was the largest political grouping in Europe but it consisted of over 300 separate units, each claiming their independence. Some were important states such as Saxony and Bavaria; many were ruled by minor dukes and counts. About 30 per cent of the Empire was owned by the Church, including large territories such as Salzburg, Trier and Münster. Lay rulers looked enviously at this Church land.

There were 65 Imperial Cities, owing obedience only to the emperor. Most were in south Germany. Each would control an area of countryside of towns and villages. The largest cities, Ulm and Nuremburg, had significant power. The cities fought hard to keep their independence from the emperor and the local rulers who wished to absorb them, but there were social tensions that made them unstable. Literacy levels and political awareness were high.

Apart from these, perhaps 1,500 Imperial Knights formed another important political group. These were lesser nobility with proud traditions and claimed to accept only the emperor's authority. Economic changes had made them a group in decline. Their land ownership might amount to no more than a neglected castle and a few square kilometres of poor land and they were threatened with extinction by cities and local rulers. They were still important as a military force although their private armies and lawless behaviour caused disruption.

The emperor – elected by seven electors – was the ruler of this complex political unit. Since 1440 the emperor had always been the ruler of the largest unit within the Empire: the Habsburg lands. This was because the Habsburgs were a strong barrier to threats to Europe from the east but would not be strong enough to dominate the Empire. A balance had to be struck – the German princes expected the emperor to be strong enough to support and defend the Empire, but not strong enough to dominate it.

Fig. 2 Europe, c. 1500

The title of emperor was a great honour but it had little real authority. There was the Imperial Diet or Reichstag where electors, princes, churchmen and cities met and common problems were discussed, but the emperor had no clear right to taxation, no imperial administration and no permanent army. Emperor Maximillian I (1493–1519) tried but failed to increase imperial power.

Since the Empire lacked any strong central authority, it was less able to resist the demands of the pope and the Church.

France

France was the greatest power in Europe, with the largest population (about 15 million). France had financial strength as the king could tax without consensus. It had the largest and most efficient army in Europe. Its Kings had claims to Milan and Naples.

Italy

Italy was a useful geographical term rather than a state. There was no central authority. Apart from the Kingdom of Naples, which was relatively weak and dominated by unruly nobles, the rest of Italy

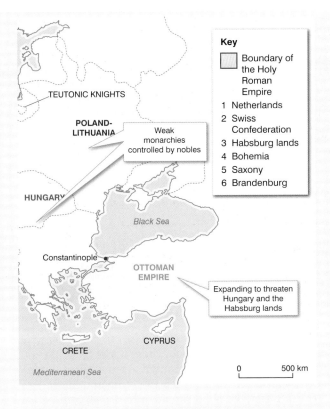

armies created Europe-wide respect. By 1500 they had conquered the last Muslim kingdom in Spain. They wished to secure their northern border with France. Ferdinand had a claim to Naples. Both aims involved conflict with France.

Poland-Lithuania

Poland-Lithuania was ruled by members of the same family (the Jagiellos) but did not have a common government. The kings were weak because they were elected and the nobles dominated government. There were racial and religious divisions and a ring of external enemies such as Muscovy and the Ottoman Empire. It was a key supplier of grain and naval supplies to Europe.

Ottoman Empire

Power concentrated in the lands of the Sultan. Advanced in the Balkans and conquered most of Hungary by 1526. In the Mediterranean its forces raided Italy. Its pirate allies attacked the coasts of Spain.

Bohemia

Bohemia was an elective monarchy dominated by the nobility. Various succession wars resulted. The crown was united with Hungary in 1490. Centre of religious disputes with the success of the Hussites. The crown of Bohemia (and Hungary) passed to the Habsburgs in 1526.

Hungary

Hungary was the major barrier to the Ottoman advance in 1500. The effective rule of Matthius Corvinus collapsed on his death in 1490 as the nobility elected weaker rules. The defeat at Mohacs in 1526 wiped out most of the kingdom.

Kingdom of Denmark

Its kings had ruled Norway and Sweden since 1397. In 1523 Sweden broke away from the union to form a kingdom under Gustavus Vasa.

was divided into smaller 'city states' that had expanded their territories over time to dominate their weaker neighbours. In northern Italy, unlike most of Western Europe, trade and industry were important. It was heavily populated, concentrated in the great cities of Florence, Venice and Milan. The wealth created by commerce meant that rulers could spend heavily on art and culture and at the same time finance warfare between the states. Types of authority differed. Some (for example, Venice) were dominated by the wealthy merchant classes but elsewhere the trend was for leading figures to emerge in control, such as the Sforza dukes in Milan and the Medicis in Florence. The popes had extended their power over the Papal States by 1513 and in this context acted as secular rulers.

Spain

Spain was a newly unified force. Ferdinand and Isabella became joint monarchs in 1479. Their

Activity

Revision exercise

Look on the internet for a map of central Europe around 1500. Locate and label the seven electors in the Holy Roman Empire and the cities named in the map on these pages. Identify lands owned by the Church.

Cross-reference

For the **popes as secular rulers of the Papal States**, refer to pages 130–3.

 Key terms

Ottoman Empire: originally a powerful tribe from eastern Turkey, the Ottoman Turks conquered most of the territory of the Eastern Roman Empire and Constantinople itself after an heroic siege in 1453. The Sultan was both head of state and head of Islam, and his specially selected forces of mounted cavalry (*siphahis*) and infantry (*janissarries*) were efficient and numerous.

Islam: the religion originating in the 7th century based on the teachings of the prophet Muhammad. The term is also used about the followers of the religion as a group.

Cross-reference

The **failure to stop the spread of Lutheranism** in the 1520s is discussed on pages 56–7 and 65–7.

Exploring the detail

The state of popular religion

Studies of the state of popular religious belief and practices have claimed that popular faith was in decline. The evidence cited for this was many examples of abuses and the growth of supposedly superstitious practices. However, historians such as Andrew Johnston in *The Protestant Reformation in Europe* (1991) argue that the laity (non-churchmen) criticised the Church because they wanted more from it; there was a tremendous interest in spiritual improvement that the Church was failing to provide. Virtually everyone accepted Catholic teaching – the threat to the Church from other beliefs was minimal.

The threat from Islam

A major factor causing fragmentation in Europe was the advance of the **Ottoman Empire.** The threat was so serious because the Sultans (rulers) of the Ottoman Empire between 1453 and 1566 were particularly able; their resources were great and, as leaders of **Islam**, they made holy war against Christian Europe.

In just over a century, the Ottoman Empire achieved an incredible expansion. Much of the south-west Balkans was lost to Christian Europe by 1500. From 1519 a powerful advance led to the conquest of Christian Hungary and the death of its king with 16,000 of his nobility at the Battle of Mohacs in 1526.

Activity

Revision exercise

Look in an historical atlas or on the internet to find information about the expansion of the Ottoman Empire in the years 1453 to 1566. Draw a timeline showing the Ottoman conquests and make a note of from whom they were conquered.

In 1529 Vienna itself was besieged. No wonder there was a fear that Christian Europe would not survive. The Ottoman armies swept down the coast of the eastern Mediterranean through Palestine and Egypt – the whole North African coast lay open. Meanwhile, a powerful navy was constructed that raided the coasts of Spain and Italy and seized island bases from their Christian defenders. Western shipping was in constant danger from pirates and Diarmaid MacCulloch in *Reformation: Europe's House Divided 1490–1700* (2004) estimates that over a million Christian men and women were snatched to become slaves between 1530 and 1640. There was a constant concern that the Ottoman Turks would overrun eastern Europe. The Ottoman advance was to play a vital role in the failure to stop the spread of Lutheranism in the 1520s.

Popular religion, ignorance and the spread of heresy

The main beliefs of Catholics c.1500

The main beliefs of the Catholic Church were imprinted on the minds of ordinary people through their regular contact with the local church and priest. The Church taught a belief in heaven, hell and purgatory and emphasised the need to participate in the Church sacraments, do good works and respect Church authority.

Churches would have had 'doom' pictures painted on their walls in which the congregation could see the awful Day of Judgement which, the Church taught, lay in wait for them when they died. It was believed that, on this day, the naked soul would be weighed on the scales of justice held by Archangel Michael. Those who had led impure lives and were 'sinners' were thought to go below to the terrible flames of hell, to be tortured by demons with long forks, while the 'saved' would be raised up to the joys of heaven. The priest would use this as a frightening visual aid. For both the higher and lower social classes, there was a real fear that the judgement would go against them. Heaven and hell, God and the Devil, angels and demons were a reality to most Catholics and people looked

Fig. 3 *Detail from the Wenhaston Doom, St Peter's Church, Wenhaston, Suffolk – devils are dragging damned sinners into the jaws of hell. Doom (or 'Last Judgement') paintings were a colourful visual aid to the Church's teaching*

to the Church to provide the answer to the question: How can I be saved and be certain that I will go to heaven?

Combined with the belief in heaven and hell went the doctrine of purgatory. Purgatory was a halfway house between heaven and hell. As it was believed that no one was pure enough to face the presence of God, the idea of an interim state, where sins could be cleansed away, had come into being. The amount of time spent in purgatory was believed to depend on the state of the soul, which would have to be perfected before it could enter heaven. Purgatory was seen as a place of fire and torment, but with a time limit – in the end, the soul would see God. Because of this, it was believed that the time a soul spent in purgatory could be reduced by doing good works, by buying indulgences or by prayers of the relatives or friends of the deceased. Many people left money in their wills for priests or monks to pray for their soul after death and the Church taught that certain prayers could reduce an individual's torments.

Cross-reference

For more on the practice of **buying indulgences**, look ahead to pages 42–3.

Key terms

Sacraments: the core services of the Catholic Church, essential to salvation. They were the channels of communication between God and humankind and the main way of making a person holy in the eyes of God.

Last Supper: Jesus's final meal before his crucifixion. The events may be read in Matthew 26.

Moment of consecration: the point in the Communion Service in which the priest says the words of Christ at the Last Supper: 'This is my body.'

The Church also offered a lifelong route to salvation through its **sacraments**. There were seven of these:

- Baptism: usually 'infant baptism', this was performed on a young baby to bring it into the 'life of Christ'.
- Confirmation: a public affirmation of faith, usually from a child, confirming his or her religious faith.
- Penance: this involved confessing sins to a priest, who then granted absolution (forgiveness) and gave out a penance (punishment). Penance was believed to give the sinner grace, but the process was a lifelong cycle as sin could not be avoided.
- Matrimony: the marriage ceremony.
- Eucharist (Holy Communion): at mass, the central service of the Catholic Church and symbolic of the **Last Supper**, the priest blessed the bread and wine using the words of Christ. It was (and is) believed that at this **moment of consecration**, the bread and wine became the actual body and blood of Christ, through the miraculous power of God, although their appearance remained the same. This is called the doctrine of the Real Presence.
- Ordination: priests and bishops received power and grace to carry out their duties.
- Last rites: given in serious illness or at the point of death, and were to forgive sins and strengthen the soul for its future life.

Catholics would have regular experience of the Mass and penance and, in attending Mass each week, they believed they witnessed a miracle performed by the priest. Consequently, the Mass was regarded as an especially powerful means of gaining God's grace and using these sacraments was regarded as a means of restoring favour with God and strengthening an individual's chance of reaching heaven.

The Church stressed that God had a great store of grace that could be earned by doing 'good works'. Good works could be simply acts of charity such as visiting the sick, but special 'good works' could be going on pilgrimages (visits to holy places such as Jerusalem or the shrines of popular saints), or exceptional devotion to particular saints or to the Virgin Mary, the Mother of God. The Church argued that humankind had free will to chose to do good and earn salvation, although it stressed that such good works without real faith were of no value.

Fig. 4 *Pilgrims visit the Church of the Holy Sepulchre and the tomb of Christ in Jerusalem, c.1410. Pilgrimages were a 'good work'*

The Church claimed that there was no salvation without its support. The Church asserted that it was the only authority to interpret the Bible and that only its priests could celebrate the Mass and give absolution. In this way, the Church held the keys to salvation. The special powers of the priesthood meant that they were the intermediaries – the middlemen – between God and the ordinary Catholic. Every attempt was made to keep the priesthood distinct from laypeople (non-churchmen). They had special church courts and were not allowed to marry, so they could devote their lives to God.

Cross-reference

The **hierarchy of the Catholic Church** is illustrated on page 14.

Evidence of the health of popular devotion

It would seem that popular devotion remained strong at the beginning of the 16th century. Studies in Germany show that the number of masses paid for steadily increased, reaching a peak in 1517. The number of religious brotherhoods in Hamburg for the purpose of paying for masses for their members increased from 5 to 99 in the period 1450 to 1517, while church building and extensions of existing churches were also highly popular. In a parish, the Church was seen as an essential part of daily living:

> The Church was a source of assistance available for everyday living. Its blessings in the form of holy water and charms could ward off fire, disease or sudden death. The ringing of church bells might prevent storms, whilst the formal curse of the priest protected crops from insects and weeds. Holy water was thought to be effective against animal disease.

1

H. G. Koenigsberger et al., *Europe in the Sixteenth Century*, 1989

There is evidence too in a growth in the veneration of the Virgin Mary, the mother of God. The people were taught that she did not die but was taken bodily to heaven. She was prayed to because it was believed she could speak directly to God through her son.

There was a story that Mary's home in Nazareth had been miraculously transported by angels to Italy and in 1507 worship by pilgrims at this house in Loreto was officially approved by the pope. A favourite topic for sculpture was a 'Pieta', which represented Mary holding her dead son. Many miracles were claimed to have been performed by Mary and men vowed to give their lives for her; poets wrote verses to her.

There is also evidence of increasing devotion to saints who, it was believed, could intercede with Christ the Judge. Churches had many images of saints. There was a belief that saints could be special protectors and work miracles for individuals. Even the 'reformer' Erasmus asked St Genevieve to save his eyesight and Luther prayed to St Anne to save him from a violent storm. St Jude was the patron of lost causes, St Bernard looked after beekeepers – saints were constantly called upon. There were many local saints and religious holidays and festivals centred on celebrating these. During the 15th century, guilds and clubs were set up and they maintained special altars to the saints of their trades. Young people took a pride in decorating these little side altars with fine altar cloths and candles. We know from wills that even the poor would leave money to pay for candles to be lit before a statue of their favourite saint.

With the growth in the veneration of saints came a huge interest in relics. There was a belief that the remains of saints and objects linked with holy events could work miracles. The Church encouraged this by offering time off purgatory for those who prayed to or touched holy relics, and it was assumed that the more relics meant the greater holiness. Nor was the cult of relics limited to the uneducated: Frederick the Wise, the Elector of Saxony, had collected 17,000 relics by the time of his death in 1525.

Cross-reference

Frederick the Wise is profiled on page 42.

Activity

Source analysis

Read Sources 2 and 3. What can we learn from these sources about the cult of relics?

Activities

Challenge your thinking

1. Why is the state of popular devotion at the beginning of the 16th century difficult to measure?

2. What type of evidence has been cited in this section? Can you think of other ways in which devotion might be measured?

Exploring the detail

Syphilis

Syphilis is a highly infectious sexually transmitted disease. It was possibly brought from the New World and was spread by French troops returning from Charles VIII's campaign of 1494–5. By 1496 it had arrived in Germany and by 1497 in England. Despite French efforts to call it something different, it was universally known as the 'French pox'.

Activity

Group activity

Working in groups, make a poster showing some of the main aspects of popular religion. You could look at religion as a part of daily life in rural areas, devotion to the Virgin Mary and the saints or relics. Use the internet to find some pictures for the poster.

Key terms

Heretical: contrary to the established teachings of the Catholic Church.

Lollards: the name 'Lollards' perhaps came from a Dutch word meaning mumbler or mutterer. Clearly it was used by their opponents.

The greatest storehouse for such treasures was Rome. Here in a single tomb 40 popes were buried and 70,000 martyrs. Rome had a piece of Moses's burning bush. A portrait of Christ on the cloth used by St Veronica to wipe his face. Rome had the chains of St Peter, a crucifix which leant over to talk to St Brigitta, the coin used to pay Judas and the beam on which he hanged himself. Above all, Rome had the entire bodies of St Peter and St Paul, which had been divided to benefit other Churches.

*R. Bainton, **Here I Stand**, 1978*

When the recently deceased Saint Elizabeth of Hungary was lying in state she was literally ripped apart by worshippers eager to get their hands on parts of her body and clothing for relics. Strips of linen covering her face were torn off, her hair was cut off as were her nails and even her nipples.

3

*A. Johnston, **The Protestant Reformation in Europe**, 1991*

Some of the evidence about popular religion, such as the trade in and acceptance of false relics, may suggest the ignorance of the ordinary people and two further developments in the late 15th century also bear witness to the strength of religious superstition and irrational behaviour in the name of religion. Jews, who were regarded as 'Christ-killers', were increasingly accused of crimes against Christians from 1450; they were expelled from Spain in 1492 and the first ghetto, whereby Jews were made to live in a restricted area of the city, was set up in Venice in 1516. A craze for persecution of supposed witches, who were nearly always women, seems also to have begun around 1500. Witches were believed to be a source of evil and evidence of the Devil in the world. A manual of how to identify witches and put them on trial (*The Witches Hammer*) was published in 1488.

However, it is important not to make value judgements about popular religion. It was not all 'bad' and the version of the later reformers all 'good'. Both the educated and the 'ignorant' accepted many Church practices and teachings unquestioningly. It is also possible that wars, plagues (a serious outbreak around 1500 caused the deaths of 10 per cent of Italy's population) and the new disease of syphilis focused people's minds even more firmly on the insecurity of life and drove them to seek more spiritual comfort at this time of change.

The spread of heresy and unorthodox movements

Heresy is a view (or views) that went against the teaching and essential beliefs of the Church. It is important to remember that before the 16th century the boundary between what was official and acceptable teaching and that which was unofficial was not always clear. The Church tolerated a wide range of views, but not attacks on essential teachings.

Lollards and Hussites

By around 1500 there were two important **heretical** groups. The first of these, the **Lollards**, developed only in England and was started by John Wyclif.

Key profile

John Wyclif (or Wycliffe)

John Wyclif (c.1330–84) was a leading professor at Oxford who made his early name for his outspoken attacks on clerics; his beliefs were condemned by the pope in 1377. He had powerful friends and so avoided punishment. He left Oxford in 1381 but his views became more radical and in his retirement he poured out a torrent of increasingly virulent and bitter writings. He translated the Bible into English.

Wyclif's views were revolutionary for their time. He believed that the Bible in English was the only source of authority and all the Church's teaching should be tested against it. He denied the authority of the pope and urged the monarch to reform the Church. He did not believe that Christ was really present at the consecration – a belief known as the Real Presence – or in priestly celibacy.

Fig. 5 *John Wyclif from an 1882 engraving*

Although Lollardy seemed to appeal to townspeople, merchants and gentry, the Lollards gained no support from the ruling classes. English kings in the 15th century strongly supported persecution (probably because they needed the support of the Church) and, although there was a revival between 1490 and 1530, it was easily controlled. The 'English heresy' remained the belief of a tiny minority.

The second group, the Hussites of Bohemia (roughly the area of the Czech Republic), had a European context and were more important. Their founder was Jan Hus (1368–1415). The result of his movement was to create a reformed Church, unique in that it was the first part of western Europe to break away from obedience to the pope.

Key profile

Jan Hus (or Huss)

Jan Hus (c.1372–1415) was a member of the theology department of the University of Prague, which was influenced by the ideas of Wyclif. In 1402 Hus began preaching in the city, demanding Church reform. He became rector of the university in 1409, but in 1411 his views were condemned and he was asked to come to Rome to explain himself – a request he refused. He attacked the sale of indulgences. He was declared a heretic but was allowed to live in safety in a castle provided by rich patrons. In 1414 he wrote his most famous works, heavily based on Wyclif's work (one had the same title). In 1414 the Council of Constance met and Hus was asked to meet Pope John XXIII to explain himself. Despite the promise of a safe conduct from the Emperor Sigismund, he was tried for heresy and burned at the stake in July 1415.

Fig. 6 *Jan Hus in prison, from an illustration of 1866*

Source analysis

Study Figure 6. What is the attitude of the illustrator towards Hus?

Cross-reference

The **sale of indulgences** is described on pages 42–3.

The Hussites' appeal was based on a national protest movement and the complex political situation of the time. Hus appealed to Czech national feelings against German domination of the Church and government and an Italian pope. He attracted support from all elements in Bohemian society, particularly the nobility. The betrayal and death of Hus in 1415 caused huge resentment and by 1420 an independent Bohemian Church had been set up which rejected the authority of the pope. It survived all attempts to wipe it out. The mainstream part of the Church had two points of difference with Rome: their services were in Czech, and they observed the practice of the worshippers receiving both bread and wine at Communion – but they did believe in the Real Presence. The Taborites, a more extreme group of Hussites, denied the Real Presence and had radical social aims such as the abolition of the death penalty.

Other divergent movements

Towards the end of the 15th century there arose in southern Germany and the Netherlands movements that caused the Church authorities great difficulties. We know, for example, that movements such as the Bundschuh, which spread rapidly throughout Germany after 1500, collected support from the urban poor, ex-soldiers and beggars as well as rural peasants.

These movements carried at least one of these messages:

■ Millenarianism: prophesies and preaching that a Golden Age was to arrive soon and suddenly. Christ was to appear on earth again and sweep away the ungodly (usually priests and landlords) and raise up the oppressed and victims of injustice. His 1,000-year reign (the Millennium) would begin. Life on earth would be utterly transformed and a classless society would be created. This was the main theme of the Bundschuh movement.

■ Messianism: the belief that a hoped-for deliverer from oppression – a saviour or champion – would arise who would punish the rich and create an earthly paradise for the poor. This figure might be a prophet from the Bible or an emperor who would emerge from a secret cave; he would be instantly recognised.

■ Egalitarianism: all authority was to be overthrown, all dues and taxes to be abolished, the rich and powerful were to be eliminated, all Church property was to be sold and the money given to the poor. Peasants would be given freedom to collect wood from forests, pasture their animals on open land and have free access to water.

The existence of heresy could throw light on the state of the Church. It could show that there was plenty of discontent with the condition of religion. Preachers seemed obsessed with heresy. Possibly it helped to undermine established teaching – the authorities were aware of the example of Hus in Martin Luther's time. On the other hand, it could show satisfaction with the Church as both Lollards and Hussites had been contained and in 1517 there was no evidence that they were winning converts.

■ Cross-reference

Movements in southern Germany and the Netherlands, including the Bundschuh movement, are discussed in the Introduction to this book, page 3.

■ Activity

Talking point

'Mass movements such as millenarianism could only happen in a gullible and superstitious age.' Do you agree?

 Summary question

How strong was the Church c.1500?

3   The beginnings of change

Cross-reference

For more on the Devotio Moderna turn back to page 10.

In 1512 Pope Julius II convened a Lateran Council. It was the last of five such meetings, held in the Church of St John Lateran in Rome, and it was to last until 1517. The opening speaker declared:

> Unless by this Council or by some other means we put a limit on our morals, unless we force our greedy desire for human things, the source of evils, to give way to the love of divine things, it is all over with Christendom.

Clearly, the need for reform was recognised at the highest level.

The beginnings of reform

There is strong evidence of protest and demands for reform of the Church at least 150 years before 1500 from both laypeople and the clergy, and the evidence suggests that the Church made some effort to reform itself. The Devotio Moderna was a good example of a 'lay' movement. Savonarola in Florence was just one example of a churchman who tried to 'reform' morality. There were also reforming bishops who attempted to raise standards for both priests and regular clergy, particularly in France and Spain. There was a tendency for breakaway groups to form, which set higher standards than the existing monastic orders and the orders of friars. In Spain strict supporters of the Franciscans created the Franciscan Observants, and the Augustinian Friars, founded in 1256, also created an 'observant' wing; Martin Luther, the Protestant reformer, joined this in 1505. Some orders, such as the Carthusians, maintained a high reputation and never needed reform.

Key profile

Girolamo Savonarola

Girolamo Savonarola (1452–98) wielded tremendous power in Florence from 1494 to 1498. At a time of a raging epidemic of syphilis, Savonarola warned the people of Florence that Judgement was at hand. The ruling family, the Medicis, were driven out. Savonarola preached simplicity of life and repentance. Bonfires were organised and the people were urged to cast their lewd fashions, pornographic books, musical instruments, make-up and trinkets (and especially mirrors, the symbol of vanity) into the flames. However, public opinion turned against Savonarola; he was condemned by the Church and burned at the stake in 1498. His views (but not his methods) were widely admired and read as an influence for reform.

Fig. 1 *The burning of Savonarola, May 1498*

The demand for reform was growing ever louder, but the popes were slow to respond to such pressures. One reason for this was the quality of the popes themselves, but the problems of Italian politics, the dangers of the Turkish threat to eastern Europe and the obstruction of the cardinals at the papal court all added to inaction. The calling of the Lateran Council was evidence

Cross-reference

The **political context** in which demands for reform were made is outlined on pages 20–2.

For the **rivalry between Francis I and Charles V**, see the Introduction to this book, page 4.

that the papacy wished to respond to the demands. It condemned the long-standing abuses of the Church, attempted to reduce the luxurious lifestyles of the higher clergy and identified the need for better education of the lower clergy. It was a wake-up call, but there was a lack of strong drive from the top to ensure its debates were turned into action.

The election of Pope Adrian VI (1522–3) was a hopeful sign. He came from the Netherlands and had no party in Rome to grant favours to nor any faction to support. Above all, Adrian had a reputation for personal holiness and integrity. He refused to sleep in the gorgeous papal apartments, preferring instead a simple straw mattress in a plain room. He frightened the life out of the cardinals by being genuinely incorruptible and, when he announced that his first task was to reform the papal *curia* (court) from where 'all evil has come', they obstructed every proposal. Already an old man, Adrian died after 18 months in office.

Progressive Church leaders hoped for a reformer but the following pope, Clement VII (1523–34) proved a disappointment. Clement was an aristocrat from the Medici family and was weak, indecisive and afraid of committing himself to reform. Like previous popes, Clement wished to keep the papacy independent. Italy in the 1520s was the battleground for the rivalry between the King of France, Francis I, and the Emperor Charles V. Therefore, although problems were emerging in Germany, where Martin Luther challenged the Church and demanded reform, Clement refused to call another council. He supported Francis I in Italy against the Emperor, which turned out badly as Francis's forces were defeated and Charles V's unpaid troops sacked the city of Rome in 1527.

Fig. 2 *Castel Sant'Angelo, the papal fortress in Rome. It was connected to St Peter's Basilica by an underground tunnel and Clement VII fled along this to the Castel to seek refuge during the Sack of Rome*

Exploring the detail

The Sack of Rome

The Sack of Rome was one of the most terrible events of the 16th century. About 20,000 imperial troops (some were Lutheran supporters) stormed the city and did not finally leave until February 1528. A participant wrote 'We took the city by storm, killed 6,000 men, plundered the houses, carried off what we could find in the churches and finally set fire to the town.' The pope fled through a secret tunnel to his fortress of St Angelo with a few cardinals. Others were pulled up the walls in baskets or committed suicide to avoid torture. After a month, the pope was captured, hiding in a storeroom. 'No age, no sex escaped the violation of the soldiers, their cruelty to kill, their lust to rape or their greed to rob and spoil.'

The Sack of Rome was a turning point in Catholic reform. Patrick Collinson in *The Reformation* (2005) comments: 'The year 1527 had an impact like that of 11 September 2001.' It was seen as a sign that God was displeased both with the morals of the city and with the pace of reform. Much of the visible wealth of the Church was looted and the pope's income halved. Some more progressive cardinals pressed for change. Clement still managed to hold out, but such cardinals were determined to elect a pope more committed to reform.

The work of Pope Paul III, 1534–40

Key profile

Pope Paul III

Paul III (1468–1549) was a member of a leading aristocratic Roman family, the Farnese. He was made a cardinal aged 25 and spent lavishly on art, building and mistresses. He had at least five children. He held famous firework displays and revived the Roman carnivals. However, in around 1520 he seems to have had a spiritual change of heart. Elected pope aged 66, he was expected to have a short reign, but he lived for 15 years. Paul had immense energy, clear and determined views, and great diplomatic skill. He commissioned Michelangelo to paint the world-famous *Last Judgement* on the end wall of the Sistine Chapel in 1534.

The reign of Paul III was a decisive turning point in the history of the papacy and the Church. Paul committed himself to the cause of reform and re-asserted the leadership of the papacy. During his reign, several key initiatives began:

- 1540: the foundation of the Society of Jesus
- 1542: the Roman Inquisition
- 1545: the Council of Trent opening session.

Paul III was a complex mixture. He did not appear to be a reformer in his personal life. One of his first actions was to make his grandsons, aged 14 and 16, cardinals and his son Pier Luigi was given his own duchy carved out of the Papal States. However, he quickly showed his support for Church reform:

- He made leaders of the Catholic reform movement into cardinals: Contarini, Carafa, Sadoleto, Pole, Morone, and John Fisher.
- He supported new orders such as the Barnabites, Ursulines and Capuchins.
- He attempted administrative reforms such as ordering 80 bishops living in Rome to return to their dioceses.
- He was determined not to take sides in the Italian wars and tried to build up the papacy's role as an international power, promoting peace.
- He was determined to call a general council. His first summons to the bishops came in 1536.
- He set up a commission to investigate the faults of the Church and to produce a report making recommendations. It was headed by Contarini and Carafa and produced the Consilium.

Key profile

John Fisher

John Fisher (c.1469–1535) was Bishop of Rochester in England from 1504 to 1535. An international academic and a saintly bishop, he made his name by his brilliant defence of Catherine of Aragon in her divorce case against Henry VIII. He supported papal authority and was imprisoned by the king in 1534. Henry was driven into a fury when Fisher was made a cardinal in May 1535 and had him executed in June.

The Consilium

The *Consilium de Emendanda Ecclesia* ('Advice on the Reform of the Church') was published after nine months of intensive work in 1537. It was a hard-hitting, radical document not afraid to criticise the very top – the popes themselves. The report began with flattery:

> Christendom ought to give thanks to God for making you Pope at this time. Christ's church, falling indeed and almost collapsed, should be restored by you and your hand should save it from ruin.

1 *From the Consilium*

Activity

Thinking point

Find pictures of Michelangelo's *Last Judgement*. Why do you think this theme was chosen?

Cross-reference

The **Society of Jesus** is detailed in Chapters 9 and 10.

The **Roman Inquisition** is covered on page 134.

The **Council of Trent** is explored on pages 136–41.

Fig. 3 *A tired-looking Paul III by Titian, 1546, with his two grandsons Ottavio (kneeling) and Cardinal Alessandro*

The cardinals warned the pope to act on their advice because previous popes had 'collected advice and not acted on it'. A start should be made with the holy city of Rome itself, where the prostitutes, rent boys and trinket-sellers must be driven out. The popes themselves were responsible for some abuses, such as selling Church offices despite the prohibition in canon law: 'flatterers have led some popes to imagine their will is law'. The report painted a detailed picture of failing pastoral care, low-quality preaching, the dire state of the monasteries and the low moral standards of priests. The Consilium went on to recommend the changes needed. For example:

- There should be no exemptions from the authority of the bishops.
- All sales of offices (simony) should stop and positions should be awarded on merit.
- Bishops should stay in their dioceses and spend their time in reform, pastoral care and educating their priests.
- Holding more than one benefice (pluralism) should be ended.
- All religious orders that are not Observant should be abolished.
- New humanist teaching should be stopped and censorship of books introduced.

The results of the Consilium were disappointing but not surprising. Carrying out these changes (if it ever was possible) would create a storm of protest, even revolution. The financial position of the papacy was made much worse by the Sack of Rome and the loss of states in Germany, so the pope could not really agree to proposals to reduce funds even more. Paul III diplomatically agreed that the principles were sound, but refused to allow publication. In 1538 the report was leaked (nothing changes!), probably by Contarini himself.

This was something of an 'own goal' as The Consilium was seized upon by enemies of the Church as evidence that they were right all along. Martin Luther translated it into German and added highly sarcastic comments in the margins. Luther also made the point that there was no mention of reform of Catholic doctrine, which was the central issue so far as he was concerned. The gulf between Luther and the Catholic Church was to remain.

The Consilium was exceptional in the severity of its criticism, but its general style and content was not much different from many denunciations of abuses in the past few centuries. Even with major problems such as control of the religious orders, the solution suggested of strengthening the bishops' authority was traditional and backward-looking.

New orders

New religious orders emerged in Italy at the start of the 16th century. Some developed from an existing order; others were of a new type. These included priests living under vows, known as clerks regular, and orders for laypeople. Some were a mixture of both. These developed for a number of reasons:

- Dissatisfaction with existing orders of monks and friars, which had become too established and had lost their original zeal.
- A wish to express a love of God in a different way than withdrawal from the world, such as caring for the sick, those in prison or the poor. There was a great tradition of laypeople working for charity. There was a desperate need at the time owing to the effects of harvest failure, plague, the wars in Italy and the syphilis epidemic.
- For centuries the way to satisfy a demand for change in the Church had been to create new styles of religious orders – for example, the great orders of friars founded in the 13th century (Franciscans, Dominicans, Augustinians) were themselves a reaction to criticisms of existing **enclosed orders**.

Question

Why do you think implementing such changes could create a 'revolution'?

Activity

Preparing a presentation

Draft your own version of advice for reforming the Church. Present your views to the class and discuss how your proposals could be carried out.

Key chronology

Main examples of new orders, 1517–35

1517 The Oratory of Divine Love
1524 The Theatines
1528 The Capuchins
1532 The Somaschi
1533 The Barnabites
1535 The Ursulines

Key terms

Enclosed order: an order of monks or nuns who lived enclosed within walls in a religious community.

It was easier to found a new order than to try to change an existing one. As it was, the established orders bitterly opposed their 'observant' splinter groups, for example the Capuchins.

The variety and number of new orders, and the energy and enthusiasm of those involved in them, were to be of great benefit to the strengthening of the Catholic Church. The new orders were important in their work for education and charity and they provided laypeople with a chance to make a contribution to the Church by making a contribution to society. They were supported by the popes, which increased their authority, and they were a clear and positive sign of renewal taking place within the Catholic Church and that the Church could adapt and evolve to face the new challenges of the 16th century. However, most of the new orders were small in terms of membership (certainly up to the 1560s) and were concentrated in Italy, mostly in the north.

The Oratory of Divine Love

The Oratory movement, which was founded by Ettore Vernazza in 1497, combined strong religious devotion with care for the sick, especially work in hospitals. Groups of lay Catholics in Italy, who did not wish to become a religious order, took vows or wore a habit, and joined together to serve God by helping the poor and disadvantaged. They were like 'holy clubs'. These oratories spread from Verona to other cities such as Naples and Bologna. The most famous was the Oratory of Divine Love, which met between 1517 and 1527, dedicated to the work of reform in Rome. The Oratory was important because:

- it provided an excellent example of holy living in its members' charitable work, which must have had an influence although this has not been evaluated
- it was a clear sign that a religious revival was taking place
- many of its members, encouraged by the spirit of the oratories, became leading figures in the Catholic renewal movement, including Gian Pietro Carafa, Gasparo Contarini, Cajetan de Thiene and Jacopo Sadoleto. One member, Reginald Pole, helped to return England to the Catholic Church in Mary Tudor's reign (1553–8)
- members were usually from noble families, which gave them a disproportionate influence, but their numbers were small – perhaps 50 members in the Roman Oratory.

Key profiles

Gian Pietro Carafa

Gian Pietro Carafa (1476–1559) was a member of a wealthy aristocratic family from Naples. He helped to found the Theatines and was appointed cardinal by Paul III. He rejected any compromise with the Lutherans and believed the only way forward was to attempt to stamp out this heresy. He became Pope Paul IV in 1555, when he became known for his energy in reform and relentless zeal to crush the heretics; possibly he bordered on madness. He said, 'Even if my own father were a heretic, I would gather the wood to burn him.'

Gasparo Contarini

Gasparo Contarini (1483–1542) was born in Venice and began a career in government. A personal crisis led him to a religious conversion and his ability was recognised by Paul III. He believed that it was possible to reach a compromise with the Lutheran reformers and organised a meeting with them in 1541.

The Theatines

The Theatines were an offshoot of the Roman Oratory, founded by de Thiene and Carafa. They were a new type of organisation in that they were priests involved in pastoral care, who took monastic vows in order to live a perfect priestly life but wore no monastic habits. The first members gave away all their property to live in total poverty. Their work involved preaching, caring for the sick and setting a public example of the highest standards of priestly life; they were a very tough, disciplined group.

The Theatines were important because they set a demanding example and future reforming Italian bishops were members. However, their influence was limited. The group's demands were so hard that there were few recruits and its leaders weeded out at the start any they thought could not keep up. Probably there were not more than about 30 members. They only had two houses in 1557. The concept was far too limited to have a great impact.

The Capuchins

Fig. 4 *Catacomb of the Capuchin Church in Palermo, 1833, with the remains of dead friars lining the walls*

The Capuchins were another important new order. They were a good example of a new order that developed from an existing one. The Franciscan Observants were a division of the Franciscan order. This group wished to live more strictly by St Francis's teaching of total poverty and simple living, preaching and helping the poor, and the Capuchins evolved from them. The Capuchins did not become a separate order until 1619.

From the first, the Capuchins lived in small communities in basic huts away from town centres. They rejected the fine town churches built by other Franciscans and lived a life of extreme poverty and fervent prayer. Sleep, food and comfort were deliberately limited and begging was only as a last resort. The communities spread through Italy after 1528.

Their extreme example attracted much support and popularity (ironically, even from women from powerful aristocratic families such as Pope Clement VII's niece – the support of these women was essential in Church politics). Their ministry was to the poorest in society and they were well known for seeking out those most desperate through disease, sickness or family breakdown. They rejected the flowery language of most preachers in favour of a simple, direct style, although they were careful not to encroach on the work of parish priests. The Capuchins were hated by the Franciscan Observants who almost got them abolished in 1534.

The importance of the Capuchins is hard to assess because there is not much documentary evidence available. A similar order for women was founded in 1538. They did not claim to be doing anything new, but in terms of numbers they were significant. In 1550 there were 2,500 members. Restrictions on expansion were lifted in 1572 and by 1640 there were 30,000 members with 1,500 religious houses. Their preaching, standards of life and charity (especially among the sick) must have had an impact on strengthening the Catholic Church. They were involved in missionary work in France, north Germany and Switzerland. They played an essential role as diplomats between Catholic States.

> They seem to have contributed to the improvement of morale. They restored the confidence of many Catholics in their Church as an organisation of which to be proud, and as a potential winner in the struggle against Protestantism. They helped to reverse the popular view of the Catholic Church as doomed to be the loser.

2

K. Randell, *The Catholic and Counter Reformations*, 1990

Other new orders

The Somaschi were founded in 1532 as an order of priests who at first did not take vows. Its founder had been a soldier and hated war with all its social results. His companions had been inspired to charity by the great plagues of north Italy in 1527–9 and their main interest was the foundation of orphanages and care for prostitutes.

The Barnabites, founded in 1533, were another group of clerks regular. They too were influenced by the miseries of north Italy and devoted themselves to pastoral care and education of young people. Their way of life was so strict and demanding that the pope himself questioned it.

In 1535 the foundation of the Ursulines marked a landmark in the history of the role of women in the Church. Some unmarried women from all social classes and age groups got together in a company living under a rule and dedicated to St Ursula. They lived with their families and did not have a habit and their aim was to teach young girls the faith and works of charity. Their education was a kind of 'Sunday school' that aimed to wipe out class distinctions and deliberately rejected the monastic approach. The Ursulines spread in north Italy and France, but having free communities of lay women was too advanced for the Church of the day and the Ursulines were gradually changed to an order with a habit, vows and strict enclosure. However, Ursuline convents were the start of many schools for the education of girls and their popularity increased. In 1750, for example, there were 10,000 Ursulines in France.

The development of printing and the new literacy

Printing was an important contributor to the religious changes of the 16th century. Without printing, words and ideas would not have spread as rapidly and changes would have undoubtedly been slower. Reformers could make their views accessible to 'ordinary' people.

Activity

Revision exercise

Copy and complete the following table to provide a summary assessment of the impact of the new orders for the Catholic Church.

Positive signs that the new orders were benefiting the Catholic Church	Limitations to the contribution of the new orders

Key
▲ Printing centre and date of first occurrence of printing

Fig. 5 *The spread of printing throughout Renaissance Europe*

Printing using moveable type was probably perfected in Mainz, Germany around 1450 and thereafter spread rapidly. Although geographically patchy, by 1500 printing was established in every part of Europe. Towns developed book fairs to exchange copies (for example, Frankfurt, where the book fair still exists) or became production centres (for example, Venice, Paris and Basle).

Fig. 6 *The printing workshop of Badius Ascensius in 1521 – probably the first illustration of the printing process. Note the female workers*

Key terms

Woodcut: a woodcut is a picture cut into the surface of a block of wood and then inked to provide a print. Woodcuts became important after 1450 and were used to illustrate books or on their own as an art form. This time was a great age of German art. Dürer, Holbein and Cranach all produced brilliant woodcuts.

A closer look

Early printing

Before 1450, printing on wooden blocks to produce **woodcuts** of short, popular works was well developed, but most books were copied by hand. Like many great inventions, printing required a number of processes to come together. The actual press (to put the ink on the paper) was modelled on those used in paper processing. To make the ink stick to the metal letters and not smudge, an oil-based ink was developed from the oils of Flemish painters. The metal type (each letter a mirror image of an actual letter) was produced using the existing skills of metal craftsmen. A crucial development was the production of cheap paper. Parchment (sheepskin) or vellum (calfskin) was very expensive and a single Bible would take 300 sheepskins. By 1400 paper-making from rags had become an established industry, at about 15 per cent of the cost of parchment.

Printing in the period to 1500 (known as the incunable or cradle period) was bound to be a transitional phase. About 30,000 titles were printed – in total, some 6 million books.

Printed works were in demand from the Church authorities, who wanted long runs of Latin Bibles, prayer books, and copies of the service books. Consequently, the earliest books followed traditionally popular themes such as saints' lives or works by writers intended to inspire the reader to a good life or death. They were produced to look exactly like manuscript copies. However, although half the output was religious books, there was also a demand for works that reflected the growth of humanism, especially in Italy. Grammars, dictionaries and texts on history, mathematics and medicine were in demand, as well as accurate texts of major Latin writers such as Vergil and Cicero for study.

In the years after 1500, books began to adopt new styles, developed by the printer Aldus Manutius (1449–1515). The heavy and hard-to-read 'blackletter' typeface was replaced by Roman and italic styles that were much lighter and in keeping with the humanist spirit of love of the classical past. Title pages with the name of the author and date of publication, indexes and shorter paragraphing became common. Printing became more concentrated in larger units and publishing – with skills of marketing and presentation – became a new profession.

Copying books by hand had always produced inaccuracies and centuries of copying had repeated errors and added others. Printing almost stopped this process, although some errors still persisted. Identical texts were now available for scholars and general readers and the researches of individual scholars were spread more quickly and their ideas could be refined by discussion.

The impact of printing

Through printing, knowledge became easier to gain. Students in lectures no longer had to copy down the texts that were dictated to them or make their own dictionaries – they could be taken home to study. Anyone who could read, and had sufficient money or access to a library, could obtain a text for study or information and, of course, religious works were heavily sought after. The new printing found a ready market in the urban centres:

> Among men who needed to read, write and calculate in order to manage their business and carry out the work of the town, who were being educated in growing numbers in schools and universities, there was a large and ready market for the printed word. Underlying this was the growth of urban populations and the spread of literacy. As townsmen grew in number, education and confidence in their abilities, their intellectual needs increased. They wanted useful and entertaining books of every kind.

3   *E. J. Rice, **The Foundations of Early Modern Europe**, 1970*

The works of Erasmus were immensely popular with publishers. Around 3,000 copies of his New Testament – with his name on the title page – were sold in the first two editions. His *Adages* went through many ever-expanding editions after 1508. His *Handbook of a Christian Soldier* (1503) became one of the most read and translated works of the 16th century.

Around 300,000 copies of Martin Luther's works were printed between 1517 and 1520 and his translation of the Bible into German sold 200,000 copies in 12 years. Books played a huge part in shaping the new religious opinion.

Cross-reference

To recap on the **growth of humanism**, turn back to page 9.

Did you know?

The following modern typefaces may be available from your list of fonts – check how they look: Times New Roman, Gothic Black Letter, Century Gothic, Antiqua.

Did you know?

A large book such as the Bible contained a few mistakes. The 'Wicked Bible' missed out the 'not' from 'Thou shalt not commit adultery' and the 'Breeches Bible' had Adam and Eve making themselves breeches rather than aprons out of fig leaves to cover their nakedness. You can look up this story in Genesis 3.

Cross-reference

For more on **Erasmus's writings**, see pages 11–3.

There is more detail about the **impact of printing on the Reformation** on page 57.

Diarmaid MacCulloch argues that as the printing presses created a vast amount of reading material, reading became an important skill. Reading involves sitting quietly and engaging personally with a text. For lay people, this could involve a more personal, inward-looking style of religious thinking.

However, the printed word was two-edged. It could glorify the Church with 'many books of heavenly wisdom', but at the same time be used to undermine it. It could increase the power of the state by publishing propaganda, but opposition to authority gained wider publicity.

Furthermore, although we know the numbers of books printed, the question of how many people actually read them from cover to cover or how much they understood what they read is difficult to answer. If a book were read aloud to others, was it all read or were the boring bits missed out? Books were expensive and it is likely that ownership marked status. The question of literacy is also important. Probably around 4 or 5 per cent of the population of Germany were literate and most of these lived in the towns. However, as 90 per cent of Germans lived in the countryside, this was still a very small percentage. Therefore, although printing was important, both as the written word and the visual images of woodcuts, its place in religious change needs to be balanced against other forms of communication, such as preaching and word of mouth.

Cross-reference

The **significance of woodcuts** in spreading ideas is discussed in more detail on page 58.

Activity

Group activity

In pairs or small groups, use a large sheet of paper to draw two columns listing the benefits and limitations of the printing revolution.

1340s
- The Black Death kills one-third of European population
- Existing Catholic practices and standards questioned

Evidence for demand for change outside the official Church
- Brethren of the Common Life
- Laypeople demand higher standards
- Christian humanism
- Savanarola

Evidence of reform from within the Church
- Lateran Council
- Bishops in France and Spain
- Older orders reform
- New orders in Italy
- Popes committed to reform: Adrian VI and Paul III
- Consilium

Influences on change
- Printing revolution
- Syphilis epidemic
- Sack of Rome, 1527

Fig. 7 *The beginnings of change in the Catholic Church*

Learning outcomes

In this section you have studied the main factors that led up to religious change in the early 16th century. You should have an understanding of the importance of humanism in promoting a more critical approach to the Church, as well as considering the arguments about whether there was a real need for change because of the condition of the Church and its leadership, the Renaissance popes. You should understand that the need for change has to be set in the political context of the growing power of rulers of important states such as France and Spain over the Church, and the weakness of other states such as the Holy Roman Empire. You have examined the state of popular religion in relation to how people regarded the Church and the quality of their religious practices, and whether the Church was in real danger from heresy. You have analysed the way in which the Catholic Church itself promoted change, how influential this was and what its limitations were. Finally, you have examined the great technological revolution of printing, which promoted the spread of humanism and the Reformation and the debate about its importance.

AQA Examination-style questions

(a)   Explain why the papacy was unable to reform the Church in the years 1500–23.

(12 marks)

AQA Examiner's tip

To answer both these questions you will need to use material from Sections 1 and 6 of this book. In part a) the task is to select reasons and not simply to describe events. A good answer might deal with the problems of the Italian wars, increasing financial problems, the reluctance of monarchs to support Church reforms, vested interests such as the cardinals in Rome who opposed change and the characters of the popes themselves. Factors will need to be linked together and lead to a conclusion.

(b)   How important were the ideas of the humanists in weakening the authority of the Church in the years before the Reformation?

(24 marks)

AQA Examiner's tip

For part b) questions a balance is needed and this might consist of pitting the ideas that humanists considered were important against the ways in which they were not, or balancing the ways the ideas of humanists were important against other factors. In discussing the humanists, you might want to include the interest in a critical examination of texts and satires such as the *Praise of Folly* and the New Testament of 1516. If you follow the second approach, you will probably want to discuss the importance of the image of the papacy, heresy, the role of secular rulers, the standards of clerical life and the impact of the printing press. You will need to make a judgement supported by evidence.

In this chapter you will learn about:

- the importance of Martin Luther

- Luther's theology of 'faith alone' and the 95 Theses

- the indulgence controversy and how it developed between 1517 and 1521.

Let none of you buy tickets of indulgence. Leave that to the lazy Christians dozing half asleep. I know nothing about souls being dragged out of purgatory by an indulgence. I do not even believe it, despite what the new-fangled professors say. On the points about indulgences [in the 95 Theses] I have no doubts at all. [Indulgences] are not based on scripture. I pay no attention to that sort of drivel, for nobody supports [indulgences] except a few dunderheads who have never smelt a Bible.

From a printed sermon by Martin Luther, 1517

Luther's sermon was written as part of his attack on the sale of indulgences, which supposedly reduced an individual's time in purgatory.

Fig. 1 *Martin Luther in middle age by Lucas Cranach (d.1533). Cranach was invited to Wittenberg by Frederick the Wise and lived near Luther. He became the great visual propagandist of the Reformation after 1519*

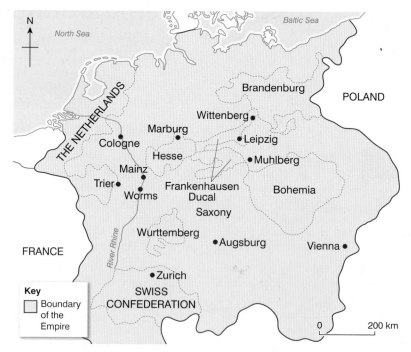

Fig. 2 *Important places in the history of the German Reformation*

Martin Luther has been described as 'the Father of the Reformation' and the recent historian Patrick Collinson has asserted that 'without Luther there would have been no Reformation, or not the same Reformation'. Luther, unintentionally at first, changed world history. He attacked many of the Catholic practices of his day and his protest demolished parts of the Catholic Church. He was an academic, but at the same time could touch the feelings of the ordinary man. He had huge energy and conviction and a powerful way with words, both spoken and written. He also knew the value of publicity and, although he lived most of his life in the insignificant town of Wittenberg, with a population of around 2,000, he made this the 'engine room' of his Reformation.

Martin Luther was typical of the recruits to the monastic and clerical life on whom the smooth running of the Church depended: a bright boy from a hard-working middle-class family with a shrewd respect for education.

2

D. MacCulloch, Reformation: Europe's House Divided 1490–1700, 2004

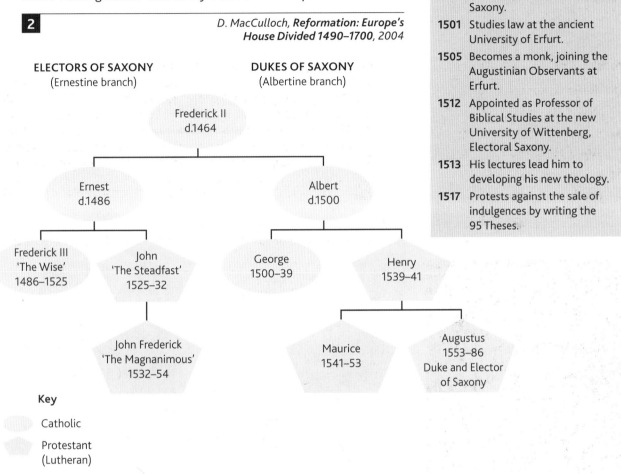

Key chronology
Luther's early life

1483 Born in Eisleben, a town ruled by the Counts of Mansfield.

1484 Moves to Mansfield, Electoral Saxony.

1501 Studies law at the ancient University of Erfurt.

1505 Becomes a monk, joining the Augustinian Observants at Erfurt.

1512 Appointed as Professor of Biblical Studies at the new University of Wittenberg, Electoral Saxony.

1513 His lectures lead him to developing his new theology.

1517 Protests against the sale of indulgences by writing the 95 Theses.

Fig. 3 *Rulers of Saxony*

Luther spent most of his youth in Saxony, which in 1485 had been divided between two brothers of the ruling family. The larger part, Ducal Saxony, was ruled by Duke George, who was to become one of Luther's greatest opponents. The smaller part, Electoral Saxony, was ruled by Frederick the Wise, the Elector of Saxony who became one of Luther's greatest supporters. In 1505, much to his father's disgust, Luther abandoned the study of law at Erfurt University to enter a strict Augustinian monastery and become a monk. He claimed this decision was taken because he had been terrified by a thunderstorm and vowed to St Anne that he would become a monk if his life were spared.

Although the Augustinians were a strict order, they were not shut off from the world and the community acted as teachers and lecturers. Consequently, Luther went on to become a professor at the University of Wittenberg, which had been founded in 1502 by the Elector Frederick as a rival to the much older and prestigious university of Leipzig in Ducal Saxony.

Cross-reference

More detail on the **support provided to Luther by Frederick the Wise** can be found on page 56.

Fig. 4 *Frederick III, the Elector of Saxony. He was the protector of Luther, although he never officially became a convert*

■ Key profile

Frederick the Wise

The Elector Frederick III of Saxony (1463–1525) was known as 'the Wise'. Without the protection of Frederick, Luther would probably have been arrested and executed at an early stage in his career. Frederick became Elector in 1486. He was highly respected in the empire for his sense of justice and wise government. He kept his state out of wars. Frederick was one of the seven electors of the Holy Roman Emperor and the coincidence of an election of an emperor in 1519 meant that those wishing to silence Luther could not risk offending Frederick. Frederick never became a Lutheran and died a Catholic in 1525. His brother, John, a Lutheran, succeeded him.

■ The indulgence controversy and the 95 Theses

Fig. 5 *Selling indulgences, from a 16th-century German woodcut*

The Church claimed that the pope could draw on a Treasury of Merits – consisting of all the merits built up by Christ and all the saints but not yet used – to reduce the time that individual souls would have to spend in purgatory. Consequently, indulgences were produced, offering varying degrees of 'time reduction'.

Such was the demand for indulgences by the late 15th century that the popes saw there were financial advantages to these and selling them became a well-organised system. From 1476 they could even be bought for a friend or relative in purgatory. The Church stressed that for the indulgence to be effective there had to be genuine repentance, but the sale of indulgences suggested that a soul could be released from purgatory for a cash payment.

In 1514 a sale of indulgences was launched to pay for building the new St Peter's Basilica in Rome. It had been agreed that profits from the sale of indulgences in Germany would be divided between Pope Leo X for the building and Albert, Archbishop of Mainz and head of the German Church, who was heavily in debt, having paid a large sum to the pope for his archbishopric.

■ Cross-reference

To recap on the concept of **purgatory**, look back to pages 22–3.

The instructions to the indulgence sellers, written by the Archbishop, pushed the teaching on indulgences to the limit. The instructions said 'it is not necessary for those who contribute to the fund to be truly sorry or go to confession'. Everyone who bought one would be granted full forgiveness of sins and indulgences could be applied to souls already in purgatory. In 1517 the sale of indulgences within the empire was entrusted to a Dominican friar, John Tetzel, whose preaching was that of the worst kind of salesman. He used emotional blackmail and was eager to persuade Germans to contribute:

> The dead cry, Pity us! Pity us! We are in dire torment from which you can redeem us for a pittance. Will you leave us here in flames? Will you delay our promised glory?
>
> As soon as the coin in the coffer rings
> the soul from purgatory springs.
>
> Place your penny on the drum
> the pearly gates open and in strolls mum!

3   *Extracts from John Tetzel's sermons*

Key profile

John Tetzel

John Tetzel (1465–1519) was a Dominican friar who trained in Leipzig (a rival order and university to Luther's). He was the chief preacher of the indulgence. His extreme claims and tasteless methods were challenged even before Luther. After Luther attacked the sale of indulgences, Tetzel pushed the Dominican order into reporting Luther to Rome. He was, however, strongly criticised for his methods by the Church authorities and died in obscurity in 1519.

The preaching of the new indulgences was banned in Electoral Saxony by the Elector Frederick because he did not want any competition for his collection of holy relics (the best of which were a thorn from Christ's crown of thorns and a nail from the cross), which were also claimed to be able to reduce time in purgatory. However, those wanting an indulgence from Tetzel could easily go over the border to the neighbouring state.

The 95 Theses

The sale of new indulgences enraged Luther. He had preached against the practice before Tetzel's arrival and eventually, in exasperation, on 31 October 1517 he wrote 95 Theses (points for academic argument) against indulgences. He may have nailed them to the church door in Wittenberg, which was the normal procedure for those wishing to display material and start a debate, although there is no proof that this happened. What we do know, however, is that they circulated quickly and became the subject of heated debate.

The timing was not accidental, as Luther would have known. In the Catholic Church, the first two days in November have a particular focus on the dead and souls in purgatory, so buying indulgences would be at its height towards the end of October. Crowds would be anticipated coming to view Frederick's relics on 1 November.

The 95 Theses were not only circulated in Wittenberg: Luther also sent printed copies to his own bishop and the Archbishop of Mainz,

Activity

Revision exercise

Make a list of the main influences on Luther between 1483 and 1517. Use two headings, **People** and **Ideas**, and briefly give a reason for including each point. Decide which influences were the most important.

Fig. 6 *The famous church door of the Castle Church at Wittenberg. The original and most of the church were destroyed by fire in 1760. The painting above the door shows Luther and Melanchthon, with the Confession of Augsburg*

accompanied by a letter making the point that people seemed to think that they were assured of salvation when their money was paid and that their souls would leave purgatory. He suggested that the instructions to the indulgence sellers, 'issued under your name', must have been 'without your knowledge and consent'.

The theses were, as James Atkinson pointed out in *Martin Luther and the Birth of Protestantism* (1968), rather disorganised and not well thought out, but the tone of them – concise and combative – caught the public imagination.

> Thesis 1: When our Lord Jesus said repent, he meant the whole life of believers should be one of repentance.
>
> Thesis 21: The preachers of indulgences are wrong when they say that a person is forgiven every penalty by the pope's indulgence.
>
> Thesis 27: There is no divine authority for preaching that the soul flies out of purgatory as soon as the money clinks in the collecting box.
>
> Thesis 43: Christians should be taught that those who give money to the poor or lend to the needy do a better action than purchasing pardons.
>
> Thesis 50: Christians should be taught that if the pope knew of the demands of the preachers of indulgences he would rather have the basilica of St Peter's reduced to ashes than built on the skin, flesh and bones of his sheep.
>
> Thesis 81: Why does the pope not empty purgatory out of holy love for all Christians? This would be a righteous reason. Meanwhile, he releases souls for sordid money.
>
> Thesis 86: Since the pope has great wealth, why does he not build St Peter's with his own money, rather than with that of his faithful poor?

4

A selection of the 95 Theses

Activity

Source analysis

Read Source 4.

1. Read theses 1, 21, 27 and 43. In what ways does Luther criticise indulgences?

2. How would the theses given in the source appeal to popular feeling against the pope?

■ Luther's ideas

As a monk, Luther had undergone years of spiritual and psychological torment. He had wanted to find the best route to heaven and he rigorously performed 'good works' such as fasting, vigils and repeating the prayers of the Church each day. However, Luther commented that he almost killed himself overdoing these rituals, 'so that the bones stood out of him'. Luther confessed his sins daily, once taking six hours, but he was not convinced he had confessed all his sins. The teaching of St Augustine, the patron of his order, profoundly influenced Luther and seemed to him evidence of an unjust God. 'This appeared completely unjust. I was myself driven to the very depths of despair so that I wished I had never been born. Love God! I hated him!'

Key profile

St Augustine

St Augustine (354–430) was Bishop of Hippo in North Africa and one of the greatest teachers of the Church. His view of salvation was coloured by the times he lived in. The Roman Empire was crumbling. Old certainties were gone. He battled strongly against a group of Christians who taught that salvation depended on their own efforts to live a pure life. St Augustine took a deeply pessimistic view of humanity. Like Luther, St Augustine was much influenced by St Paul. He argued that all humankind was corrupted by the sin of Adam and Eve (Original Sin), so how could persons so mired in sin do anything to save themselves? Everything depended on God's grace and the power of God who decided who should be saved. It followed that as God's will was unalterable, a person's salvation was predestined. It has been argued that the views of St Augustine – as developed by all the reformers – destroyed the old Catholic Church.

Luther was helped through his crisis by Johannes von Staupitz, a member of Luther's Augustinian order and a mentor for younger monks. Staupitz was in charge of the theology faculty at the University of Wittenberg and arranged for Luther to teach there to help him develop his thinking. He advised Luther to learn more about God through biblical study and encouraged him to focus on the love of Christ for humanity rather than on God the stern judge.

Between 1513 and 1520, in periods of intense study and contemplation of the texts (particularly Paul's letters and the study of St Augustine), Luther developed a theology that was to bring him inner peace and be the basis of Reformation Europe. He was influenced by humanist ideas and used Erasmus's New Testament in Greek when it was published in 1516. Luther argued that the words of Scripture were the only guide to the knowledge of God and not the authority of the Church. Furthermore, he concluded that God was not an angry God but a God of mercy, and that mercy was available to all. Mercy was not, he argued, dependent on 'good works' but on a person's faith – a doctrine sometimes referred to as justification by 'faith alone'. God had sent Christ into the world to save sinners, Luther argued, so there was hope for everyone. Faith alone was the essential element for salvation.

Luther summed up the insight that lifted his anxieties when he wrote, 30 years later:

> My situation was that, as a perfect monk, I stood before God a sinner. I had no confidence that my good works would satisfy him. I did not love a just and angry God but hated him. Night and day I studied, then I saw the connection between the justice of God and the just shall live by faith. A Christian had all that is needed in faith, and needs no good works to make him righteous.

5 *Luther's reflections on 'faith alone'*

Luther was not actually saying anything new. 'Faith alone saves' is in the New Testament and in the writings of St Augustine. In a way, Luther's theology was a revival of early Christian teaching. Even so, the great Reformation battle cry became 'faith alone saves'. This belief caused great controversy because it made much of the Church's teaching on salvation irrelevant. Good works such as pilgrimages, the cult of the saints and the Virgin Mary, the sacraments themselves and indulgences were, according to Luther's thinking, of no help in gaining salvation. Indeed, to the reformers they were not harmless but a positive danger to a Christian soul.

Exploring the detail

Key biblical texts

Paul's letters in the New Testament contain the two key texts for the reformers: 'For by grace you are saved, it is the gift of God: not through works, lest any man should boast' and 'We conclude that a man is justified [made right] by faith, without deeds.

Luther's writings

Luther set out his ideas in some detail in three important works:

- *Address to the Christian Nobility of the German Nation*, August 1520
- *The Babylonish Captivity of the Church*, October 1520
- *The Freedom of a Christian*, November 1520.

In these publications he detailed his views about man's relationship with God and the nature of the Church. The main points advanced in these works were:

- faith alone saves ('*sola fide*')
- Scripture alone: the test of the truth of the Church's teaching was the evidence found in the Bible. As a result of his study of Scripture, Luther rejected purgatory, the power of the saints and the pope's power that supported them.

Address to the Christian Nobility of the German Nation

The *Address to the Christian Nobility of the German Nation* was an appeal to the Emperor Charles V and the rulers of Germany to lead a reform of the Church. It launched an attack on the abuses and corruption of the Church and dismissed the power of the pope as being based on lies. To support the role of secular rulers, Luther argued in favour of 'the priesthood of all believers' – that priests were not a special group set apart to be the middleman between God and humankind, since faith alone saves. There was no need to confess your sins to a priest. It followed then that, for example, priests could marry. It certainly meant that the monastic life was useless.

The Babylonish Captivity of the Church

The *Babylonish Captivity of the Church* was the most revolutionary of the three writings. It focused on the Church's teaching on the sacraments. The whole sacramental system, according to Luther, was a fraud imposed on Christians by the popes. He said that there was no evidence in Scripture for four sacraments and only allowed three (baptism, the Eucharist and penance – but later penance was dropped), which destroyed the whole sacramental system and the power of the priest to deliver it. He also denied two features of Catholic teaching on the Mass, claiming that:

- the faithful should have both the bread and the wine at Communion, whereas it was customary for only the priest to take the wine
- the Mass was not a re-enactment of Christ's sacrifice carried out by a priest. It was not a good work for the merit of laypeople.

However, Luther *did* accept that Christ was actually present at the moment of consecration at the Mass – the doctrine known as the Real Presence – but not the Church's explanation of how this happened, which was based on a teaching known as **transubstantiation**. He did not accept that a miracle had taken place, but that the bread and wine remained on the altar, existing together with Christ's body and blood.

The Freedom of a Christian

The Freedom of a Christian was not so controversial. By accepting that freedom exists in submission to the will of God and trusting in His mercy for salvation, Christians were released from the rituals of the Church. This trusting faith would show itself in love for other people and by doing good works. Luther tried to share his own sense of freedom when he first accepted these views:

Key terms

Transubstantiation: this theory was based on the idea of the 'schoolmen' that all material things had a substance – a kind of essential quality as well as an external appearance. Transubstantiation implies that the substance of the bread and wine changed miraculously at consecration into the body and blood of Christ, although the appearance remained the same.

I begin to understand that the just man lives through God's gift, that is by faith. Here I felt that I was altogether born again and had entered paradise itself through open gates.

6 *From The Freedom of a Christian, 1520*

 Activity

Revision exercise

Using the information in this chapter and Chapter 2, draw a table contrasting the Catholic doctrines of the time with Luther's ideas. You could use headings such as:

- the Sacraments
- the Mass
- the Scriptures
- the importance of the priest
- the pope
- how to reach heaven.

The outcome of the indulgence controversy and Luther's protest

When Luther prepared his 95 Theses, he was hoping to correct the abuses of the indulgence system, not attack the authority of the pope or purgatory in general. However, the Church was alarmed by Luther's protest as it affected powerful people: the Archbishop of Mainz, the Dominican order to which Tetzel belonged and Pope Leo X who authorised the sale of indulgences.

Although the Church and some secular authorities were concerned over the financial results of attacking indulgences and theologians feared the religious implications, many ordinary people were delighted by them. For some Germans, they were further evidence against the influence of an Italian pope, who just seemed to be making money out of Germans, and very quickly the 95 Theses were translated from the Latin into German and spread widely over Germany and Switzerland.

As the debate raged, a storm of **pamphlets** was produced, giving the views of both sides. Backed by the Dominican order, Tetzel produced a paper supporting indulgences. Luther's response, 'A Sermon on Indulgences', was a best seller.

The Church authorities were quick to appreciate the importance of Luther. The Archbishop of Mainz sent a file of his writings to Rome for Leo X to read. The pope saw the dangers at once, but decided to let Luther's Augustinian order deal with the controversy. However, Staupitz sympathised with Luther and the Augustinians moved to the defence of Luther, to protect one of their own order against Tetzel's Dominicans.

Pope Leo ordered Luther to Rome but he declined to leave Germany – considering what had happened to Jan Hus this was wise. Luther had a powerful protector in Frederick of Saxony and the Elector's secretary, Spalatin, was also on his side.

Consequently, the pope decided that the issues should be settled in Germany. He asked Sylvester Prierias (1456–1523), a papal theologian, to prepare a case against Luther. In his 'Dialogue', he said that to deny the authority of the pope to issue indulgences was heresy and that the pope cannot err. In his 'Reply', Luther rejected this, distancing himself

Key chronology

Key events arising from the 95 Theses

Oct 1517	95 Theses issued.
Oct 1518	The Augsburg Meeting: Luther meets Pope Leo X's representative, Cardinal Cajetan.
Jul 1519	The Leipzig Debate: Luther debates his views with John Eck.
Jun 1520	Pope Leo X issues the papal bull of excommunication *Exsurge Domine*.
1520	The 1520 Writings: Luther publishes 24 books setting out his views on doctrine and reform of the Church, including *The Address to the German Nobility*, *The Freedom of a Christian* and *The Babylonish Captivity of the Christian Church*.
Dec 1520	Luther burns the papal bull in public at Wittenberg.
Apr 1521	The Diet (or Reichstag) of Worms. Luther states his case before the Emperor Charles V. The Edict of Worms declares Luther an outlaw.
May 1521	Luther leaves Worms but is taken to Wartburg Castle.

Key terms

Pamphlet: a short work of 8 pages of about A4 size (or 16 pages of A5), which was not bound like a traditional book. Usually, pamphlets were controversial, dealing with a topical issue.

Cross-reference

To recap on **Jan Hus**, return to page 27.

See pages 42 and 56 for more on **Frederick of Saxony**.

even further from the orthodox view. An Imperial Diet was meeting in Augsburg and the pope's representative, Cardinal Cajetan, was sent there in October 1518 with the task of reconciling Luther to the Church or, in the event of failure, ensuring Luther's arrest. Frederick of Saxony acted as Luther's protector and ensured that Luther was given a safe conduct from the Emperor to attend the Diet.

Key profile

Cardinal Cajetan

Cardinal Thomas Cajetan (1469–1534) was a great Dominican theologian and supporter of the scholastic school of theology. He was a strong supporter of papal authority, but not a narrow-minded one. He probably agreed with Luther's views on indulgences. Later he supported attempts to compromise with the Lutherans.

The meeting at Augsburg, October 1518

Cajetan represented the voice of the pope himself. He had not come to argue about indulgences, but to get Luther to admit he was wrong and was defying the authority of the pope. His insistence pushed Luther further away and led him to deny the pope's authority over indulgences. Luther claimed that Church doctrines needed to be tested by reference to the Scriptures, whereas Cajetan accepted papal authority without question.

Public feeling was already at boiling point and Luther was soon receiving public acclaim as the 'honest German' against the 'Italian' pope. In such circumstances, it was impossible for Cajetan to think of arresting Luther, let alone taking him from Germany.

The Leipzig Debate, July 1519

From questioning the authority of the pope over indulgences, Luther began to question the whole basis of the papal primacy. He studied the Bible intently and came to the conclusion that a general council of the Church should have supreme authority and that 'faith alone saves' rather than faith *and* good works, which was the Church's teaching. However, because the pope was anxious to get the Elector Frederick to vote for his candidate in the imperial election of 1519, he was content to leave Luther to the German authorities.

A public debate on Luther's teaching, to be held in the presence of Duke George (who opposed Luther), was arranged at Leipzig University. The debate lasted 18 days. Luther's opponent, John Eck (1486–1543), was a highly respected Dominican friar and, although concerned to correct abuses, was a dedicated defender of the teachings of the Church and a man who had made it his life's work to combat heresy. He was considered the best debater in Germany and his brilliant tactical display forced Luther to declare his position openly.

Forced into a corner, Luther effectively condemned himself as a heretic by saying that faith alone saves, that Scripture alone was the test of what to believe and that the authority of the pope was based on a lie as there was no evidence for a pope (or purgatory) in the Bible. Luther was explicitly stating his agreement with many of the views of the notorious heretic Jan Hus, who had been condemned by the Council of Constance in 1415. Therefore, there was no option for the Church but to excommunicate him and remove him from Christian society.

Cross-reference

Luther's views on **'faith alone saves'** are discussed on page 45.

Exploring the detail

The imperial election of 1519

The Emperor Maximillian had worked hard make certain that his grandson, Charles of Habsburg, was elected Emperor after his death. As the seven electors were the key to this, he tried to make certain which way they would vote. The Elector Frederick had a crucial vote, so this was not the time to displease him. On the other hand, the pope worked hard to defeat the election of Charles. The Elector Frederick therefore had to be flattered and kept onside by the pope. Indeed, Pope Leo promised him a decoration – the 'golden rose' – with requests not to vote for Charles of Habsburg and to crush Luther, 'that only son of Satan'.

Luther's bull of excommunication, June 1520

Fig. 7 *Luther burning the papal bull of excommunication, 1520. The picture is from a 19th-century work called the* **Heroes of the Reformation**

Although Cajetan's report to Rome had been fairly balanced, Eck's was much more aggressive and a new committee in Rome produced the **bull of excommunication** *Exsurge Domine* ('Arise O Lord') in June 1520. The bull condemned 41 of Luther's views as heretical; it was forbidden to read his works and his books were burned in a public square. He was given 60 days to deny (or recant) his views and banned from further preaching and writing.

John Eck was made responsible for publishing the bull in Germany, but there was serious resistance in north and central areas. When Duke George published the bull in Leipzig, it was ripped down in the night. Luther himself wrote a sarcastic parody of the document and was prepared to resist. On 10 December the students of Wittenberg prepared a huge bonfire to burn copies of the canon law, anti-Lutheran books and papal decrees in revenge for burning Luther's books. Luther attended the bonfire and, in a dramatic gesture, burned a copy of the papal bull. Burning the bull was symbolically seen as burning Pope Leo himself, so it is hardly surprising that in January 1521 Luther's excommunication was finalised.

> The breach was complete; from now there could be war or surrender. The quarrel had moved out onto the stage of European politics. 'All Germany is in revolution,' wrote the pope's representative Alexander. 'Nine-tenths shout Luther! as their war-cry: the other tenth cares nothing about Luther and cries "Death to the court of Rome!"' The peasants near Wittenberg, when they met a traveller on the road, would ask 'Are you for Martin?' and beat him if he said he was not.

7 *O. Chadwick,* ***The Reformation***, *1972*

Key terms

Bull of excommunication: the most serious sanction the pope had. Someone excommunicated was cast out of Christian society and banned from receiving any sacraments of the Church. Their soul would be sent to hell. A bull is the term given to the most important papal instructions and decrees and is usually referred to by the first words in Latin of the document. The name comes from the impressive lead seal fixed to it (the Latin word for 'seal' is *bulla*).

Question

Why was Luther excommunicated in 1521?

The Diet of Worms, January to April 1521

Charles V had been elected the new Holy Roman Emperor in 1519 and he decided to give Luther a hearing despite the Church's opposition. His motive seems to have been his own sense of fair play, but he was not blind to the faults of the Church. Pope Leo formally appealed to the Emperor to take action to enforce his condemnation, but Charles could not upset the German princes and electors and public opinion was so pro-Luther that arresting him would have been difficult.

Charles offered Luther a safe conduct to and from a Diet attended by the Emperor Charles V and the princes, electors, dukes, imperial cities and other groups within the empire. Although Jan Hus had been given a similar document in 1415 by a previous emperor and it had not been kept, Luther had too much public support to be in danger from attending.

A closer look

Luther and the Diet of Worms

Luther's appearance at the Diet of Worms was a piece of high drama and a decisive moment in Luther's life, although it is hard to get an accurate picture as there are various versions of what happened.

The huge hall was crammed with hundreds of representatives in a stifling heat. The highest in the land were present. After a series of delays creating massive tension, Luther entered – his supporters created an image of a humble monk from a poor background. Luther stressed his ignorance of court etiquette. The popular image became Luther defying all the powers of the world to stand for truth. In his own mind it was a struggle between the truth and the Devil and he was confident of his success.

On the other hand, Worms seems a pointless occasion because Luther was not asked to explain or debate his views publically. He was asked if the writings that were in his name were really his (no argument – his name was on the covers) and if he was prepared to give up the opinions given in them. Luther asked to be allowed overnight to think about his answers – once again, the tension built up.

Next day he agreed with the first question but could not give up his views on the great evils of the papacy or supporters of the papacy. He invited anyone to argue the issue with him and prove him wrong, but this did not happen.

The Diet ended with Luther's famous words:

> Your Imperial Majesty demands a simple answer. Here it is plain and unvarnished. Unless I am guilty of error on the evidence of Scripture or reasons based on the Scriptures I cannot and will not retract anything, for to act against our conscience is neither safe nor open to us.

8 *Extract from Luther's speech at the Diet of Worms*

The final well-known words – 'Here I stand, I can do no other' – were probably added later. All sources agree that Luther ended with 'God help me. Amen.' This was a statement of the power of individual belief and it seems very modern. The reply of Charles V, delivered the next day, was just as impressive, making the case for authority:

A single monk, led astray by private judgement, has set himself against the faith held by all Christians for a thousand years or more, and impudently concludes that all Christians up till now have erred. I have therefore resolved to stake upon this cause all my dominions, my friends, my body and my blood, my life and soul. After Luther's stiff-necked reply yesterday, I now repent that I have so long delayed proceedings against him and his false doctrines. I have now resolved never again, under any circumstances, to hear him.

9   *Adapted from Charles V's reply to Luther*

Charles made it clear to the princes there could be no compromise. By the Edict of Worms, Luther was declared an outlaw and anyone who gave him support or shelter was liable to be punished for aiding heresy. Part of the text said, 'we forbid anyone from this time forward to dare, either by words or deeds, to receive, defend, sustain or favour the said Martin Luther. On the contrary, we want him to be caught and punished as a notorious heretic, as he deserves, to be brought personally before us. Those who help in his capture will be generously rewarded.' In a way, the political history of the next 34 years in the empire was an attempt to enforce this Edict of Worms.

Fig. 8 *Luther at Worms*

Under the terms of the safe conduct (which Charles did not break), Luther was allowed to return to Wittenberg. However, on the journey he was 'kidnapped' when he reached Saxon territory by men who were under the orders of the Elector Frederick. He was taken to the Elector's castle at Wartburg, where he remained for the next 10 months. However, the Emperor made no attempt to arrest him and Luther enjoyed some welcome reading, writing and thinking time there. The castle was not an isolated prison; it was 1.5 km from the large town of Eisenach, where Luther had been born. Consequently, he was able to produce pamphlets that were published there, despite the ban of the Edict of Worms, and he was able to study and begin a translation of the New Testament into German.

Summary question

Why did Luther's protest attract so much support in the years 1517–21?

Question

Is it ever right to resist established authority?

Exploring the detail

The Wartburg captivity

Luther's 'kidnap' has become a legend. Supposedly, Luther rode for hours to shake off pursuit, but was eventually taken. The Elector Frederick's motives are unclear. It is possible that Frederick acted because he feared that Charles would go back on his word and have Luther arrested and executed. However, as it suited Charles V to have Luther out of the way, without being forced into further action, it has been suggested that Frederick may have been acting in agreement with Charles.

5   The growth of Lutheranism, 1521–55

In this chapter you will learn about:

▪ the development of Luther's ideas after 1521

▪ the reasons for the success of Lutheranism, including the support of the princes and the Holy Roman Emperor's absence

▪ the part played by printing, the spoken word and Luther's preaching in the spread of Reformation ideas

▪ the reasons for and the results of the Peasants' War of 1524–5 in affecting the spread of the Lutheran Reformation in Germany

▪ the conflict between the Emperor and the German princes and the compromise Peace of Augsburg.

▪ Key chronology

Events in Luther's later life

1522 Returns to Wittenberg to take charge of a reformation; translates and publishes the New Testament in German.

1525 Marries a former nun, Catherine von Bora – six children born between 1526 and 1534; criticises the Peasants' War.

1526 Publishes the German Mass, to be used in Saxony.

1529 Takes part in the Colloquy at Marburg.

1529 Publishes the Great Catechism and Small Catechism, statements of his beliefs and how Church services should be organised.

1534 Publishes the Old Testament in German.

1546 Dies at Eisleben.

Fig. 1 *The Emperor Charles V by Titian, 1548. The Emperor is shown as a crusader defeating the forces of Protestant heresy*

▪ The development of Luther's ideas after 1521

While Luther was in Wartburg, others began to take up his views and create change within Germany. For example, Andreas Carlstadt carried forward what he thought were Luther's views in Wittenberg by supporting clerical marriage, and he himself married a 15-year-old girl in December 1521. He also got rid of the rituals in the Catholic Mass by giving the laity bread and wine and wearing ordinary clothes instead of vestments. Carlstadt encouraged the removal of all sacred images and statues as the work of the Devil, but this led to the desecration of Wittenberg's churches. This iconoclasm, together with a frenzy of monks and nuns getting married, seemed to show that public order was breaking down. The Elector Frederick was deeply displeased, while Duke George appeared delighted.

Key profile

Andreas Carlstadt

Andreas Carlstadt (1486–1541) was a fellow Augustinian monk. He believed it was his mission to interpret Luther's views. He was a friend of Luther (he was involved in the Leipzig Debate), but was given to wild enthusiasms and lacked common sense. After 1522 he was excluded from university life and left Wittenberg in 1524.

The town of Wittenberg was attractive to others with a more extreme message. Most important were a group from Zwickau, a large town in Saxony, who were nicknamed the Zwickau prophets. This group preached that there was no Real Presence, and that as there was no example in the New Testament for baptising infants, the reformers should only carry out adult baptism.

Luther decided to return to Wittenberg in March 1522. He saw that the changes that were being carried out in his name could not go uncontrolled and that he needed to make his views clear on issues such as clerical marriage, baptism and the organisation of the Church. He decided that clerics should be allowed to marry, but confirmed that infant baptism should not be changed. In support of this belief, Luther married Catherine von Bora in 1525.

Cross-reference

For more on the arguments surrounding **infant baptism**, see Chapter 8.

Key profile

Catherine von Bora

Catherine von Bora (1499–1552), from an upper-class family, was sent to a convent aged 10 when her father married again. She took her vows at 16, but did not like convent life. In 1522 Catherine and others fled from her convent in Catholic Ducal Saxony. Luther seems to have arranged their escape from Saxony (possibly in a covered wagon or a herring barrel) and the group arrived in Wittenberg. Luther took it upon himself to find partners for the ex-nuns and married Catherine as part of this plan. It was a happy marriage despite Luther's early doubts. Catherine proved a highly capable organiser, bringing up five children (one died in infancy) as well as looking after a home with 40 rooms excluding the bedrooms. Luther's home was always full of visitors wining and dining. Luther loved a good meal and, as the drink flowed, the table talk became more earthy. Thanks to Catherine, a great contrast can be made between the lean portraits of his youth and the man who became the model for a proverb 'As fat as Martin Luther'.

Activity

Thinking point

Research Luther's views on women, marriage and family life. They reflect the traditional attitudes of men in the 16th century.

Luther said there was nothing wrong with sacred art and statues in churches so long as they were not excessive. Furthermore, he confirmed that the body and blood of Christ was really, physically present on the altar during Communion – so services had to show reverence. In 1526 Luther published the German Mass and, in 1529, the Great **Catechism** and Small Catechism, providing statements of his beliefs and how Church services should be organised. Finally, he made it clear that it was the duty of the secular ruler to impose discipline on the Church.

Key terms

Catechism: a series of questions and answers – the Small Catechism was an excellent innovation with language at a simpler level, which showed that Luther knew the importance of communication. The idea was later copied by Catholics.

Cross-reference

For **Zwingli's reformation in Zürich**, turn to page 95.

In developing his ideas, Luther showed that he was a conservative reformer at heart and this led to major disagreements with some of the other reformers, who had begun to go further than him in their thinking. For example, in Zürich, Zwingli had ordered the removal of images from churches and claimed that the bread and wine were only bread and wine and that there was no Real Presence.

A colloquy (discussion) was organised by Philipp of Hesse at his castle at Marburg in 1529 between Luther and Zwingli. It was decided to focus on the nature of the bread and wine. Luther wrote in chalk on the table 'This is my body' – the words of Christ over the bread at the Last Supper – and covered them with a velvet cloth. 'Is' to him meant 'really is'. Zwingli was reduced to tears by Luther's refusal to look at alternative possibilities and a disastrous split opened up between the Protestant reformers.

Why was Lutheranism so successful?

A peaceful Lutheran Reformation took place in Denmark, Norway and Sweden, which was completed in the 1540s. The 1530s saw further conversions including Württemberg (1534), Holstein and Pomerania (1535), Brandenburg (1539) and Ducal Saxony, the state of Luther's old enemy, Duke George. The reasons for Lutheran success include the following:

- Philip Melanchthon balanced Luther's passion and violent enthusiasm. He acted as a conciliatory force, trying to moderate some of Luther's more extreme statements and attitudes and excusing Luther's rather earthy expressions. In 1521 he brought together Luther's scattered theological writings into a clear statement of doctrine – the *Loci Communes*. A gentle, moderate and academic man, his talent was his learning: he had no great enthusiasm for politics or conflict and could not stop Carlstadt in the 1521–2 period. He was keenly interested in preventing extremism and hoped to reunite the Church if an acceptable formula could be found. He was present at Marburg (1529), wrote the statement of faith at the Diet of Augsburg (1530) and led talks at Regensburg (1541) with Catholic bishops to try to heal the schism.

Fig. 2 *'Heroes of the Reformation'. From the left: Martin Luther, John Oecolampadius, John Frederick of Saxony, Zwingli and Melanchthon*

Cross-reference

The **Diet of Augsburg** and the **talks at Regensburg** are outlined on pages 66–7.

Key profile

Philip Melanchthon

Philip Melanchthon (1497–1560) was a brilliant scholar who had been appointed professor of Greek studies at Wittenberg University at the age of 21. Like other humanists, he translated his real surname, Schwartzerd, into Greek. He was converted by Luther in 1518 and became his chief lieutenant and disciple. He attended all the great occasions between 1518 and 1521. He belonged to the liberal wing of Lutheranism and towards the end of his life was disowned by the hardliners. He wrote the first biography of Luther.

- John Bugenhagen (1485–1558), who changed his name to Pomeranus but this did not catch on, was a valuable force in the spread of Lutheranism. Sent from Wittenberg to north Germany, his energy, determination and effective preaching established the new Church. King Christian II invited him to Denmark and he was influential in the conversion of Scandinavia. He believed strongly in education and established schools in Hamburg and Lübeck.

- By 1524 friends and disciples of Luther had spread the word to many other German cities and founded schools to secure the young for the new faith.

- Luther's personality was critical for the way his protest developed. If he had been a retiring academic, shrinking from his perceived task, the Reformation would have been very different.

- The strength of Luther's teaching should not be underestimated. Although many welcomed his appeal to bring down the papacy, the stress on the Scriptures, the end to the power of priests and the simplicity of 'faith alone' appealed to many.

Luther's German translation of the Bible was his masterpiece, becoming one of the foundations of the German language. Its style was direct and used everyday words that ordinary people could appreciate. He also wrote over 20 hymns, the most famous being 'A Safe Stronghold our God is Still'. Songs and hymns were an effective way of spreading Lutheran ideas.

The support of the German princes

There is no doubt that the political, religious, social and economic situation of the Holy Roman Empire was highly favourable for the spread of Luther's teaching. The political situation meant that the Emperor had little control over the princes, although he needed their support for his wars and dared not risk offending them. There was also a strong tradition of anticlericalism and dislike of an Italian pope, which encouraged the princes to see the opportunity to assert their independence by supporting Lutheran ideas. Of course, not all princes were politically motivated in offering their support to Lutheranism and many were genuinely persuaded by Luther's religious arguments, but there were many advantages to be gained by following the new-style religion:

- The Church owned about 30 per cent of the lands of Germany. The land and property of the Church would be a great temptation to seize and convert for their own use. As Luther argued that monastic life was unnecessary, he had given the sanction to secularise Church property. Papal taxation could also be diverted to the use of the prince.

- The removal of the authority of the Church would increase the power of the ruler, as there was no longer a need to defer to the authority of the pope. For example, bishops could be appointed and Church revenues collected to benefit the state.

- Luther's own teachings, such as his writings of 1520, suggested that the influence of the Church should only be in spiritual matters. He gave the rulers the task of reforming the Church, supervising its organisation and preserving order. This would be an attractive option.

- Balanced against such factors were the concerns of the princes in terms of Lutheran teachings creating social disorder. Some were initially wary as Luther, in his 1520 Writings and in *The Freedom of a Christian*, seemed to be advocating that the peasants should be given more freedom and that all were equal under God. However, when a revolt broke out among the peasants in 1524–5, Luther gave his support to the princely authorities and the peasants were crushed. Once it was clear that Lutheranism was on the side of order, more princes were ready to accept Lutheranism.

Did you know?
'A Safe Stronghold our God is Still' is still in many hymn books and, with its stirring music, it became almost the anthem of the Reformation. The composer Mendelssohn used the theme in his 'Reformation Symphony'.

Cross-reference
For the **political situation in Germany**, revisit pages 20–1.

Cross-reference
The **Peasants' War** is covered later in this chapter, on pages 62–4.

Consequently, after 1529 the Lutheran princes were to provide organisation, discipline and, more importantly, military protection for the new Church. The Reformation therefore became more political and its survival a matter of European politics.

The princes who supported Lutheranism included Frederick, the Elector of Saxony (1463–1525), who protected Luther at critical moments in his early career. He even gave Luther a home – part of the Augustinian monastery where Luther used to work. It was the Elector's support for Luther that prevented him from being arrested. Frederick's support for Luther may have stemmed from a number of reasons:

Cross-reference

Frederick the Wise, the Elector of Saxony is profiled on page 42.

- The Elector was respected for his wisdom and sense of justice, and he may have wanted to give Luther a fair hearing and a chance to explain himself.
- Frederick's bitter rivalry with his brother George probably played a part – Duke George was against Luther, whereas Frederick was in support of him; Wittenberg was 'Frederick's university' and one of his professors was being accused of heresy; Luther's opponent Tetzel was working for the Archbishop of Mainz, a rival family.
- Frederick was almost certainly motivated by a sense of nationalism. There was strong anti-papal and anti-Italian feeling in Germany, with resentment against Italian interference in German affairs and against papal taxation – many felt that the pope was taking huge sums out of Germany, which would not have happened in France or Spain. Frederick sympathised with these views.

Philip of Hesse (1504–67) was an early supporter of Luther. His motives were not entirely political. Using money gained from the takeover of Church property, he founded a new university at Marburg – the first purpose-built Lutheran university – and built hospitals and schools as well as other charitable works. He arranged the Colloquy of Marburg in 1529 and was one of the six Lutheran princes who signed the protest at the Diet of Speyer against attempts to stop Lutheran services in Catholic states. He tried to prevent splits in the Protestant movement and organised the Schmalkadic League in 1531 to defend it. His bigamy and defeat at Mulhberg weakened Lutheranism.

Cross-reference

Philip of Hesse's bigamy is covered on page 67.

In 1525 John Frederick, the new Elector of Saxony, converted to Lutheranism, together with Duke Albert of Hohenzollern, who converted his Prussian lands. The alliance of Hesse and Saxony became the main support of the Lutheran movement. Together with other minor princes, about half of Germany was Lutheran by 1555.

The absence of the Emperor

In theory, Charles V, the Holy Roman Emperor, should have been able to prevent the spread of Lutheranism – by force if necessary. His failure was a reason for Luther's success. Although Charles was only 19 when he became Emperor, his family inheritance seemed to make him the most powerful ruler for 700 years.

Cross-reference

For **Charles's answer to Luther at the Diet of Worms**, see pages 50–1.

Charles was the natural defender of the Catholic Church for both personal and political reasons. He spent the first 17 years of his life in the Netherlands, where his tutor was Adrian of Utrecht (later Pope Adrian VI). Charles went to daily mass and made frequent confessions. His answer to Luther at the Diet of Worms in 1521 was evidence of his religious sincerity. He had the task of defending the Church and he took this pledge in his coronation oath very seriously. As the Catholic Church stood for a single undivided faith and its influence was international, it

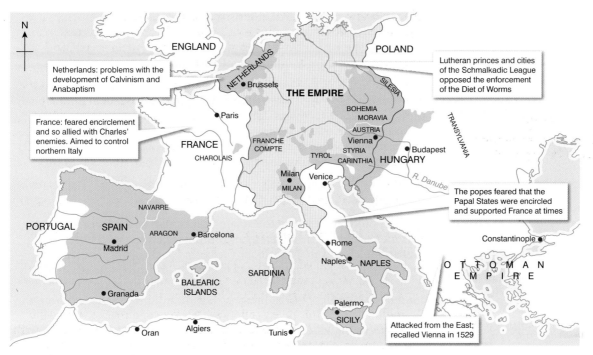

Fig. 3 *The empire of Charles V and his enemies*

helped to preserve order and authority. Finally, the unity of Christendom was essential in the face of the external pressure of the advance of Islam in eastern Europe.

However, the sheer size of Charles's empire created a variety of problems and meant he was absent for critical periods. The permanent hostility of France and the advance of the Ottoman Empire, the suspicion of the papacy and occasional revolts such as in Spain (1522) and the Netherlands (1541), as well as constant shortage of money and colossal debts by 1555, meant that Charles never had time to solve any one issue. In Germany there was a power struggle between the Emperor and the princes, who wished to increase their authority. This was happening without Luther, but Luther made it more difficult because the princes could claim that supporting Luther was sanctioned by God. Charles could try to crush Lutheranism by force, but he needed the princes to fight the French and the Turks. Charles's own strong Catholic belief and the unity of his empire meant he was reluctant to compromise.

Charles was absent from Germany after 1521 and did not return until 1529, distracted by the long war with the French, which was almost continuous from 1521–9, and by the need to defend his eastern frontier against the Ottoman Turks, who had conquered Hungary in 1526 and laid siege to Vienna in 1529. In that crucial period, the new faith attracted great support including leading princes and imperial cities and it proved impossible to reverse this process.

The impact of printing and the spoken word

The printed word

Until recently, it had been taken for granted that the spread of Luther's Reformation was based on the growth of the printing press. Luther was the first major challenger to the Church after the development of the printing press and there were large numbers of his works, such as the Bible and the catechisms, printed. The 95 Theses were printed

Cross-reference

This section should be read together with the information on the **development of printing** on pages 35–8.

Exploring the detail

The boom in publishing

Between 1518 and 1525, there were 1,465 German editions of Luther's works – perhaps 3 million copies. Other pro-Lutheran writers perhaps added about 2.5 million; Luther was a publishing sensation, but he was not alone. If we add pamphlets to the total, perhaps another 6 million works could have been printed.

Key terms

Evangelical: the belief that the message of the Christian gospel should be spread to all; belief in faith alone and the authority of the Bible alone. Evangelicals is often used as another word for Protestants.

Polemicist: someone who enjoys arguing and debating, usually in a hostile, aggressive way.

in German (together with Luther's letters to leading churchmen) and quickly distributed throughout Europe. The 1520 Writings were snapped up and analysed by a waiting public. The sheer speed of this dissemination was unprecedented, as was the war of words that accompanied Luther's career.

Pamphlets were important in the first wave of **evangelical** enthusiasm from 1518–25, which was dominated by pamphlet argument – especially the main events of Luther's protest. Luther himself was a brilliant **polemicist** and he was expert in writing shorter pamphlets. He developed a non-theological, homely style that appealed to the ordinary reader.

Printed images

A major problem of trying to explain the success of the Reformation is how its ideas could be understood by ordinary people with little or no education. They were hazy about the basic beliefs of Christianity, let alone new evangelical ideas. The Lutherans (like the Catholic Church) thought much about how to teach people. Pre-Reformation Catholic churches were full of visual imagery. Historian Robert Scribner wrote a ground-breaking study on the importance of printed images, especially the woodcut, in which he argued that the woodcut was a vital way to engage 'simple folk' in the meaning of Luther's ideas – it was crude, cheap and effective.

Activity

Thinking point

Research the works of Dürer, Holbein and Cranach. Try to find some examples relating to the work of the reformers.

Fig. 4 *A woodcut called 'The Seven Heads of Martin Luther', a link to his attack on the seven sacraments*

Woodcuts usually reduced Luther's message to a few simple points that ordinary people could understand. The most common themes were the doctrine of 'Scripture alone' – an easy slogan that could be pictured as Luther holding a Bible – and the corruption of the Church. Luther was portrayed as a saint, complete with halo, which was ironic as the evangelicals were attacking the Catholic cult of the saints. Contrasts were made between the simplicity of Christ and the Apostles and the pope and his corrupt, loose-living cardinals. Attacks on the papacy went down well, as did evil-living monks, nuns and priests who were often shown getting amusing, if cruel, punishments from the Devil and his assistant demons. The complex issue of 'faith alone' was rarely a subject for woodcuts.

There is debate over the importance of woodcuts. Their greatest use was in a short period, perhaps 1518–24, and they are not easy to interpret. Visual images are difficult and many people would have been pushed to understand the complex imagery. (Even today, visual historical sources are considered hard for many students to interpret.) Most woodcuts needed a detailed text to explain them or words on the picture. This was hard for those who could not read.

Activity

Talking point

How important was printing for the spread of the Reformation? Remember the press had existed for 60 years before 1517 and great ideas had spread across Europe long before the press was invented – Christianity, for example.

A closer look

The importance of the cities: the powerhouse of the early Reformation?

Historians such as Stephen Ozment and Euan Cameron have stressed the importance of the 'city reformation', based on the evidence that 51 free imperial cities out of 65 became Protestant. A. G. Dickens called it an 'urban event'. Part of the reason for this was the ease with which the printed word spread in the cities. There tended to be a higher degree of literacy in cities and there was often a printing house. It was easy to buy pamphlets or listen to someone reading them in the central square. Cities were tight communities and new ideas could spread rapidly. They were also often wealthy through trade or were financial centres and open to many influences from the outside world.

Cities under the control of a local bishop or lord may have seen the Reformation ideas as an opportunity to break free from control and strengthen their independence. Some may have wanted to eradicate the constant friction between the Church and town councils, while the revenues confiscated from the Church would have been a useful addition to city funds. Furthermore, the townsfolk would have been more involved in the life of the parish than in rural areas, while the life of the clergy would be more public in towns than in rural areas and abuses more common knowledge.

However, there were regional variations. In north German cities such as Lübeck and Stralsund, widespread pressure from below forced unsympathetic city councils to make changes or they were replaced. In south and central Germany there were small groups receptive to reform. They could, for example, be intellectuals who had read humanist literature or anti-clericals who had some grievance against the Church. Some councils were receptive to reform anyway, such as Breslau and Nuremberg, but they needed to avoid disorder. For example, at Nuremberg the city council (strongly supportive of humanism) invited Lutheran preachers to proclaim their ideas. However, the councillors were afraid of the wrath of Charles V if they proceeded too quickly. In 1525 they held a 'religious conversation' between Catholics and Lutherans. The result was a 'win' for the Lutherans and only then did the council allow the Mass to be abolished.

Despite the many variations, a general pattern emerged. A Lutheran preacher would arrive and there was a popular response. A meeting would be called to discuss a change – at the time this was called a 'religious conversation' – and sooner or later the council would decide to back the new faith. After that, the powers and rights of the Church were abolished, monastic houses closed and there could be some attacks on Church property and the destruction of images.

Activity

Group activity

In groups, research and present information on how the Reformation developed in various cities such as Strasbourg, Augsburg, Regensburg and Breslau.

Fig. 5 *The rich German Imperial Free City of Nuremburg, one of the first city councils to accept a Lutheran Reformation in 1525*

Key terms

Sermon: a talk on a religious theme, often explaining the Bible or giving a guide to conduct. All the reformers were tireless preachers. Two thousand of Luther's sermons survive in print, perhaps one-third of the total he preached.

Activity

Thinking point

What are the problems of assessing the impact of sermons that only survive in print?

The spoken word

Preaching the Word of God was the major mass medium of the 16th century. Luther may have said 'the Word did it all', by which he meant the power of the Gospel message, and it can be strongly argued that the **sermon** played the most important role in the immediate success of Lutheranism. Robert Scribner and Andrew Pettegree have researched the impact of the sermon in detail.

The sermon was important to the Catholic Church long before 1517. Towns paid preachers to deliver regular sermons and there were plenty of star preachers. Handbooks were printed with model sermons. Sermons were often informal, given in churchyards or under trees, and would have great novelty value. Evangelical preaching styles now stressed an explanation of the biblical texts and were suited to the less educated listener, with plenty of lists, repetition and quick summaries. Preaching was important because it bridged the gap between town and country as evangelical ideas were spread by word of mouth.

However, the impact of the sermon was not always positive. Preachers had their personal style so that the way a doctrine was put over was not necessarily consistent. Listening is hard and people often change what they have heard into what they thought they had heard. By the very violence of the language used, people were fired up to the need for change. This could lead to abuse of Catholic Church, attacks on Church property, turning out monks and nuns to beg in the streets, mockery of religious ceremonies and destroying images. It is no surprise that city councils supported the Reformation, if only to preserve order.

Luther's impact as a preacher

Luther was a working preacher and teacher. Until within a few days of his death, he was writing books and pamphlets, teaching in the university and preaching sermons. He regarded his preaching on the Word of God as his most important task and there are more than 3,000 written copies of the sermons he gave. Echoing slogans such as 'Scripture alone', he said that 'ears alone' would be the way to spread the Reformation. His impact as a preacher was critically important in 1522 when the Reformation in Wittenburg was going beyond his original intentions thanks to Andreas Carlstadt and the Zwickau prophets. Luther returned from Wartburg to Wittenburg and, deliberately dressed in his former habit of an Augustinian monk, he preached a decisive set of sermons in the town church. Delivered over a period of eight days, the sermons took back control of the reform process: Andreas Carlstadt left the city and the Zwickau prophets were driven out of town. The public now accepted Luther's more conservative approach to reform.

Michael Mullett in his book *Martin Luther* (2004) comments that this set of sermons was a masterpiece and typical of Luther's style as a preacher. They addressed the hearers in a language familiar to the urban population and gave simple insights into his own life and habits. All hearers agreed that his voice was compelling ('this man is kind, gentle and cheerful. His voice is sweet and sonorous') and he had a conversational style, sometimes portraying himself as just an ordinary *Kerl* – a bloke.

Fig. 6 *A woodcut of Luther preaching. The power of preaching the Word of God was central to his message*

> Take myself as an example. I opposed indulgences and all the papists, but never by force. I simply taught, preached and wrote God's Word; otherwise I did nothing. And while I slept or drank beer with my friends, the Word so greatly weakened the papacy that no prince or emperor ever inflicted such losses upon it. I did nothing, the Word did everything.

1   *Extract from one of Luther's sermons*

The consequences of the Lutheran Reformation

Although Luther saw his ideas as bringing about religious change, it is impossible to separate religion from politics or social and economic problems. In the 1520s the Imperial Knights and the peasants used Lutheranism to further their own agendas. After 1525 Lutheranism would be forced into a political struggle to defend itself against the Emperor Charles V and the Catholic princes.

The Knights' War, 1522–3

The Imperial Knights were under the direct authority of the Emperor but their status was under threat. The knights seemed to want political change to restore their former prestige. Their leaders were Ulrich von Hutten (1488–1523) and Franz von Sickingen. Hutten became known for his skilful writings against the pope and produced propaganda appealing

Cross-reference

Andreas Carlstadt and the **Zwickau prophets** are outlined on page 53.

Activity

Source analysis

Read Source 1 and Source 1 on page 40.

1 How does Luther try to create links with his listeners?

2 How effective would such sermons be?

Cross-reference

For the **threat to the status of the Imperial Knights**, refer back to page 20.

to Germans to join Luther's cause. Von Sickingen had had a long career in minor wars and offered his services to Luther in 1520 as a protector of the new movement and, for a while, Luther went along with this.

Key profile

Franz von Sickingen

Franz von Sickingen (1481–1523) made his name in private warfare between 1513 and 1517. He became the self-styled champion of Luther and promoted a strong German nationalism. He was killed at the end of the Knights' War.

In 1522 the knights attacked the city of Trier, which was owned by the Catholic Church, claiming this was being done in the name of the Lutheran Reformation. The attack failed. German princes attacked the knights and dispersed them. Many were hunted down and killed – the Imperial Knights were no longer a political force. Luther now made it clear that he would have nothing to do with violence and that his programme was religious change. However, the printers linked Hutten with Luther, especially in visual imagery, portraying them as comrades fighting the pope on behalf of the German people. This encouraged others to believe that Luther's teaching was about opposition to authority.

The Peasants' War, 1524–5

Did you know?

Allegedly, the Peasants' War was sparked off because the Countess von Lupfen made her husband's tenants spend a holiday gathering snail shells on which to wind her wool.

Fig. 7 *The Peasants' War*

Cross-reference

The **Bundschuh movement** is outlined on page 3.

The Peasants' War was a series of serious outbreaks of violence – the largest ever revolt of the German masses before the 20th century. Although peasants formed the main element of the revolt, townspeople and nobles also participated.

Its causes were linked to a number of issues:

- The protests were part of a long series of outbreaks of violence since 1450 such as in the Bundschuh movement.
- Bad harvests and famines between 1500 and 1524 had led to utter misery. Protests were often the only way to express discontent.
- In the south and west of Germany, landlords were restricting peasant freedom. It was hard to move from one estate to another, it was forbidden to seek food in the lords' forests and labour service on the lords' land was increased.
- Rapid population increase led to the division of existing plots of land. In parts of central Germany, about half of the peasantry had not enough land to feed a family. At the same time, heavier taxes were imposed.
- Peasant complaints seemed to focus on the grasping demands of landlords who were members of the Church. Peasants had to pay tithes (one-tenth of their products a year) to support the Church.
- Many peasants were still serfs, their lives controlled by the landowners – their freedom was restricted and their status degrading.

Peasant protests seemed to begin in southern Germany and rapidly moved to central Germany. Although many were orderly, the protests increasingly turned to violence as monasteries and convents, churches and castles were looted. The peasants (whose numbers in fact included urban craftsmen and more wealthy peasants) had no clear aims and no coordinated leadership. Where their aims were written down, as for example in the Twelve Articles of Memmingen and the Tyrolean Constitution, they were a mixture of detailed economic changes and religious demands possibly inspired by the views of Luther. However, after the initial wave of destruction, the peasants did not have a definite programme.

When the local rulers recovered from the shock, both Philip of Hesse and the Elector Frederick acted decisively to crush the rebels. Fanatics such as Thomas Münzer, who preached that a kingdom of God would be set up on earth preceded by an orgy of violence against the Church, really alarmed them. He was defeated at Frankenhausen in 1525. The local rulers, both Lutheran and Catholic, carried out terrible reprisals and the Peasants' War – a very one-sided affair – was over.

Luther and the Peasants' War

Although Stephen Ozment has argued that Luther's Reformation was powered by the cities, Peter Blickle has put forward the view that Luther appealed greatly to the rural populations. This is supported by the following points:

- Lutheran preachers in cities attracted great crowds from the surrounding rural areas. Such would witness a Lutheran service and report back – thus the Reformation would be spread.
- Luther's message seemed to be that the 'common man' was the ideal Christian. Christian liberty was open to everyone and the Bible provided ordinary people with a weapon of protest when it was heard in German. Jesus had critical things to say about the rich and property owners.
- Information about how much the peasants understood of Luther's views is limited. They thought they understood his social views, but probably did not grasp salvation by 'faith alone'.
- By studying the content of the cheap woodcuts that were published for those who could not read, much of the message the peasants received was a negative view of the pope and monks rather than a positive view of Luther's teachings.

Activity

Revision exercise

Create a poster or flyer advertising the grievances of the peasants.

Exploring the detail

The Twelve Articles of Memmingen

These contained demands such as the rights of the poor to choose their own ministers, the abolition of most tithes, the abolition of serfdom, the restoration of common lands, and free access to fishing, hunting and wood gathering.

Cross-reference

Thomas Münzer is explored on page 98.

Fig. 8 *German peasants arming for war. The risings seriously threatened the authorities in the Church and struck fear in local rulers*

■ Luther's message seemed to say that, with the power of the pope broken and authority cast down, now was the time for the poor to rise up and change the social order. The hundreds of Lutheran ministers who marched with the rebels seemed to back this up.

Luther's attitude to authority and rebellion, however, was consistent. In his 1520 Writings he said he would always side with those in authority, although he urged rulers to treat the common man with fairness and consider the burdens they faced, blaming them for taxing the poor too much. In the 1524–5 rebellion he first advised conciliation, but then demanded swift action to end the rebellion quickly:

> If a peasant is in open rebellion, then he is outside the law of God. Rebellion brings with it a land full of murders and bloodshed. Therefore let everyone who can, smite, slay and stab, secretly or openly, remembering that nothing can be more poisonous, hurtful or devilish than a rebel. It is just as when one must kill a mad dog.

*From Luther's pamphlet **Against the Murderous and Thieving Hordes of Peasants***

Although the rest of the pamphlet advises more caution, this 'smite, slay and stab' pamphlet caused a storm of criticism and dismayed Luther's friends. The Peasants' War and Luther's reaction to it was a critical turning point because it turned peasants away from Lutheranism while helping to convince the princes that Luther was not a dangerous revolutionary and was on their side.

Question

Why did the Peasants' War break out in 1524?

Did you know?

The civil war in Germany is usually known as the Schmalkaldic War, after the League of Schmalkalden.

Cross-reference

The **alliances of the Lutheran princes** are explained on page 66.

Civil war and the religious Peace of Augsburg, 1555

In the next 30 years the success of Lutheranism became a political issue, ultimately decided by war – a German civil war. Charles V made war on his own rebellious subjects in an attempt to enforce the Edict of Worms. The princes who became Lutheran were forced to defend themselves by creating alliances between themselves such as the League of Schmalkalden and received backing from foreign powers such as France and England. However, not all the Lutheran princes and cities supported such alliances or fought for them. The Catholic princes were in a difficult position. States such as Bavaria supported Charles V's attempts to control Lutheranism, indeed creating their own leagues and fighting the Lutheran princes who took up arms against the Emperor, but they did not give him complete support as they were afraid of increasing his power.

Civil war

When Charles left the empire in 1521, he left his brother Ferdinand as his deputy as President of the Regency Council. Ferdinand's task was to enforce the Edict of Worms.

Key profile

Ferdinand I

Ferdinand I (1503–64) was ruler of the Habsburg lands from 1521 and Holy Roman Emperor in the years 1556–64. Ferdinand took a more flexible approach than his brother to dealing with religious issues within the empire because he needed the military and financial support of the princes in his struggle to protect the Habsburg lands from the Turks. Although he was a loyal supporter of Charles, they fell out in the 1540s over Charles's plan to reunite the Habsburg possessions under the rule of his son. Ferdinand refused to accept this and did not help Charles in his final wars 1551–5. Ferdinand realised that there was no chance of defeating the Protestant princes and negotiated the compromise Peace of Augsburg in 1555.

The early 1520s showed the futility of attempts to enforce the Edict of Worms. At the Diets of Nuremburg in 1522 and 1524, the papal representative demanded the arrest of Lutheran preachers and the capture of Luther who was 'worse than the Turks', but there was great hostility to the pope. The 1524 Diet used two arguments, saying it would enforce the Edict if the pope would first reform the Church and stop taking money out of Germany and also that a German national council should be called to settle the problems of the Church. Both were unacceptable to the papacy but were used frequently in the coming years.

Pope Clement VII rejected the idea of a council and had a clever move of his own. He called a meeting of the Catholic princes at Regensburg in 1524 with a view to enlisting their support. Dukes John and William of Bavaria attended with Ferdinand of Austria. The reward for support was generous – all received one-fifth of the revenue of the Church in their lands. For them, there was not much financial reason to support Luther.

The meeting decided to enforce the Edict of Worms, but called for the reform of abuses. Regensburg was important because it led to the Catholic princes forming the defensive League of Dessau in 1525. In response, Saxony, Hesse and Brandenburg formed the League of Torgau in 1526. Already Germany was starting to divide along religious lines.

The First Diet of Speyer, 1526

Charles V was unable to deal effectively with the Lutheran problem because of wars with France and the Turks, which had started in 1521. However, his great victory over the French at Pavia (1525) gave him space to order Ferdinand to call another Diet in 1526. Charles demanded that those who broke the laws of the empire should be punished. By the time the Diet met, the Turks had begun their advance into Hungary and the French had declared war again. Instead of obedience to the Emperor, both Catholic and Lutheran princes passed the suitably vague declaration that 'each one should conduct himself towards the Edict of Worms as he should answer for it towards God and the Emperor' – in other words, each prince could do as he liked with regard to religion.

The issue of enforcing the Edict of Worms was put on hold. However, the League of Torgau opened negotiations with enemies of the Habsburgs such as France and Denmark for help in the future.

The Second Diet of Speyer, 1529

By 1529 Charles's position had greatly improved. Peace had been made with France and the pope, Ferdinand had been crowned King of Hungary and the Turks had been stopped at Vienna. The spread of Lutheranism to north Germany had alarmed the Catholic princes.

The Diet was made to give up its declaration of 1526 and a proposal was issued to stop Lutheran services in Catholic states. A group of 6 Lutheran princes and 14 imperial cities signed a protest about these points, hence the name 'Protestants'.

Did you know?
Luther himself was displeased that his followers were called Lutherans; he thought they should simply be called Christians. The word 'Protestant' originally covered only those rulers who 'protested' at the decisions of the Diet of Speyer in 1529. Later, the meaning widened to include other groups founded by, for example, Zwingli and John Calvin. Lutherans are Protestants, but not all Protestants are Lutherans.

Charles left Germany in a rage, but after he had been officially crowned Emperor by Pope Clement VII in Italy (the last emperor to be so) he returned with another attempt to bring the parties together as he called another Diet.

The Diet of Augsburg, 1530

The business of the Diet was to find a common ground between Lutherans and Catholics. As Luther was an outlaw under the Edict of Worms, Luther did not attend. This was probably a good thing because he had already decided that no compromise was possible. Instead, Philip Melanchthon was invited to present Lutheran doctrines to the Emperor. He was ideal as he was a natural conciliator. Melanchthon drew up the Confession (a statement of beliefs) of Augsburg in the hope of bringing the sides together. Its 28 Articles were written in a non-controversial style and many articles were matters of faith common to both Catholics and Lutherans. Where there were differences, moderation was attempted. For example, although veneration of saints was not acceptable, their images in churches were. Clergy were allowed to marry, but celibacy was not condemned. However, the number of sacraments was fixed at two; the Mass was not a sacrifice; Communion in Both Kinds was allowed (but not insisted on); justification by 'faith alone' was defined; and the 'abuses' of the Catholic Church condemned. The authority of the pope was not absolutely accepted. On the other hand, Anabaptist teaching on adult baptism and their refusal to take part in civic affairs was denounced. Zwingli would not accept the teaching on the Mass and images in churches. Catholics rejected the Confession, while the more radical groups felt there was too much given away. Even so, it was an important statement of Lutheran belief and helped to restore unity after the Marburg discussions of 1529.

The Emperor, however, declared that he would enforce the Edict of Worms and gave the Lutherans six months to return to the Church.

The success of Lutheranism, 1531–41

Despite this bold declaration, Charles's position weakened. The Turks resumed their attack on Hungary and he desperately needed money and men to defend the Habsburg lands. In the Mediterranean the Ottoman navy was becoming dangerous. The Catholic princes had shown that they would not side totally with the Emperor's wishes. Lutheran organisation was becoming stronger and, in March 1531, 8 princes and 11 city states met at Schmalkalde to form the Schmalkaldic League led by John of Saxony and Philip of Hesse. Although this was defensive, it promised to protect any state where the true gospel was under threat. The League claimed to control 12,000 men. Under threat from the Turks, Charles declared at the Diet of Nuremberg (1532) that he would take no action against the League in return for men and money. An imperial truce was declared and the emperor rode out against the Turks, with both Lutherans and Catholics in his army.

After 1532 Lutheran successes continued. In 1534 Philip of Hesse organised the invasion of Württemberg to restore its exiled ruler. The Schmalkaldic League was greatly expanded when more cities joined. Francis I of France joined it and Henry VIII of England became its protector. It now claimed to control an army of 20,000 men. Even Ducal Saxony became Lutheran after the death of Duke George.

Inevitably, a Catholic league was formed to resist the Lutheran one in 1538. However, it seemed that by 1541, as other states became Lutheran, nothing could stop the movement sweeping across Germany.

■ Activity

Challenge your thinking

Research the terms of the Confession on the internet. They are written in clear language and give an insight into the moderation attempted.

■ Cross-reference

For more on **Anabaptism**, see Chapter 8.

Charles made another attempt to find a solution by bringing Catholic and Lutheran theologians together at Regensburg in 1541. The failure to reach a compromise led him to believe that force was the only answer. The political situation was turning in his favour:

- The bigamy of Philip of Hesse was a huge propaganda coup for the Catholics.
- A war with France from 1542–4 ended with the Peace of Crépy – France agreed not to support the Schmalkaldic League.
- In 1545 a truce was organised with the Turks.
- In 1545 the general council of the Church, which had been demanded for decades by Catholics and Charles V, finally had its first meeting.
- In 1546 Pope Paul III made an alliance with the Emperor, offering him money and men to support a war against the Lutherans.

Charles had managed to weaken the Protestant Schmalkaldic League by dividing it, although it was never a united organisation. The League did not represent all the Protestant side; Brandenburg, for example, did not join. Some of the younger Lutheran princes tended to put their political ambitions before their support for Lutheranism. The most important of these was Duke Maurice of Saxony as he had military ability gained in fighting for the Emperor in the early 1540s, ambition and ruthless political skills. He refused to join the League. He hoped for better from the Emperor.

Key profile

Maurice of Saxony

Maurice of Saxony (1521–53) became Duke of Saxony in 1541. His uncle was Luther's early opponent, the Catholic Duke George. His father became a Lutheran and Maurice inherited the bitter feud with the Electoral branch of the family, especially the present Elector, John Frederick. In 1541 he married Agnes, daughter of Philip of Hesse. Despite the links with the Schmalkaldic League, Maurice supported the Emperor in the war of 1546–7 and then the Emperor's enemies after 1551. He was regarded either as a Judas or a supreme example of political realism. He died from his injuries in battle in 1553.

Exploring the detail

The bigamy of Philip of Hesse

Philip of Hesse was the political leader of the Lutheran side but his personal life was a mess. He had made an unhappy marriage in 1523 to Christina, daughter of Duke George of Saxony, but he had many affairs and dealings with prostitutes. Recovering from syphilis in 1539, he met a 17-year-old noblewoman half his age, Margaret (strangely, distantly related to Luther's wife) and insisted on marrying her. Her mother wanted some official approval and Philip wrote to Luther, asking for approval of a bigamous marriage. It seemed to Luther that Philip was going to go ahead anyway and there was a threat that Philip would leave the Lutheran cause. Luther gave his approval for the bigamous marriage. A complication was that the Diet had passed a law making bigamy punishable by death. There was a tremendous scandal and Philip had to beg the Emperor for mercy.

Cross-reference

See the rulers of Saxony on page 41.

Backed by the large numbers of Spanish and Italian troops coming to his support and with the help of his brother, Ferdinand, Charles felt strong enough for a showdown. In July 1546 the Diet of Regensburg put John Frederick of Saxony under the Imperial Ban and he was ordered to give up Lutheranism. Maurice of Saxony was promised the lands and title of the Elector in return for his support.

War with the Schmalkaldic League began in September 1546. Only Hesse, Saxony and Württemberg and four imperial cities actually fought. Maurice occupied John Frederick's lands in December 1546, but the League forces drove him out. However, he was able to unite his forces with the Emperor and in April 1547 the forces of Charles V routed the troops of the League at Mühlberg. John Frederick was captured, Philip of Hesse surrendered in July and was imprisoned, despite a promise from Charles. Maurice was granted Electoral Saxony. Charles had gained control of much of Germany.

Collapse and compromise, 1547–55

However, Charles's triumph proved short-lived because the scale of his success created enemies. In 1548 he forced the Diet at Augsburg to accept a new statement of faith: the Interim. This gave a few concessions to the Protestant side such as allowing Communion in Both Kinds (that is, both the bread and wine) and clerical marriage, but otherwise confirmed Catholic teachings. The Protestant leaders condemned it, especially Lutheran cities such as Magdeburg, which led resistance. Pope Paul III condemned even the small concessions made, while both Catholic and Protestant rulers were dismayed at the treatment of the defeated at Mühlberg. Ferdinand withdrew his support when Charles tried to have his son Philip recognised as ruler of all his empire, thus excluding Ferdinand.

Catholic princes in Germany feared Charles would assert his authority over them, while in Europe the new King of France, Henry II (1547–59) viewed the Emperor's success as a danger to the balance of power and began to create a coalition against him.

In 1550 the Baltic princes – an area not under imperial control – formed the Second League of Torgau to defend their rights and the Lutheran faith. Maurice, dismayed that he had not received all he was promised for supporting Charles, changed sides and joined the League in 1551. The League made the Treaty of Chambord in 1552 with France. Charles's enemies had gathered against him, his friends did not give him support – even the pope and his brother stood aside. He could only rely for money on Spanish taxation.

French troops and the forces of Maurice of Saxony overran southern Germany. Taken by surprise, and in declining health, Charles was forced to flee to the Austrian lands. It was essential to buy off the German princes. Once again, Maurice changed sides. Realising he had not enough troops to force the issue and breaking with Henry II, he reached agreement with the Emperor at the Treaty of Passau in August 1552. The Lutheran princes would be allowed freedom of worship until the next Diet and John Frederick and Philip of Hesse were released.

Maurice had been an important force in the survival of Lutheranism. On his death, the Electorate and the Duchy were granted to his brother, Augustus.

The Peace of Augsburg, 1555

Charles left Ferdinand to negotiate a compromise at the Diet of Augsburg, which Charles did not attend. He abdicated his titles in 1556 and retired to a Spanish monastery. The terms of the Peace of Augsburg were:

- Catholics and Protestants were to be equally represented on the Imperial Council.
- All property of the Church taken over before 1552 was to remain Protestant, but no further secularisations of Church lands were allowed.
- Every secular prince should decide on the religion of the people of its territories. This principle of *cuius regio, eius religio* ('whoever ruled a state should decide its religion') was the cornerstone of the religious settlement. People could move freely to a state of their religious choice. This principle did not apply to the cities.

The Peace of Augsburg lasted over 60 years and it gave legal force to the reality that Lutheranism could not be crushed by force. It marked the

Cross-reference

For the **First League of Torgau**, see page 65.

failure of Charles V to preserve the unity of the empire; the unity of Christian Europe had been destroyed. The peace did not give freedom of worship to any other religion. There was no mention of Calvinism, which was developing rapidly. The period after 1555 opened a new and more bitter religious conflict between the forces of a revived Catholic Church and a tough dynamic Protestant faith: Calvinism.

Cross-reference

Calvinism is the subject of Chapters 6 and 7.

The **revived Catholic Church** is explored in Chapters 9–11.

Summary question

Why was Charles V unable to prevent the spread of the Lutheran Reformation in the 1520s?

Learning outcomes

In this section you have developed an understanding of Luther's background and ideas, why he challenged the Catholic Church in 1517 and how and why that challenge, as expressed in the 95 Theses, led to his condemnation as a heretic and his final break with the Church in 1521. You have also examined the reasons for the success of Lutheranism after 1521, examining factors such as the roles of Luther himself, the princes and the cities as well as the problems of Charles V. The ways in which Luther's message was spread have also been evaluated. Finally, you have studied the political outcome of Luther's protest, involving the competing interests of the Emperor, the Catholic and Protestant princes, and foreign powers, and analysed why Lutheranism was able to survive until the compromise of 1555.

Activity

Thinking point

Write a speech that Charles V might have given to defend his policy in Germany. To begin, you could try to get hold of a copy of the speech Charles gave when he abdicated in October 1555. Everyone present was moved to tears – including Charles himself.

AQA Examination-style questions

(a) Explain why the Diet of Worms took place. *(12 marks)*

AQA Examiner's tip Part a) does not need description so all of focus should be on the reasons why the Diet took place. You might like to consider the motives of Luther, Charles V, the Elector Frederick and the Church authorities.

(b) How important was the sermon in the success of the Lutheran Reformation to 1555? *(24 marks)*

AQA Examiner's tip Part b) requires balance, analysis and judgement. The focus is on the sermon and perhaps the most straightforward way to tackle this is to look at ways in which the sermon was, or was not, important. Another approach would be to balance the part of the sermon against other reasons for the success of the Lutheran Reformation to 1555, such as its basic appeal, the opportunities afforded by the printing press, the support of the princes, the position of Charles V and the parts played by negotiation and by warfare. You might conclude that methods of spreading the word were less important than practical issues such as political rivalry and organisation.

John Calvin (1509–64) and the Genevan Reformation

The establishment of Calvinism

In this chapter you will learn about:

- Calvin's writings and theological ideas

- his first and second Genevan ministries and the conversion of Geneva

- the organisation of the Genevan Church

- the role of the Consistory, pastors and Grabeau.

Activity

Thinking point

You are invited to form your own opinion of Calvin and his work as you study this chapter, so note down as much evidence as you can find about what might have won him friends and made him enemies in the 16th century.

Fig. 1 *John Calvin, from a 17th-century engraving*

John Calvin is best remembered for the religious reforms he carried out in Geneva, but not everyone who lived there loved him:

> One named his dog after him, rude papers were left in his pulpit. Songs were written against him, men abused him as a hypocrite and a tyrant, thirty tennis players chose for their game the square outside the church where he was teaching. Someone offered money to anyone who would assassinate him.

1　　　　　　　　　　　　　*Adapted from O. Chadwick, **The Reformation**, 1972*

Key profile

John Calvin

John Calvin (1509–64) was born at Noyon, northern France, the eldest of three brothers. In 1523 he entered the University of Paris to take a BA, intending to study theology, but five years later his father changed him to a law course at Orléans. In 1531 he returned to Paris on his father's death and the following year he published his first work, a humanist study of the Roman thinker Seneca.

Calvin was a brilliant linguist in Hebrew, Greek and Latin. He was influenced by French Lutherans and seems to have had a quiet conversion in 1533. After the Day of the Placards in 1534, the French authorities began a persecution of suspect reformers and Calvin left France for the Swiss city of Basle, where in 1535–6 he published *Institutes of the Christian Religion*.

In 1536 he was returning to Paris from a visit to Italy when he stopped off in Geneva, where William Farel persuaded him to stay to help reform the city. In 1537 he presented reform proposals to the city council, but these were rejected, and the next year Calvin and Farel were asked to leave Geneva. From 1538–41 Calvin stayed in Strasbourg, where he married Idelette de Bure, but in 1541 he returned to Geneva where he established the Ecclesiastical Ordinances. By 1555 opposition to his reforms had been defeated. Calvin died in Geneva in 1564.

Calvin's writings and religious ideas

Institutes of the Christian Religion

It was in the Swiss city of Basle, where he had fled from possible persecution by the Catholic Francis I of France, that the French scholar and reformist thinker, John Calvin, wrote one of the most influential reference works in religious history – the *Institutes of the Christian Religion*. This was first published in Latin in 1535–6. A more accurate English translation of its Latin title would be 'Introduction to Basic Christian Piety', which perhaps better explains its contents. Calvin's book was a six-chapter introduction to the Christian faith. It was not an outline of Calvinism; its purpose was to explain the evangelical Protestant faith and at the same time show that it could be well organised and effective. No other Protestant reformer had produced such a book. Although its essential features were not changed, the final version of 1559 contained 80 chapters. Its lucid style and clear structure made it influential, especially in the French translation of 1541. In the opening chapter Calvin sets out his subject: he will deal with the Creator God and those He created, humankind itself. To gain knowledge of God should be the aim of humankind and God's greatest act is the creation of humankind. The book was arranged in a traditional structure: the 'Knowledge of God the Creator'; 'the Knowledge of God, the Redeemer in Christ'; 'the work of the Holy Spirit'. Calvin's starting point was that God held supreme power:

> God is omnipotent [all-powerful] and omniscient [all-knowing]. God is the fountain of all goodness and we must seek nothing elsewhere but in him.

2   *From **Institutes of the Christian Religion**, 1535–6*

God intervened in the life of the world and would come to judge all humankind. The sinner should attempt to know God through the Scriptures, but it was important to accept that God was the righteous judge and so the sinner must throw himself on His mercy. The only thing that sinners could do was to 'beg, grovel and abase themselves' before the throne of God.

Calvin's theology was not new and he accepted much of the work of the Lutheran reformers: salvation by faith alone; the Bible as the basis of all belief; the priesthood of all believers; predestination. He was a fierce critic of the papacy and wanted to root out any thought or practice that seemed to hint at support for the Catholic Church even on the Protestant side.

On the issue of the sacraments, Calvin asserted that infant baptism was the only acceptable form, thereby distancing himself from Anabaptism. On the Communion, Calvin tried to find a middle way over the problem of what was the nature of the bread and wine. Catholics claimed that Christ was actually present on the altar by a theory called transubstantiation; Luther had stated that Christ was actually present but denied the theory of transubstantiation. However, Calvin argued that Christ could not really be in the bread because Christ was in heaven. However, he rejected Zwingli's teaching that the bread and wine were merely symbols. Instead, he taught that Christ was really present but in a spiritual sense and the bread and wine remained the same. This seemed a good compromise, although the Lutherans and Zwinglians rejected it.

> From the physical things shown in the sacrament [the bread and wine] we are led to spiritual things by a kind of analogy. Thus when bread is given as a symbol of Christ's body it nourishes and keeps the life of our body, but as it is Christ's body it is the only food to enliven our soul.

3   *From **Institutes of the Christian Religion**, 1535–6*

Fig. 2 *A page from Calvin's highly influential **Institutes of the Christian Religion***

Cross-reference

To recap on the doctrines of **salvation by faith alone**, the **Bible as the basis of all belief**, the **priesthood of all believers** and **predestination**, look back to page 44.

Cross-reference

The issue of **infant baptism** is discussed on page 96.

The debate as to the nature of **bread and wine** of the Communion is outlined on pages 46 and 54.

The Ecclesiastical Ordinances

The organisation of the Church was a vital point for Calvin and this differed from Luther's, who left organisation to the princes – in effect, state control. Calvin said the Church must have a structure, which meant that properly appointed ministers must preach the Word and administer the sacraments. In 1541 Calvin drafted an ecclesiastical constitution for Geneva. His condition for taking on responsibility for the spiritual welfare of the city was that these Ecclesiastical Ordinances should be accepted. With some modifications, this draft was approved by the political authorities. This constitution set in place a Calvinist Church order. In terms consistent with Calvin's theology, it established a ministry which, instead of having bishops, was based on four offices: pastors (or ministers), doctors (or teachers), deacons and elders. A strict Church discipline was called for and those who failed to keep to the high standards required of Calvinists were disciplined by a court that was a unique feature of Calvinism: the Consistory of pastors and elders which, after 1555, possessed the right to excommunicate (ban from Church membership) persistent sinners.

The most difficult problem for Calvin was the relationship between the Church and the civil power of the Genevan Council, but he believed strongly that the Church should work in harmony with, but be independent of, the civil power. It should also be able to enforce its views on social and moral issues.

The Ordinances set up four orders of ministers:

- Pastors: the duties of the Venerable Company of Pastors were to teach, preach, administer the Word of God and 'admonish and correct people's conduct in public and in private'.
- Doctors: these were to teach true doctrines and to act as teachers in the schools.
- Deacons: chosen by the Little Council, deacons were to care for the poor, needy and sick.
- Elders: these were to 'supervise every person's conduct, and to warn backsliders and those of a disorderly life. After that, where necessary, they should report to the ministers who will arrange for correction' – in fact, to enforce the discipline of the Church. The elders were 12 laypeople from different parts of the city, so that everyone could be checked. They were selected by the Little Council and chosen for their good lives.

The Ordinances set up schools in each parish for children of primary age. Schoolmasters were appointed to the boys' school and the separate girls' school; appointments were confirmed by the Little Council. Sunday schools continued to strengthen Calvinist teaching. Calvin supervised the standards of education and there was soon a generation who knew nothing but his teaching. This strengthened his support and his detailed curriculum and regulations show that he saw the importance of indoctrinating the young as well as teaching them. However, there was no college for higher education until the Genevan Academy in 1559.

The Ecclesiastical Ordinances provided the first example of a clear, well-defined structure of government for a Protestant Church. It was hard to improve on this model; the structure claimed to mirror the organisation of the early Christian Church and was based on the Scriptures. It was widely copied.

■ Cross-reference

More details on the **Consistory** can be found later on page 78.

■ Exploring the detail

The Church

For the reformers, the Church meant the whole number of believers gathered together. For Catholics in the 16th century, it meant the hierarchical structure of pope, bishops and parish clergy.

■ Cross-reference

The **structure of the Genevan government**, including the two councils, is discussed on page 76.

For more on the **Genevan Academy**, see page 88.

The changes that the Genevan Council made to Calvin's original draft showed that its members were determined to keep their authority and this was written into the final version. In particular, the Consistory had to report offenders to the Little Council for judgement and sentence. Clearly, there was potential for clashes between Church and Council, as Calvin identified his views with the voice of God and expected the Council to carry them out.

Double predestination

Calvin's most famous and controversial doctrine is 'double predestination'. He believed that God had predestined, or already decided before their birth, that some people should be saved ('the elect') and some should be damned ('the reprobate'). According to his views, there was nothing anyone could do to change this. Although the idea of an 'elect' that would be saved had already been accepted by other reformers such as Luther and Zwingli, they stressed 'single predestination' – that God elects those to be saved. Calvin went further. He drew the logical conclusion that most would be damned – hence 'double predestination', meaning that a few were predestined to eternal life *and* many to eternal damnation.

The idea of predestination came from St Paul in the New Testament and St Augustine and it had been an issue since early Christianity. Once again, it relates to the problem of free will and St Augustine's view that our ability to choose the good is limited. 'Faith alone' stressed that nothing could be done to earn 'the grace of God'; so God must select those to obtain grace. As God is all-knowing, He will know who has been selected ('predestined').

However, Calvin's stress on the all-knowing nature of God led him to state that, before time began, God created all things in the full knowledge of what would happen in human history and to each individual. Mankind is saved or lost through the choice of God:

Fig. 3 *Calvin, Luther and the pope engaged in a theological discussion, from a French cartoon of 1600*

> Cross-reference
>
> **St Augustine** is profiled in more detail on pages 44–5.

> As Scripture shows, we say that God from the first set up his eternal and unchangeable plan, and decided once and for all and long before those who were to receive salvation, and those whom, on the other hand, he would give over to destruction. He chose the elect through his freely given mercy, but by his just and blameless decree, he has given over others to damnation. This decree, I admit, is a fearful one, but it is impossible to deny that God had foreknowledge what the end of man was to be before he created him

4   From *Institutes of Christian Religion*, 1535–6

Double predestination was not at first central to Calvin's theology; in the 1536 edition of the *Institutes*, it is mentioned twice. His views were gradually expanded, partly as a defence against those who attacked them. The doctrine raised all sorts of problems that are impossible to answer. How could a God of goodness decide on eternal damnation? What is the point of trying to be a good person?

Calvin always taught that no one could know whether they were the elect or the reprobate, but that everyone should live their lives in the hope of salvation. Historian Geoffrey Elton argues that, however, in practice true Calvinists came to think it was possible to know you were one of the elect on earth and that this belief created great self-confidence. Success on earth seemed to imply 'election'.

The Bible as the basis for all belief

As with the other main Protestant reformers, Calvin acknowledged the Bible as the final authority and the complete revelation of God's purposes. According to Calvin, the Bible alone defined all theology and human institutions and all doctrines had to be tested against it. This marked out Protestants from Catholics (who gave equal weight to the authority of the Church) and Anabaptists (who supported personal interpretations).

His own doctrinal statements were based on these Scriptures. Calvin did not believe that every word of the Bible was literally true, but he tried to limit speculation on religious matters by insisting on the primacy of the Word of God. By using the Bible as a basis for all belief, he believed the Church could recover its original vitality and purity.

> The Scriptures, gathering together the knowledge of God in our minds which is otherwise confused, disperses the darkness and clearly shows us to the true God … nothing is omitted which is necessary to know, and nothing is taught except what it is of advantage to know.

5   *From **Institutes of Christian Religion**, 1535–6*

However, the Scriptures could not simply be read without commentary and analysis. Much of Calvin's writing and preaching was devoted to explaining the books of the Bible, trying to define the correct texts and interpretations to help believers. Consequently, his insistence that the Bible was correct led others to suggest that it was a belief in his own interpretation of the Bible that drove his faith.

Calvin was different from the other Protestant leaders in that his attitude to the Bible was more hardline. Some felt that parts of the Scripture had less status than others (Luther called the Epistle of St James 'an epistle of straw' because it puts a case for good works) or even that some books should not have been included. Calvin was outraged at these suggestions, which implied that all the Bible was not the complete way in which God spoke to humankind. This explains his attitude to Castellio.

Cross-reference

Calvin's attitude to **Castellio** is outlined on page 85.

The conversion of Geneva and the structure and authority of the Genevan Church

Calvin's first ministry in Geneva, 1536–8

Calvin was returning to Paris on family business when he stayed the night in Geneva in 1536. He was approached by William Farel, who had already begun a reformation in the city and had suspended the Mass, to aid Farel in the task of reform. Calvin comments that he wished to continue an academic life, but that Farel 'who burned with an extraordinary zeal for the Gospel' said that God would curse him if he did not stay and help. So began Calvin's association with Geneva.

Fig. 4 *Old Geneva (modern photo). Calvin lived here in the Old Town in the Rue des Chanoines*

Key profile

William Farel

William Farel (1489–1565) was a French reformer who was initially interested in Catholic reform but later joined Lutheran sympathisers. He was a fiery critic of the Catholic Church. In 1532 he became a minister in Geneva and in 1536 persuaded Calvin to come to develop a reformation. Both were expelled in 1538 and Farel persuaded Calvin to return again in 1541. He was a close friend of Calvin.

The political context is important. Geneva was in a state of confusion. It was a city of about 10,000 people (about five times the size of Wittenberg). Its population was French-speaking. Geneva was technically under the authority of the Duke of Savoy, but authority was disputed between the Bishop of Geneva and the city council, who claimed it was an independent republic. Geneva was positioned between France and Berne and Geneva allied with Berne in a bid for independence. In 1527

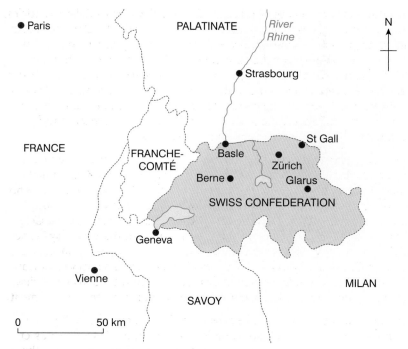

Fig. 5 *Geneva and its neighbours in the mid 16th century*

the bishop was driven from the city and his troops were defeated by 1536. Berne decided to support a reformation and Geneva followed suit led by Farel. Supporters of the Savoy, French and Berne factions were still causing trouble in the streets when Calvin arrived. The city wanted to free itself from interference by Berne. By 1536 the city had already agreed to its own Protestant Reformation; it was Calvin and Farel's task to organise it. In 1536 Calvin presented a Confession (statement) of Faith to the Little Council and, in January 1537, 21 Articles on the Organisation of the Church.

Geneva had a complex structure of government and the actual power was in the hands of old-established families who made the final decisions. Unlike some Italian city states, which were controlled by a single family, the Genevan system (with annual elections for the Syndics) made it impossible for one group to dominate. This helped Calvin as his opponents were never in power for long.

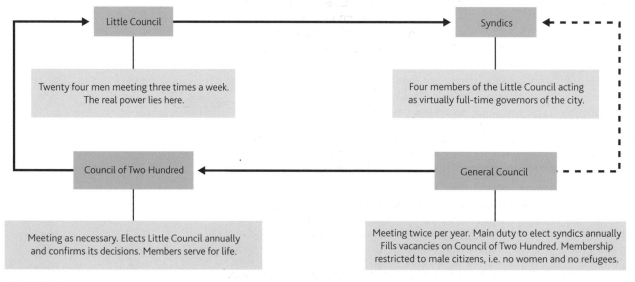

Fig. 6 *The Genevan government*

The Little Council and the Two Hundred Council agreed to Calvin's Articles, but they were cautious about giving power to the hands of a Church. Calvin wanted the power to excommunicate those who disobeyed the rules of his Church – a vital demand if the Church was to be independent – but the Little Council insisted on having a say. In the same way, Calvin's Confession of Faith was accepted but, when Calvin insisted that each person had to sign it, this was too much and many refused to sign. It was more than the former Catholic Church had asked and as Farel and Calvin were French, they appeared to be foreigners telling the city what to do.

Calvin and Farel had devised a clear system of reform, but it seemed that they had little political sense. In 1538 Syndics opposed to Calvin had achieved power, but they did not tone down their demands. Anyone who did not sign the Confession was stopped from going to Communion, but the Council refused to allow this without the Council's permission. The Council even decided to accept Church services drawn up by Berne. Calvin and his supporters were hardly tactful. In a sermon, Calvin called the Little Council 'a council of the Devil' and one of his supporters was jailed for calling them 'a council of drunkards.' From their point of view, they were God's instruments and must proclaim the truth as they saw it.

This was a struggle for power between the Church and the civil power. When Calvin and Farel refused to hold Communion services on Easter Sunday, with angry mobs roaming the streets, the Council ordered them to leave. Calvin accepted the invitation of Martin Bucer to come to Strasbourg, to become a pastor to the French exiles there.

A closer look

Calvin and Bucer in Strasbourg

Calvin had intended in 1536 to settle in Strasbourg and in 1538 he joined Martin Bucer there. Bucer (1491–1555) was a former Dominican friar who was influenced by the writings of Erasmus. Becoming a minister in Strasbourg, he had established an effective reformed Church there after 1527 and he had an important influence on Calvin. He favoured a middle way between Luther and Zwingli and played a leading role in all attempts to compromise between Catholics, Lutherans and Zwinglians. He was a master at phrasing statements of faith that blurred any differences and his system of Church government was similar to Calvin's in 1541. In Strasbourg, Calvin learned from Bucer the need to compromise over such key issues as the relations between the Church and the civil authorities. In 1540 Calvin married the widow of an Anabaptist with two children.

Calvin's second Genevan ministry, 1541–64

In 1541, following the establishment of a pro-French faction, Calvin was invited to return to Geneva and, after a year of persuasion (he was reluctant to exchange a peaceful life for a stressful alternative), he and his family returned to Geneva in September 1541.

Before his return, the Little Council agreed that it would draw up plans for a structured organisation for the Genevan Church. It accepted many of Calvin's proposals, put into law by the Ecclesiastical Ordinances of 1541.

Calvin would not have succeeded at all without the backing of a majority of the Little Council and it did take him until 1555 until he was almost

Fig. 7 *The death of Calvin, by a 19th-century artist. Calvin wished to be buried in an unmarked grave*

■ **Source analysis**

Study Figure 7. Do you think the artist was in favour of Calvinism?

completely unchallenged. The Council was needed to enforce the discipline that Calvin believed was necessary, but it seems in some ways odd that it was prepared to support him despite the fact that, week after week, its aristocratic members sat in the front pews as Calvin blasted their failings in his sermons.

The Council's major concern was to avoid civil unrest in Geneva. It did not want the Genevan Reformation to collapse or be threatened by a powerful neighbour such as Berne. Calvin himself had a European reputation and a brilliant mind – it did not wish to lose him, despite occasional quarrels. He was supported by many influential churchmen and citizens and his personal authority was immense, as is shown by his delivering 260 sermons without notes, each 2 hours long, each year.

The role of the Consistory, pastors and the Grabeau

Once established again in Geneva, Calvin set about changing Genevan society by working through the pastors and the Consistory.

The Consistory

The Consistory was made up of 12 lay elders and all the pastors. The balance changed over time: in 1542 there were 9 pastors but by 1564 there were 19, which shows how the relationship with the civil authorities had changed in Calvin's favour. The Consistory met most Thursdays. The meetings were chaired by one of the Syndics and every punishment had to be approved by the Little Council.

The Consistory had the duty to enforce high standards of religious and social behaviour and there are detailed records of its activities. Calvin hoped for a reformation of manners as much as doctrine. At first, most cases concerned religious issues such as missing Sunday services or sermons, or survivals of Catholic practices. People were checked to see if they knew the basic prayers. By 1550 these accounted for only 14 per cent of the cases and there was far more concern with moral and personal standards: more than one-third of cases dealt with sexual misconduct and about half with family or neighbour disputes.

Calvin was particularly concerned with public behaviour. He denounced the latest fashions and enforced a simple, unadorned dress code. He condemned singing and whistling, and was incensed by dancing, even in private houses. He argued that enjoying such things showed an inner lack of seriousness and vanity. Gambling, drunkenness, swearing, cursing and fortune-telling were prohibited. Sexual crimes such as adultery and relationships involving a wide age range were punished heavily, and he attempted to drive all prostitutes from the city. In 1550 the pastors were given permission to make an annual visit to each house to see that the rules of the Church were being kept.

The Consistory dealt with many issues that did not appear religious, but were in fact moral issues such as giving short weight, charging too high fees (e.g. lawyers), the price of bread, controlling imports, defrauding widows and orphans, what level of interest to charge and even plans for a better refuse system. Punishments could include public humiliations such as being put in the stocks, walking through the streets wearing a penitent's outfit, periods in prison, excommunication or even execution.

Pastors

Calvin intended to create a society based on the reformed faith and he enforced and structured the practice of religion. Pastors were elected from the Venerable Company of Pastors and appointments were confirmed by the Little Council. They were expected to preach, administer the sacraments and assist in the exercise of discipline. Unlike Catholic priests, the pastors were not a separate order from laypeople. They were kept busy as all Genevans were expected to go to church on Sunday and, if possible, hear a sermon each day. These were given throughout the day so no one could be 'too busy' to attend. In addition, pastors were to hold weekly classes to teach children the catechism. Attendance at Sunday service was compulsory, hearing a sermon was expected and children were trained in the catechism that Calvin produced in 1542; a thorough knowledge of beliefs was provided. The sermon was the central part of the Calvinist service and Calvin expected high standards from the pastors. The typical content and delivery of his sermons indicates what was expected of the pastors.

Calvin was a superb preacher, speaking directly and passionately, without notes but displaying great learning. He preached almost every day and twice on Sundays. Most of his sermons explained the Bible or Christian teaching, but he used the occasion to attack what he considered vices such as women wearing provocative clothes and the singing of bawdy songs. A modern biographer of Calvin, T. H. L. Parker, claimed that the really important changes in Genevan society were caused by the preaching of Calvin and the pastors. It was hard to avoid sermons. Genevans probably had more knowledge of the Bible than any other similar group.

A great contribution to Calvinist worship was the *Book of Metrical Psalms*, written by Clément Marot. Psalm-singing was the only form of singing Calvin approved of and congregational singing was a good way of creating community spirit.

Key profile

Clément Marot

Clément Marot (1497–1544) was a poet with a national reputation in France. He became a Protestant exile in Geneva. In 1541 he had published metrical translations of 30 psalms (i.e. psalms given a rhythm so they could be sung) and in Geneva wrote 20 more. Calvin gave him support and the psalms fitted the needs of the Reformed Church – scriptural but 'no frills'. In 1543 he was accused of playing backgammon by the Consistory and left Geneva. The composer Philippe Bourgeois provided the stirring yet dignified music that Calvin required.

Calvin had a poor opinion of the pastors and wished to give them more cohesion and training. They had to attend a weekly Bible study session and every three months attended a meeting called the Grabeau.

The Grabeau

The Grabeau (from a French word meaning 'to examine') was a session in which each pastor faced criticism of his ministry and conduct from the other members. It was a 'session of mutual frank and loving criticism' in which the pastors criticised themselves as well as each other.

> The quarterly meeting was a little day of judgement when, flattery laid aside, each man saw himself through the eyes of his fellows and, if he were wise, harboured no resentment but knew the joyful release of voluntary humiliation.

*T. H. L. Parker, **John Calvin**, 1975*

In theory, the Grabeau would make the pastor more effective by keeping him up to the mark and motivating him to try to avoid criticism. This encouragement to criticise and correct others was a typical feature of Calvinism, the aim being to raise standards by encouraging people to be honest and open to the accusations of others.

Activity

Thinking point

How effective do you think the Grabeau would be? Imagine its methods were regularly applied to your school or college. Would it help to raise standards?

Summary question

How important were Calvin's theological ideas to his success in Geneva?

The success of Calvinism and its influence on the European Reformation

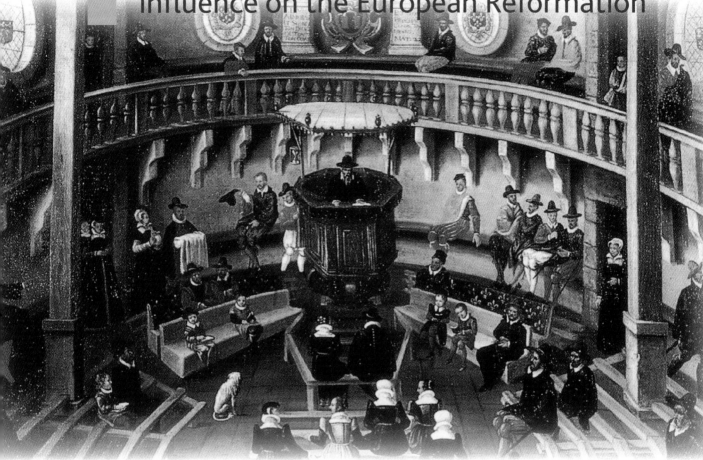

Fig. 1 *A Calvinist 'temple' in Lyon, France, c.1570*

In this chapter you will learn about:

- the reasons why Calvin and his reformed faith were successful in Geneva
- the problem of the theocratic state
- how Calvin dealt with opposition
- the Genevan Academy
- the international spread of Calvinism and the extent to which it was established as an alternative faith.

Cross-reference

For more on the **reasons for the success of Calvinism**, see Chapter 6.

In 1558, the English Catholic Bishop of Winchester gave a bleak warning of the horrors ahead:

> The wolves be coming out of Geneva, and have sent their books ahead of them, full of pestilent doctrines, blaspherny and heresy to infect the people.

1
*J. H. Elliott, **Europe Divided**, 1968*

This chapter explores why the 'wolves of Geneva' – this 'second wave' of the Reformation – created so much fear in the hearts of its opponents.

Activity

Thinking point

Study Figure 1. Compare this 'temple' with Figure 2 on page 146, the Jesuit church in Vienna. What differences can you identify?

Why was Calvinism successful in Geneva?

Calvin himself was central to the success of the Genevan Reformation. Without his enormous personal authority and charisma it would not have succeeded. Calvin was never an ordained minister and was paid by the city; technically he was not even a citizen of Geneva until 1559. He was a member of the Company of Pastors, in theory having equal status with the rest. In some ways, Calvin does not seem good leader material. He was very much an intense scholar and was in poor health for most of his life, which in his letters he writes about in great detail: the gout, ulcers on the legs, kidney stones and piles to name the main ones. As a personality, he had few light-hearted moments and he inspired admiration rather than affection, even from his supporters. His comment about the citizens of Berne – 'they have always feared me rather than loved me' – could equally apply to Geneva. Calvin was completely confident that he was working under the guidance of the Holy Spirit – this explains his temper and intolerance when he was opposed. This is demonstrated by the force of his language when attacking even small faults.

Calvin's conviction of his mission gave him the courage to press on despite the opposition and his single-minded, totally focused approach partly explains his success. As a theologian and debater in the 'religious conversations', he had no equal. The Council would be impressed by the force of his arguments and his learning although perhaps they did not understand them. He gave himself a huge workload: preaching 4,000 sermons between 1538 and 1564, writing thousands of letters and many pamphlets, carrying out weekly teaching of the Company of Pastors. His organisational skills were also important – he was careful, for example, to recruit highly educated French pastors from the upper social classes, who inspired respect in a class-conscious society and could be relied on not to support revolution.

After 1555 his authority was unchallenged. The Syndic who chaired the meetings of the Consistory no longer brought his baton of office with him (the symbol of the Council's authority) and the Little Council even adopted the practice of the Grabeau by having a private session in which its members in charity declared their faults and those of others. The Council no longer challenged decisions of the Consistory. Visitors to Geneva, such as the admittedly biased John Knox, claimed it was a superb example:

> Geneva is the most perfect school of Christ that was ever seen on earth since the days of the Apostles. In other places, I admit Christ to be truly preached; but manners and religion to be so sincerely reformed, I have not yet seen in any other place.

2   *John Knox's views on Geneva*

Key profile

John Knox

John Knox (1505–72) was an inspiring firebrand Scottish preacher who was at the head of reformation movements in Scotland and then England under Edward VI. When Catholic Mary succeeded to the throne in 1553, he fled from England to Geneva. He tried to return to England when Elizabeth was crowned in 1558, but he had written a book in 1557 denouncing female rulers – *The First Blast of the Trumpet Against the Monstrous Regiment of Women* – which meant he was barred. He returned to Scotland (where Mary Queen of Scots ruled) and carried out a Calvinist Reformation in 1559–60.

Signs of Calvin's influence were everywhere. Clothes were simple and without ornament. There was no singing, dancing or public entertainment. There were no taverns filled with a drunken rabble and prostitutes were banned from the city. The whole population was obliged to go to church or hear sermons most days of the week. Children had to chant their catechism and people were expected to go about their business in a quiet and reflective way.

However, a balanced judgement on Calvin's success needs to put Geneva into context. The city seems to have had a 'sin city' reputation for its low moral standards prior to Calvin's arrival, with high levels of gambling, drunkenness, prostitution, casual sex and adultery. Possibly its citizens were far too easy going, but there are no statistics available for comparison with other cities. Geneva's image has been seen through the eyes of the hyper-sensitive reformers and Calvin's attacks on all its failings have been accepted as accurate. The appalling moral standards and gross excesses of city life were common themes of moralists long before Calvin – for example, Savonarola on Florence and Erasmus on Rome.

Before Calvin's arrival, the City Council had already passed laws controlling drunkenness and prostitution, although these laws were not enforced. Just before his arrival, the Council tightened things up by, for example, ordering those who had sex before marriage to be publically whipped. Although it was easy to control public displays of behaviour, we have no statistics to prove Calvin controlled promiscuity and sexual misconduct. The return of former prostitutes showed they had a client base. His own step-daughter and sister-in-law were expelled for adultery and, despite the passing of a law forbidding older men to marry young girls, William Farel, aged 69 and his oldest friend, married the teenage daughter of his housekeeper.

Finally, Calvin had the charisma to enforce his model community, but by the 1570s standards were in decline once more. Even the Genevan Academy was losing its reputation.

Previous exposure of Geneva to Protestant ideas

Calvin did not have to start a reformation. There was much exposure to Protestant ideas when he arrived in Geneva in 1536. In the 1520s there were small numbers of evangelical reformers, including William Farel and Pierre Viret. Both the Lutheran and Zwinglian reformations were making great progress. The city of Berne, Geneva's ally, had carried out a reformation in 1528. However, despite pressure from Berne and the evangelical preachers, the Council still could not make a decision. This lack of certainty was causing discontent. In 1535 there was an attempt to poison Viret by one of his servants, who claimed he was acting under the orders of the Catholics. This led to a 'religious conversation' between the Catholic side and that of the reformers which lasted two months. The Council still delayed a decision and mobs attacked the churches and destroyed images – the Mass was eventually suspended, the cathedral clergy left, the other religious agreed to attend reformed services. In May 1536 Geneva voted to become an evangelical city. Three months later, Calvin arrived for his 'one night' in Geneva. The Catholic Church had been broken, but there was a fear or apathy about what to put in its place.

> When I first arrived in this church there was almost nothing. They were good about seeking out idols and burning them, but there was no reformation. Everything was in turmoil.

3 *Calvin's recollections 30 years later*

Activity

Talking point

1 Why do you think that the citizens of Geneva accepted Calvin's changes?

2 As a class, discuss what rules you might enforce to reform public behaviour.

Cross-reference

The **Genevan Academy** is discussed later on page 88.

Cross-reference

For more on '**religious conversation**', see page 59.

Cross-reference

Lutheranism is covered in Chapters 4 and 5.

The **Anabaptists** are explored in Chapter 8.

Calvin offered Geneva a truly reformed faith that was well ordered and supported authority. He offered an alternative to Lutheranism, which he felt had not gone far enough in ridding itself of the taints of Catholicism. His unique difference to previous Protestant ideas was a product between conservative Lutheranism and radical Anabaptism.

The theocratic state

The theocratic state is a state ruled by its priests or ministers, in which the laws are obeyed as commands from God. Getting a balance between the powers of the Church and the secular power has created constant friction as to which should be the master. For example, by 1300 the papacy claimed it had the power to depose any monarch who opposed the wishes of the Church. On the other hand, some rulers completely controlled the Church, such as the eastern Roman Emperors; Henry VIII became Head of the Church; non-Christian rulers, such as the Ottoman sultans, combined the roles of religious and political leaders. Historian Keith Randell points out that the label 'theocratic state' is always used in a hostile way by western historians. The attempt to create a theocratic state in Münster was not a good example. Today, there is often resentment at 'religious interference' when the Churches criticise laws made by the state on moral issues such as embryo research and abortion or whether Churches should have their own schools. However, a theocratic state is not necessarily 'wrong'. States can work with powerful religious leaders, as for example in Iran, and Islam does not have a church–state distinction.

The accusation that Calvin created a dictatorship in which he took over powers that should rightly belong to the secular authorities was often made by his enemies and by later historians. Although he had no official title, he ruled through his personal magnetism, the creation of fear through public denunciations, his ruthless crushing of opposition, punishments such as exile and excommunication, encouraging citizens to report each other's failings, and the indoctrination of young people. Geneva was unique among reformed states because it allowed so much power to its ministers. Calvin himself had such great personal authority that he was able to force through plans for a reformed society through the support of a willing Council who were afraid of the consequences of opposition. Calvin's treatment of his opponents could be seen as vindictive and the practice of visiting every household to enquire about its conduct could be viewed as intrusive. After 1555 his authority was virtually unchallenged and the rights of the Consistory to excommunicate were increased.

Cross-reference

More detail on **Calvin's treatment of his opponents** is provided on pages 85–8.

The **Consistory** is outlined on page 78.

On the other hand, the Church was not in control of any of the structures of government and they remained unchanged. The Council cooperated with Calvin for good reasons. Without him, Geneva was just another small, undistinguished city that probably would have been dominated by Berne. Calvin, the greatest biblical scholar of his age, gave Geneva fame and international prestige. The Council were not forced to obey him, but they were attracted by his teaching and the discipline he imposed. A 'Godly society' also meant social peace. Calvin was not a revolutionary in a political or social sense.

Lay elders chosen from the magistrates were members of the Consistory (although they were outnumbered by the pastors by 1564) and a Syndic always attended its meetings until 1555. Calvin only rarely attended Council meetings, but he was often *asked* by the Council for his advice, for example for a list of unsuitable Christian names and if it was

was appropriate to allow religious plays. Calvin did fail in some areas. His wish for a Genevan Academy was opposed until 1559. He wished Geneva's taverns to become places of polite conversation where people could hear Bible readings, but public pressure forced him to abandon this although the taverns were less disordered. Ministers tried to stop the use of non-biblical or fashionable Christian names, but this did not succeed. Calvin did little to intervene in financial and economic issues; he had little to say, for example, about the prosperous 'luxury' industry of Geneva – silk production. Although Calvin was successful within Geneva itself, research on the parishes beyond the city limits has shown that standards of moral conduct and religious zeal were nothing like so high.

The suppression of opposition

Calvin's victory in overcoming opposition was an important reason for his success. It took him 14 years (1541–55) of constant struggle. This opposition was of two kinds: those who opposed his religious views and those who opposed him for political and social reasons.

Religious opponents

Calvin's religious opponents probably caused him the most fury and, although they were not his most serious problem, they attacked him in a field where he hated to be challenged.

- In 1542 Sebastian Castellio, whom Calvin had appointed head of the Genevan college, claimed that a book in the Old Testament, the Song of Songs, was in fact an erotic poem not inspired by God and should therefore not be included in the Scriptures. Calvin felt this was an attack on the Scriptures. Castellio left Geneva but returned in 1544 and criticised his former colleagues. Calvin now made the Syndics see that they had to expel him.
- In 1546 Ameaux, a respected councillor who made toys and playing cards, and whose business had been badly affected by the ban on gambling, said at a dinner that Calvin taught untrue doctrine. The Council suggested an apology in private, but Calvin demanded that he should walk through the city carrying a taper and asking for Calvin's and God's mercy – perhaps an unnecessary humiliation.
- A more serious challenge came from an able theologian, Jerome Bolsec, who gave a lecture to the Company of Pastors in 1551 denying double predestination as it made God into a tyrant, consigning many to damnation on a whim. Although it did not seem a good idea to challenge Calvin in his home territory, his doctrine of predestination was on shaky ground. In a public debate, Calvin's knowledge of the texts was far superior to Bolsec's and the Council agreed that Bolsec should be expelled, giving the reason that disharmony might result if there were doctrinal differences.
- The Michael Servetus affair was important for the effect on the political situation. Servetus was a Spanish theologian who adopted extreme views and took it badly when others did not accept them. Probably he would be described as extremely confrontational, but among other views he condemned infant baptism and the **Doctrine of the Trinity** – a core belief for nearly all Christians. Suspected of heresy, he went undercover at Vienne (actually working as a doctor for the archbishop) in eastern France. There he worked on a book setting out his views, but he had the audacity of someone with total belief in himself and sent a copy to Calvin. Calvin recognised

Cross-reference

The **Genevan Academy** is outlined on page 88.

Exploring the detail

The Song of Songs

The Song of Songs (or the Song of Solomon, although Solomon is not the author) has been part of the Scriptures since the first century, but its place there has often been questioned as it is a cycle of love poems.

Cross-reference

Calvin's doctrine of **double predestination** is described on page 73.

Key terms

Doctrine of the Trinity: this doctrine holds that God comprises three persons: God the Father, God the Son and God the Holy Spirit. Each 'person' is equally God, unique but undivided. Servetus rejected the 'three persons' doctrine, which opened the debate that had divided the Christian Church from the start about the relationship of Christ to God.

Fig. 2 *The burning of Michael Servetus, 1553*

■ Activity

Talking point

Discuss the view that Calvin's religious opponents brought their troubles on themselves.

the work as that of Servetus and allowed a fellow minister to tell the French authorities where he was. He was arrested as a heretic in 1553 but escaped and incredibly turned up in Geneva at one of Calvin's sermons. He was arrested again and put on trial, with Calvin as the expert prosecution witness. At this point, Calvin's political opponents, the Perrin family, thought they could use Servetus to bring Calvin down. The trial dragged on for two months, but Servetus was so extreme in his views that he lost any support that he might have had. He was not a good choice to use against Calvin and the Perrin faction was weakened. The opinion of other Swiss Churches was that Servetus should be executed as a heretic. He was burned at the stake in 1553.

Calvin's attitude to religious opposition has caused historical debate. He presented himself as the upholder of truth and moderation (he asked that Servetus be executed instead of burned and claimed he did not wish to expose him). It has been argued that it was the Council putting Calvin's opponents on trial in a criminal court, with Calvin only acting as the expert giving his opinion. In the case of Servetus, it can be said that his heresy would have been given the same punishment by any religious group at the time. He was the only person burned for heresy in Geneva, an excellent record compared with most states (over 350 were burned in England in the years 1555–8). On the other hand, Calvin could be accused of at best not acting with Christian charity and at worst acting with vengeful ruthlessness. As with the other religious issues, he could not let things rest and said, for example, that he would not preach until his views prevailed. There was a personal hatred of Servetus (maybe something to do with their being at college together years before) and he said that if Servetus appeared in Geneva he would 'never let him get away alive'. 'If he once gets his knife in you, you do not stand a chance' commented a pastor.

Calvin was successful in defending his authority against religious opposition and after 1555 he was unchallenged. Although it could be argued that Calvin's victories increased his authority as a theologian, his opponents were not in his league to begin with.

Social and political opponents

Calvin's social and political opponents were more difficult to deal with. Diarmaid MacCulloch argues that many people opposed Calvin simply because they detested him:

> If you could anticipate having a good night out in the company of Martin Luther, the same could not be said of the buttoned-up Frenchman who wanted to stop the citizens of Geneva dancing. Calvin was in delicate health from his youth, and did not enjoy good cheer; his only recorded light-hearted activity was shove ha'penny. He did, however, enjoy getting his own way, which he identified with doing the will of God.

4

*D. MacCulloch, **Reformation: Europe's House Divided 1490–1700**, 2004*

Above this basic level, there were those who objected to Calvin's methods on the grounds that they had removed the Catholic Church only to replace it with a much more dictatorial system; those who objected to the abolition of what they thought of as harmless simple pleasures such as dancing and singing; and those who feared that the authority of the **magistrates** was being taken over by the Consistory.

There was also an element of dislike of foreigners. Large numbers of persecuted French refugees were coming into Geneva. In 1540 they made up about one-third of the population, perhaps a half by 1560. Although many were ordinary laypeople, there were also plenty of religious enthusiasts wishing to experience the 'school of Christ'. The Council was anxious enough about the incomers to pass a law banning membership of the Councils to any but native-born Genevans.

The opposition was based on the important principle of who was in charge. The civil government of Geneva was run by Genevan aristocratic families and the Church government of Calvin was run by a highly educated intellectual French elite backed by the immigrant population. The key battlegrounds were who should be allowed to excommunicate wrongdoers and who should decide on punishments.

The Perrin, Berthelier and Favre families emerged as a strong faction in the Council after 1546. Ami Perrin had supported Calvin in 1541 but probably feared his political influence. Calvin called them the **Libertines**. They were opposed to the power of the Consistory and Calvin's uncompromising policy on public behaviour – they would not have minded if Calvin could have been more tolerant. This group were a majority of the Syndics in 1547.

Members of the Libertine faction, especially Ami Perrin, were constantly called before the Consistory because of bad conduct such as dancing, making obscene gestures during sermons and exaggerated coughing, playing darts instead of attending Easter Communion, gambling and immodest dress. (The wife of Ami Perrin – who had also been criticised for dancing in public at a wedding – was a particular target of the Consistory in this respect.) Perrin was an able politician and when he became Syndic and captain-general of Genevan forces in 1553 he was in a strong position. He insisted that one of the Libertines who had been excommunicated should be allowed to take Communion; at the same time he supported Servetus and enflamed public opinion about the influx of French immigrants. Perrin's bid for power created resentment and after the failure of the Servetus case he lost his office as Syndic in 1555. All four Syndics now supported Calvin and they removed the Libertines from all the Genevan councils. The Libertine party made a clumsy attempt to create an armed rising but it did not work. Perrin and Berthelier fled; other supporters were tortured and executed. About one-third of the former ruling families went into exile. The power of the Libertines was broken.

The year 1555 was a turning point. Before then, Calvin had been brought before the Council three times between 1548 and 1553 for making offensive remarks about the magistrates, including calling them 'gargoyle monkeys' that 'vomit forth their blasphemies as supreme decrees'. After 1555 the Consistory was given power to put people on trial and the Little Council mostly supported its decrees.

Calvin has been accused of a ruthless and unforgiving approach in his dealings with opponents and it can be argued that punishments were excessive, even in the context of the 1540s. He was enraged, for example, by what he thought were lenient sentences for adultery and the Council agreed that serial adulterers would face the death penalty (the men were to be beheaded, the women drowned). However, this penalty was never

Key terms

Magistrate: a magistrate in the 16th century was anyone with the power of putting laws into practice and giving out punishments (e.g. this could be a king). The word today describes a much less important official.

Libertines: literally, those who had loose morals and were free thinkers in religion. A highly misleading label used brilliantly by Calvin to blacken his opponents.

Did you know?

Not one minister between 1542 and 1594 was a native of Geneva.

Cross-reference

The **civil government of Geneva** is covered on page 76.

The **Church government of Calvin** is outlined on page 72.

Cross-reference

To recap on the case of **Michael Servetus**, read pages 85–6.

Cross-reference

For the results of the **power of Consistory to hold trials**, see page 78.

carried out. There were punishments such as having the tongue pierced for anyone criticising Calvin or the Consistory. Jacques Gruet, a member of the Libertine group, expressed the views of many moderates in a letter to the Little Council:

> If one man murders another, he deserves punishment, everyone who maliciously and willingly hurts another deserves to be punished. But suppose I am a man who wants to eat his meals as he pleases, what business is that of others? Or if I want to dance, or have a good time, what is that to do with the law? Nothing.

5   *Jacques Gruet, 1547*

Further evidence for the increasing authority of the Consistory can be found in the increasing number of excommunications: in 1553 there were 16, in 1560 around 100.

The Genevan Academy

Geneva lacked a place of higher education to train future ministers and the elite of Calvinism, but it was only after the defeat of Calvin's opponents in 1555 that the Council made funds available to build the Genevan Academy, which opened in 1559. (Much of the money came from the sale of land owned by the Perrin family.) It was a mix of a boys' grammar school (the College) and university (the Academy). The curriculum for the College involved the study of classical writers and classical history, strongly influenced by humanism; the Academy was more demanding, with a greater emphasis on theology, which Calvin regarded as the heart of all study. His aim was not to train students for careers but to be effective preachers and missionaries. Calvin was lucky because an academic row at a similar college at Lausanne meant all the professors there resigned and were headhunted to come to Geneva by being offered better pay and conditions. He appointed Theodore Beza, who became his successor in Geneva, to lead the College.

The Academy was intended to serve local people, but its reputation attracted students from all over Europe; by 1564 there were around 300 in the Academy and 1,000 in the College. The College attracted large numbers of French students and the main aim was to convert France. Missionaries were sent to French-speaking Calvinist churches in Switzerland to improve their skills before being sent to France.

According to Ulinka Rublack in *Reformation Europe* (2005), the great days of the Academy lasted only a few years. It was never a top-class university. Other universities were founded to teach the reformed faith and fewer French students arrived in the 1570s. Its degrees were not internationally recognised and its courses were not innovative. It was not at the cutting edge of debate, nor was it intended to be. Students were sent there because they gained reliable doctrinal teaching and their private lives were closely controlled, much to their parents' approval.

Cross-reference

More details on **French Calvinism** can be found on pages 89–90.

Activity

Talking point

What arguments could be made against Gruet's views?

Fig. 3 *Theodore Beza, from an engraving made in 1861. Beza became Calvin's successor as leader of Calvinism*

Activity

Thinking point

In this activity you will consider the question: Was Calvin a dictator? You will first need to define a dictator. You could group your answer under headings such as:

- a cult of personality
- control over all aspects of behaviour
- control over minds through indoctrination
- surveillance of all members of society
- propaganda
- creating a culture of fear and suspicion.

Questions

1. How successful was Calvin in removing opposition to his authority?
2. How far did he establish total control over Geneva?

The extent to which Protestantism was established as an alternative faith

The spread of Calvinism

Calvin's Geneva would have probably remained an interesting but isolated experiment, slowly losing its unique character after his death. However, he deliberately looked beyond Geneva to the creation of a reformed faith in every part of Europe. Its character changed as it spread to established states rather than containment in a small city. It became dynamic, confident of its beliefs and certain to win over many converts. It challenged Lutheranism, Catholicism and the Radicals. International Calvinism after 1550 was the main Protestant movement and a highly important feature of the next half century. It has sometimes been called a 'Second Reformation'.

It was different to the Lutheran experience because it was a reformation from below, not sponsored by the state. However, by 1598 the attempt had failed. Calvinism remained the faith of a minority.

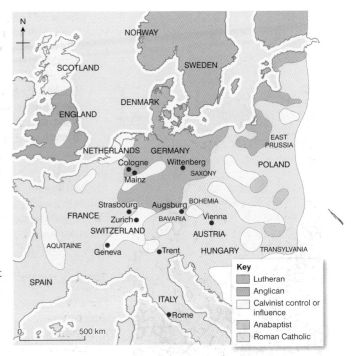

Fig. 4 *Religious divisions in Europe, c.1560*

Key
- Lutheran
- Anglican
- Calvinist control or influence
- Anabaptist
- Roman Catholic

A closer look

The growth of Calvinism in France

Calvin aimed to convert his native land of France. His writings were mainly in French; Geneva was the base for a large French community; Frenchmen formed the personnel of the Church; Calvinist organisation was directed to gain that result. The French kings had been inconsistent in enforcing their laws against heresy, but Henry II (1547–59) was determined to rid France of heretics, even setting up a special agency (the *Chambre Ardente* or 'burning tribunal') to arrest and, in the worst cases, burn offenders. Calvinism, however, grew strongly after 1555 and congregations were set up in many parts of France. By 1559 the structure of a national Church existed in France. It has been estimated that there were about 1,750 congregations comprising about 10 per cent of the population. More significant was Calvin's success in converting the nobility. Over one-third of the pastors sent to France were of noble birth and by 1559 about half the nobility had accepted Calvinism. These included the highest in the land, notably the Bourbon and Chatillon families. With the support of these powerful allies, Calvinism had military protection and could resist royal orders against it, especially in the south and west of France. This defiance of royal authority was a danger for the

Fig. 5 *The massacre of St Bartholomew, 1572 – an atrocity of the French Wars of Religion, in which many French Calvinists were killed*

Crown. At this critical moment, Henry II was mortally wounded at a tournament and his heirs were four young children. The Crown was weakened. The Catholic party in France, led by the Guise family, dominated the young king Francis II, who vowed to crush Calvinism. Despite attempts to compromise between 1560 and 1562, civil war broke out when the Duke of Guise fired on Calvinist worshippers at Vassy. For the next 30 years, the survival of Calvinism depended on the Calvinists' military strength.

In the 1550s Calvinist preachers appeared in the Netherlands. However, the authorities were successful in controlling its spread and perhaps 2 per cent were Calvinist by 1560. Its influence was greatly increased in the later 1560s when sections of the nobility adopted Calvinism to give a religious reason for their political opposition to Spanish rule.

In Germany 28 states became Calvinist, but most were very small. The exception was the Palatinate in north-west Germany, where the Elector Frederick III (1559–76) modelled his churches on Calvinist lines in 1562. His capital, Heidelberg, became a leading intellectual centre and a place of safety for exiles.

In Scotland the Reformation was led by John Knox, who established Calvinism when the Scottish parliament accepted a Confession of Faith in 1560. The power of the Crown in Scotland was weak, and although the Regent Mary of Guise and her daughter Mary Queen of Scots were Catholic, sections of the nobility supported Knox to strengthen their influence. Parliament accepted some aspects of Calvinism, but not the system of Church government in its entirety including the Consistory. Calvinism in Scotland was a lasting compromise. In England under Queen Elizabeth I the **Puritan** movement was constantly demanding the removal (or purification) of Catholic influences from the English Church, but it never achieved widespread popularity and royal authority was strong enough to resist change.

Elsewhere, Calvinism expanded where central authority was weak. For a time, 10 per cent of the Polish nobility became Calvinist, although the Jesuits re-established the Catholic Church later and there were minorities in Hungary and Bohemia.

Lutheranism had become well established by 1560. Its main appeal was to north Germany and Scandinavia and one of the reasons why Calvinism failed in these areas was the strength and well-established organisation of the Lutheran Church. There were several important new gains after 1560 such as consolidation in Sweden and the city of Strasbourg, as well as smaller states such as Brunswick. New Lutheran universities were opened. There were divisions within the Lutheran Church: there were those who felt that Lutheranism was perhaps too conservative, relying on the local princes for organisation, and its acceptance of the Real Presence was a problem for many reformers. There was no powerful leadership. This could explain why Calvinism appealed to those looking for a third way. However, Owen Chadwick in *The Reformation* (1972) comments that the Lutherans were strongly consolidating their territories up to 1618 and that the traditional image of a Church stagnating or in decline is no longer accepted.

Calvinism had a strong international appeal for a number of reasons:

- In the 1520s the reformers had expected the Word of God to sweep all before it and that the Catholic Church would collapse in the face of its

Key terms

Puritan: the name 'Puritans' was the critical label given to a wide range of opinions. The group that appeared most dangerous was headed by Field and Cartwright, who wished to abolish bishops and introduce a Calvinist system of government and Genevan services. They opposed the settlement of the English Church by Elizabeth I. In the 17th century Puritans played a leading role in events leading up to the English Civil War in 1642. Oliver Cromwell was a Puritan statesman.

Cross-reference

John Knox is profiled on page 82.

The **Jesuits** are discussed in Chapters 9–11.

Activity

Thinking point

Examine in more detail the role of Calvinism in France in the period to 1564, in Scotland to 1561 and in the Netherlands to 1566. In each case, Calvinism increased despite the opposition of the secular ruler. Does this mean that Calvinism was a revolutionary faith?

Cross-reference

For **Lutheranism**, refer to Chapters 4 and 5.

For the doctrine of the **Real Presence**, look back to page 24.

clear error. When this did not happen there was disappointment. The appearance of a dynamic, well-organised Calvinism gave new life to the Reformation movement.

- Calvinists had a strong belief that they were guided by the spirit of God. Although the doctrine of double predestination offered only the *hope* of salvation, most Calvinists believed they were the 'elect'. This gave them great certainty, especially in the face of opposition. Calvin encouraged his missionaries to be martyrs for the faith. Many people accepted Calvinism because it insisted on high ethical standards.

- Calvin himself played a crucial role in the spread of Calvinism. From 1541 he raised his sights from Geneva to the project to convert France and beyond. He dedicated his writing to leading members of French society; began a correspondence with potential supporters from Italy to Poland; and became the adviser to several aristocratic French ladies. He used the immigrants who came to Geneva as missionary workers in their own countries: between 1555 and 1559 there were 120 missions, including 32 to France; one was even sent to Brazil.

- The Genevan printing presses were central to the whole international project. Between 1536 and 1550 there were only two printing presses. The years 1550–60 saw a massive expansion, partly because of Calvin's international reputation and his vast output. If you count the work of other Genevan authors, the presses could not cope. The arrival of the leading French printers Jean Crespin and Robert Estienne turned Genevan printing into a mighty industry. They attracted print workers from France and by 1564 there were 34 printing presses. (As with so much else in Geneva, only one was run by a Genevan.)

- The marketing of the books was essential to mission work. An old friend of Calvin's, Laurent de Normandie, was a superb businessman and organiser who revolutionised the spread of printed material. He controlled a network of suppliers and salesmen and promoted sales through a network of bookshops. The *colporteurs* (bookcarriers) ran the great risk of arrest by hostile governments which were banning the import and reading of heretical books: the penalty was death. When de Normandie died, his stock totalled 35,000 books (10,000 by Calvin). Andrew Pettegree comments that his achievement in getting round controls on books and setting up a network that worked in parallel with the open one was a model wherever the trade in Protestant books was under threat.

- The organisation of Calvinism abroad provided a strong basis for expansion:

> When a few Calvinists, perhaps ten or twelve, had been converted in one place, they gathered together in a conventicle for Bible reading and worship. Once there was enough to form a congregation, a pastor was requested from Geneva and a full parish organisation was set up, including a consistory. Calvinist leaders met in a colloquy [meeting] to discuss common problems and policy. Beyond that, when there were enough churches in a province, a provincial synod would be called, and ultimately a national synod.

6   J. Lotherington, *Years of Renewal 1470–1600*, 1988

Did you know?
The sheer scale of Calvin's writing (considering his health and other duties) was amazing. Each year after 1544 he wrote four or five new works of at least 100,000 words each (about twice the length of this book), as well as constant rewrites of the *Institutes* which was about 400,000 words. His best sellers were the Genevan Bible in French – the standard Protestant text – and the Genevan Psalms.

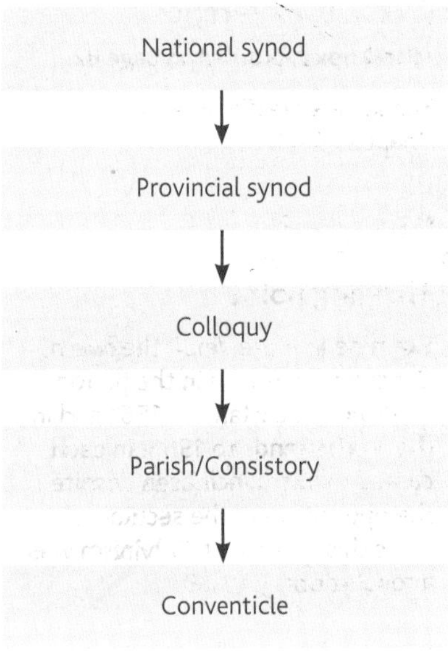

National synod
↓
Provincial synod
↓
Colloquy
↓
Parish/Consistory
↓
Conventicle

Fig. 6 *The structure of the Calvinist Church*

- Luther depended on the local princes to support the organisation of his Church, but Calvinism could thrive where the secular authorities opposed it (as in France and the Netherlands) because its organisation was founded on individual congregations rather than a hierarchy of bishops. It could exist in secrecy (the National Synod of France met in one room in Paris in 1559) and was difficult to eliminate entirely. However, it could also be imposed from above, such as in the Palatinate.

Calvin aimed to convert the middle and upper classes of society, who had most influence. Studies of the congregations have shown that he appealed – as a religion of the book – to the literate and educated classes such as lawyers and professional men, and skilled artisans rather than labourers or peasants who clung to the old Catholic ways. Genevan ministers were all drawn from the upper classes and in France his particular target was the nobility.

Activity

Source Analysis

Study Figure 7. Highlight two reasons that you consider are the most important in the spread of Calvinism.

Activity

Revision exercise

Write a diagrammatic comparison of Luther and Calvin. You could use the following headings:

- character and personality
- religious ideas
- organisation of the Church
- to whom did they appeal?

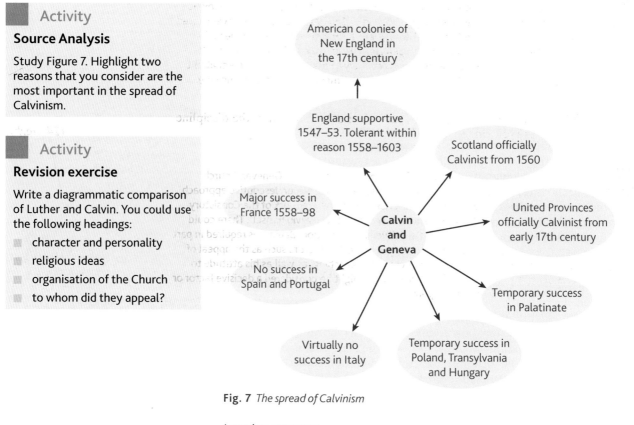

Fig. 7 *The spread of Calvinism*

Learning outcomes

In this section you have studied Calvin's writings and ideas, as well as the organisation and structure that he imposed on the Genevan Church. You have examined how Calvin changed Genevan society and how, through the pastors and Consistory, he transformed that state. You have also examined the reasons for the success of Calvinism both in Geneva and internationally and have been invited to assess the significance of the movement to the wider Reformation in Europe.

AQA Examination-style questions

(a) Explain why the Ecclesiastical Ordinances were passed in 1541. *(12 marks)*

In part a), the focus is on explanation not narrative of the Ordinances. You might consider factors such as this was a condition of Calvin's return and they were based on his experiences with Bucer; Calvin was in a strong position because he had been asked back; there was a need for a clear structure to bring discipline to the disorderly Genevan Reformation. You should try to make some judgement about the factors you give, perhaps stressing the most important and explaining why.

(b) How far was Calvin's success in Geneva the result of the discipline of the reformed Church?

(24 marks)

Part b) requires good knowledge of how the discipline of the Genevan Church produced the outcome of a reformed society – a narrative or descriptive approach must be avoided. There should be a concentration on the work of the Consistory and the Company of Pastors, as well as the impact of Calvin himself. There could well be some reference to Calvin's attitude to opposition. Balance is required in part b) answers, so consideration must be given to other factors such as the appeal of Calvin's religious views and his preaching and teaching, as well as his attitude to education. The support of the Little Council might be considered a decisive factor or the influence of French immigrants.

8 The Radical Reformation

All the leaders of Anabaptism in Münster perished. Rothman is believed to have died fighting. The queen Divara, having refused to renounce her faith, was beheaded. As for Bockelson, he was for some time led about on a chain and exhibited like a performing bear. He was finally brought to Münster, and there he and two other leading Anabaptists were tortured to death with red-hot irons. Throughout their agony the leaders uttered no sound and made no movement. After the execution the three bodies were suspended from a church tower in the middle of the town, in cages which are still to be seen there today.

1

*N. Cohn, **The Pursuit of the Millennium**, 1970*

Fig. 1 *The cages of the Anabaptists in the tower of St Lambert's Church, Münster*

The origins and ideas of the Anabaptists and other radical groups

The brutal end of the 'New Jerusalem' of Anabaptism in Münster in 1535 is the most famous episode of the **Radical Reformation**. The treatment of these Anabaptist leaders reflects the fear in which the authorities, both Catholic and Protestant, held them.

The radicals wanted to push beyond the more conservative and cautious reformations of Luther and Zwingli, who worked with the existing authorities. They wished to create what they felt was a Church truly reflecting the Gospel. Although most radicals had a common belief in **Anabaptism** (and so were called Anabaptists, rather than radical reformers, at the time by their enemies), the radicals held a wide variety of views. There was no single leader or commonly accepted doctrines.

A closer look

Zwingli and the Swiss Reformation

Huldreich Zwingli

Huldreich Zwingli (1484–1531) was the 'father of the Swiss Reformation'. He was well-educated, studying at Basle and Vienna before being ordained in 1506. From 1506–16 he was a parish priest at Glarus (eastern Switzerland). He was much influenced by the Christian humanism of Erasmus, especially the New Testament. Zwingli claimed not to have been influenced by Luther and does not seem to have read his works until 1519. In 1518 he became a priest at the Great Minster in Zürich and by 1525 had completed a reformation in the city. Zwingli's enthusiastic wish to spread his reformation to other cantons of Switzerland created a political issue as some wished to remain Catholic. The conflicts that resulted led to Zwingli's death in battle in 1531.

The reformation in Zürich

Zürich was one of the 13 independent cantons of Switzerland. It was ruled by a council of 200 wealthy citizens who were in favour of a reformation but wanted any changes to be carried out gradually. When Zwingli became a priest in Zürich in 1518, he began to attack the abuses of the Catholic Church such as indulgences, the cult of the saints and monastic life, and his preaching was popular and effective. However, he was concerned to keep the support of the Council and little progress was made until 1522 when a protest was staged against the Catholic Church's ban on eating meat during Lent. This led to a public debate with the Catholic authorities and the Council accepted Zwingli's views on reform. Monasteries were closed and all images removed from churches. In 1525 the Mass was abolished. Zwingli differed from Luther in that he disapproved of images in his churches and on the nature of the Mass. He believed that the bread and wine were simply bread and wine – there was no Real Presence. To make his point, the bread came from an ordinary loaf and the wine was served in wooden beakers. The Colloquy of Marburg resulted in a complete break with Luther. Zwingli also believed that the Church was responsible for all aspects of

Key terms

Radical Reformation: historians today prefer to use the term Radical Reformation because there were a number of different strands of radicalism, including the rejection of infant baptism. The radicals ranged from moderates to wild extremists.

Anabaptism: this means 'baptism again'. The Anabaptists believed that only adult baptism (only after someone was old enough to proclaim their faith) was warranted in the Scriptures *and* that those who had been baptised as infants must be baptised again to join an Anabaptist community.

Cross-reference

The **Christian humanism of Erasmus** is described on page 10.

Fig. 2 *Zwingli depicted in a 17th-century engraving*

Cross-reference

Lutheran theology, including the debate on the **Real Presence** and the **unsuccessful attempt to reconcile Luther and Zwingli at Marburg,** are described in Chapters 4 and 5.

For similarities between **Zwingli's concern with community life and the concerns of Calvinism,** compare pages 72 and 86.

Activity

Thinking point

You have now read about the Catholic, Lutheran, Zwinglian and Calvinist views on the nature of the Communion. Why did this issue matter so much? Draw a table setting out the four views.

community life (such as caring for the poor and sick) and that the Church should be completely under the control of the civil authorities. The Church and the Zürich Council worked together.

There were many strands of the Radical Reformation, all independent of each other and with differing beliefs (Figure 3).

15th century context
- Peasant discontent
- Visionary movements
- Popular religion
- Millenarianism
- Dreams of a fairer society

Reformation
- Destroys Catholic authority
- Encourages personal interpretation of Scripture

Group	Places	Names
Swiss Brethren	Zürich, western Germany	Felix Mantz, Conrad Grebel, Balthasar Hubmaier
More radical than Luther	Wittenberg, Zwickau, Mühlhausen	Andreas Carlstadt, Thomas Müntzer
Upper Germany and Moravia	Moravia, Bohemia	Hans Denck, Hans Hut, Jacob Hutter
Northern Germany and the Netherlands	Strasbourg, Emden, Münster, Amsterdam	Melchiar Hoffman, Jan Matthys, Jan Bockelson (or Beukels)

Fig. 3 *The strands of the Radical Reformation*

The reformation radicals emerged because the destruction of the authority of the Catholic Church was bound to encourage movements that now had the freedom to express their views. The views of Luther and Zwingli were certain to be challenged. In addition, the spirit of the Reformation encouraged a personal religion. Luther had praised the 'liberty of the Christian man' and, now that every family could potentially read the Bible in their own language, the plain words of Scripture were enough. There was no need for an academic education or books of commentaries – everyone could interpret the plain words of Scripture for themselves. For example, the radicals argued that Scripture said that graven images were forbidden, so images of saints and stained glass in churches should be destroyed. The radicals demanded genuine religious change and they would not get this from Luther, Zwingli or Calvin, who were supported by established authority.

The radicals also gained their inspiration from ideas that predated the 'official' Reformation and lay deep in popular religion. The present age of injustice and the power of the Devil would be destroyed – and the Millennium, Christ's 1,000-year reign, created – by those whom God had chosen for the purpose. The chosen ones were in direct and constant communication with God, so no power on earth could challenge them. It was their mission to destroy the established powers that supported injustices. By implication, there was a social aspect too. When the Millennium came, the poor would inherit the earth and the rich would be cast down. The radicals believed that the work of reformation was not complete and, as they were sure that the **Second Coming** was imminent, there was a sense of urgency for change.

There were a number of reasons why the radicals were persecuted by both the secular and religious authorities:

- Although not a great issue today, Anabaptism was seen as a highly dangerous doctrine. It was completely different from the traditional teaching of the Church (both Catholic and Protestant) and it threatened

Cross-reference

For **radical ideas that predated the 'official' Reformation**, see page 28.

Key terms

Second Coming: the expected second return of Christ to earth, after which would come the Last Judgement, in which both the living and the dead would be finally judged and sent to heaven or hell. Many religious sects have predicted the date of this as part of their beliefs.

the whole existence of the Christian community into which all were included by infant baptism. Adult baptism meant that, unlike a child, you could chose to join or *not* to join – so you would have divided communities with an exclusive group of baptised. Also, rebaptising had been condemned as serious sacrilege in the 4th century.

- Anabaptists claimed they should mix with only the baptised few. They stopped paying tithes to support the Church and wanted to chose their own ministers without reference to any other authority. A fairly accurate statement of their beliefs, the Schleitheim Confession, confirmed the fears of the political establishment.

- Although Anabaptism in general was a pacifist and spiritual movement, the actions of extremists, the wild claims of some of its supporters who said they had a direct line to God, isolated examples of violence and sexual excesses blackened the name of Anabaptism in the eyes of honest Christian people and their rulers.

- The radicals were strongly associated with the poor:

> Radicalism was the religion of the poor, of those who stood outside the establishment of the powerful, the priests and the learned. While at first the 'anabaptist' movements attracted people of all classes (though the majority of the membership was poor) by the end of the sixteenth century, after so many persecutions, only the poor remained.

2   *H. G. Koenigsberger et al.,* **Europe in the Sixteenth Century***, 1989*

- Any movement that tried to energise the poor was to be feared by rulers. Some radical movements argued that wealth should be equally distributed and that there should be no rich or poor. This was a threat to social order. Others supported the destruction of all images, altars and distractions from true worship – an encouragement to rioting and disorder.

- Mainstream Protestant groups supported the persecution of Anabaptists because they wished to prove their conservative and respectable credentials to the established authorities in cities and secular states. One of Calvin's motives, for example, was to show that the establishment of a truly reformed state need not be accompanied by disorder.

- The radical groups were geographically divided from each other and lacked effective leadership, inter-communication, control of a printing press and a common statement of belief. It was easy for the authorities to pick off each group separately.

- Stories of their more extreme activities gave propaganda to their enemies. Quite apart from the events at Münster and elsewhere, an example of radical activities in 1524 at St Gallen in Switzerland particularly frightened the chauvinist 16th-century male – women taking a leadership role:

> St Gallen women decided to cut their hair short because they said it provoked lustful thoughts in men and so was responsible for sin. Magdalene Muller applied the words 'the way, the truth and the life' to herself, whilst a servant girl, Frena Bumenin proclaimed herself the new Messiah and gathered disciples. In her delusion, she became convinced she was going to bear the Antichrist. To the authorities a new horror emerged when the women began to offer themselves sexually to the men in their circle. 'Why do you judge?' they replied to the appalled townsfolks' rebukes.

3   *D. MacCulloch,* **Reformation: Europe's House Divided 1490–1700***, 2004*

Exploring the detail

The Schleitheim Confession

The Schleitheim Confession was put together by the scattered groups of Swiss Brethren in 1527. Its seven points drew a clear line between them and the mainstream reformers who had mixed the Church with the world. True Christians separate themselves from a corrupt world and must not use law courts, fight wars or swear oaths. In fact, the marks of the true Church would be that it must suffer persecution, fire and death to reach salvation – not marks of Luther and Zwingli's state-supported reformations. The Confession was widely known in the 16th century. Zwingli, Luther and Calvin all read copies.

Cross-reference

For the **events at Münster**, look back to page 94.

The development of the Radical Reformation and the extent of its success

The Swiss Brethren

Fig. 4 *The spread of Anabaptism*

Luther had called Zwingli a 'fanatic' and 'dreamer', but he was not a radical reformer. Some felt Zwingli's approach was far too slow and conservative. Zürich radical groups led by Conrad Grebel, Balthasar Hubmaier and Felix Mantz felt that Zwingli was not following Scripture and condemned him as a false prophet because he opposed adult baptism. Grebel and his followers went out into the rural parishes and told the people not to accept infant baptism and to stop paying tithes. In 1524 one of their followers destroyed a roadside crucifix saying there should be no graven images; this led to attacks on churches. They publically quarrelled with Zwingli. These radicals (labelled 'Anabaptists' by their enemies) held unacceptable views but, despite being given every chance by the Council to stop their activities, adult rebaptism continued. The Council had little choice but to act. The leaders of the Swiss Brethren were put in prison and Hubmaier expelled. In 1526 the Council ordered that the Brethren should be shown no mercy – the penalty was death by drowning (an ironic take on their belief in adult baptism). Mantz, who had promised twice to stop his activities but broke his promises, was drowned in 1527. Grebel had died of disease in 1526. Hubmaier escaped but was arrested by the Emperor in 1528 and burned at the stake. His wife was thrown into the Danube with a millstone round her neck.

The remaining Swiss Brethren scattered to remote mountain areas and northwards into Germany, where they attracted supporters. One leader, Conrad Grebel, was in contact with Andreas Carlstadt and Thomas Münzer, who had caused Luther much trouble in the 1520s.

More radical than Luther: Carlstadt, the Zwickau prophets and Münzer

While Luther was in Wartburg, the Reformation in Wittenberg was directed by Andreas Carlstadt, whose views were far more radical. In 1522 a group of radicals, the Zwickau prophets, entered Wittenberg proclaiming that there was no miracle of the Real Presence and that there should be adult baptism only. Luther's return ended this radicalism. One of the 'prophets' was Thomas Münzer, who became a key figure in early Anabaptism. He went first to Prague and then to Saxony – a thorn in Luther's side.

Cross-reference

Luther's captivity at Wartburg is described on page 51.

Andreas Carlstadt is profiled on page 53.

Key profile

Thomas Münzer

Thomas Münzer (c.1489–1525) was born in central Germany and trained for the priesthood. A brilliant humanist scholar, he was fluent in Latin, Hebrew and Greek. He became a priest and from 1517–19 was in Wittenburg, a fervent disciple of Martin Luther. In 1520 he was priest at Zwickau (Saxony) and was converted to Anabaptism; he criticised Luther, calling him Dr Liar, Father Pussyfoot and the Wittenberg Pope. His views became more extreme and he preached a sermon before the electoral court that described his visions of the rulers slaughtering the evildoers without mercy. Such extremism got him expelled and at Mühlhausen he joined the Peasants' War. After the defeat of the peasant forces at Frankenhausen, he was executed in 1525, dying bravely.

Cross-reference

For the **Peasants' War**, see page 62.

Münzer's ideas were particularly influential. Apart from his Anabaptism, he believed that Christ was about to return to establish an age of the Holy Spirit. He also claimed that the Scriptures were not as important to convey God's message as direct links from the Holy Spirit to the believer through voices, visions and spiritual messages. His preaching became more **apocalyptic** as he prophesied the coming end of the world.

In 1524 Münzer became a minister at Mühlhausen in Thuringia and linked his own views on the coming end of the world to the growing tensions of the Peasants' War. His fiery preaching gained him a number of zealous followers, impressed that such a famous preacher should live among them. Up to this point, there had been little peasant protest in the area. It seems that Münzer's programme of revolutionary change and proclamation of the Millennium sparked off widespread disorders. He gathered together a fanatical 'Elect of 300'. The peasants had gathered an 'army' of about 8,000 together at Frankenhausen and Münzer was invited to lead them. Meanwhile, the forces of John of Saxony and Philip of Hesse concentrated against them. The princes offered to spare the peasants if they handed over Münzer:

> The prophet [Münzer] made a passionate speech in which he said that God had spoken to him and had promised victory; that he himself would catch the enemy cannonballs in the sleeves of his cloak; and that God himself would transform heaven and earth rather than allow his people to perish. The appearance of a rainbow, the symbol on Münzer's banner, was seen as a token of divine favour.

4 *N. Cohn, The Pursuit of the Millennium, 1970*

On the basis of this speech, Münzer was not given up, but the princes' cannon scattered the peasants. About 5,000 were killed and Münzer was found hiding in a cellar, tortured into making an apology for his rebellion and executed.

Münzer was a danger because he was a brilliant man who tried to make his apocalyptic obsessions a reality by working on social discontent to create rebellion. He had no interest in improving the condition of the poor. Martin Luther's writing against him was particularly harsh because he was against the social order that Luther supported and his moderate reforms. In practice, Münzer would never have gained the support of more influential people but, as the Anabaptist movement spread, he was regarded as a martyr to the cause.

Anabaptism in Upper Germany and Moravia

Although the Anabaptists had some common features such as adult baptism, a lay ministry and an exclusive group of believers, the Anabaptist movement suffered from lack of unity, no clear leadership and fragmented groups. Partly this was the result of encouraging each individual's interpretation of the Bible and of its own rejection of any oversight by authority.

Small numbers of Anabaptists, dominated by leaders such as Balthasar Hubmaier, Hans Denck and Hans Hut, set up a group in Augsburg. Because of persecution, Hubmaier moved to Moravia (on the eastern border of the Holy Roman Empire), where he began the most successful Anabaptist experiment. He gained the support of the local nobility and built on the past traditions of Hussite protest. A printing press was set up by refugees from Zürich and over 6,000 adults were rebaptised. The arrival of Hut shows how divisions were quickly created. Hut,

Key terms

Apocalyptic: visions predicting the end of the present world. The four horsemen of the apocalypse (Pestilence, War, Famine and Death) would bring destruction, the end would be preceded by the appearance of the Beast – whose number was 666. The prophesies can be read in Revelations 6.

Activity

Thinking point

Münzer's views are worth more detailed research. Try to find out more about the origins of his millenarianism and why he was praised as a champion of the people by former communist governments in the 20th century.

Question

Explain the importance of Thomas Münzer to the development of the Radical Reformation.

Cross-reference

For the **Hussite protest**, re page 27.

Did you know?

Jacob Hutter was dipped in freezing water (another parody of adult baptism), his skin slashed and rubbed with brandy, and set on fire. The authorities made a practice of extremely cruel deaths for Anabaptists – maybe a measure of their fear of them.

Question

Explain why the Hutterites were able to establish successful communities in Moravia.

Exploring the detail

The Bruderhofs

The Bruderhofs worked the land together and pooled all the members' skills. They laid great stress on education (every member had to read and write) and children did not live with their families. From the age of two, they lived in dormitories looked after by designated women. There was no university education as this would involve corruption by the wider world. Married couples also lived in dormitories, not separate houses. Marriages were arranged when the elders gathered the young men and women together and presented two or three men for the woman to choose from.

Exploring the detail

The rebellion in Amsterdam, 1535

Seven men and five women stripped off their clothes (to show they spoke the naked truth) and ran through the city shouting 'Woe! Woe! The Wrath of God will fall on this city!' They were seized and beaten to death by the people. This was another example of how the whole movement was blackened by atypical and probably deluded fanatics.

whom historian Geoffrey Elton describes as 'a formidable man, big, loud and persuasive', supported the visionary 'end of the world' wing of Anabaptism and proclaimed this would happen in three and a half years. At the same time, he said that no one should obey the civil authorities or pay tithes and taxes. Hubmaier's followers now flocked to him. Anabaptism lost the support of the civil authorities and persecution began. Hubmaier was executed and Hut died in prison in 1527.

The arrival of a brilliant organiser, Jacob Hutter, preserved the Moravian Anabaptists. He rejected the extreme views derived from Münzer and Hut and created pacifist communities called the Bruderhofs. After 1528, 86 such communities of perhaps 2,000 adults were created. In the persecutions that followed Münster, Hutter was captured and killed in 1536.

Even though they rejected civil authority, gradually the Moravian Brethren gained acceptance as their pacifism became evident. The communities contributed much to the local economy as they traded in local markets and gained fame as skilled craftsmen and textile workers. Their industry and quiet, dignified spirituality gained them many supporters by 1600.

Northern Germany and the Netherlands

Strasbourg, with its large Anabaptist community of about 10 per cent of the population, was the base from which Anabaptism spread to northern Germany and the Netherlands. The nature of the movement was very much the result of Melchior Hoffman. Hoffman at first supported Luther's views, but by 1529 had rejected most of them. Influenced by local Anabaptists and the ideas of Thomas Münzer, he came to adopt apocalyptic views such as the belief that the world would end in 1533 and would be heralded by a war between pope, emperor and false prophets (for example, Luther and Zwingli), after which 144,000 true apostles would rule. However, he did not support violence from his followers.

In 1530 Hoffman asked the Strasbourg authorities to give the Anabaptists their own church, but when his arrest was ordered he fled to Emden in the Netherlands. Here, he created a mass movement that spread throughout the territory. He was successful in Emden for a number of reasons:

- His message of the Second Coming was extremely popular.
- There was a lack of organisation for an 'official' reformation.
- The notion of social justice for the poor was attractive because of high food prices and unemployment.
- There were 'signs' of the end of the world, which he had predicted, because 1531–3 witnessed the appearance of three comets as well as floods, plagues and famine in the Netherlands.

In 1533 Hoffman returned to Strasbourg on the basis of a prophecy that he would be imprisoned for six months and then his teaching would be spread worldwide. He died in prison in 1543. The leadership of the movement was taken over by a Haarlem baker, Jan Matthys, and his chief lieutenant, Jan Bockelson (or Beukels) of Leyden. Both preached a revolutionary form of Anabaptism.

The authorities of Charles V, ruler of the Netherlands, stepped up their persecutions and, although some Anabaptists tried to find a safe haven out of the Netherlands such as in Münster, others believed they should stay and create rebellion. There were futile attempts to take over Dutch towns such as Amsterdam and Leyden, which only increased persecution.

The Münster experiment

Fig. 5 *A late 16th-century engraving of the city of Münster, which was controlled by Anabaptists from February 1534 to June 1535 in an attempt to create a theocratic state*

Münster was a north German town near the Dutch border. It had broken free from the authority of its Catholic bishop and had asked for the protection of Philip of Hesse. In 1531 the Catholic bishop had been forced out of the town and Lutheran preachers began a reformation. A visit from Anabaptist missionaries in January 1534 led to the baptism of leading Lutheran members of the town council. By February 1534 an Anabaptist council had been elected and when Matthys and Bockelson arrived in the town they took control and proclaimed Münster as the 'New Jerusalem' that had been prophesied. However, by this time the Bishop of Münster had organised forces to recapture the town.

Matthys began to create an Anabaptist state. All citizens had to be rebaptised or else be excluded from the town. About 2,000 left, but many more Anabaptists arrived. In April 1535 Matthys, believing he had a message from God that he was invincible, was killed in an attempt to break the siege and Jan Bockelson became leader. Under his rule, Münster reached a pitch of extremism. Bockelson proclaimed himself a prophet and the king of the world and created a court with guards, a nobility and splendid ceremonies. His 'court' lived off every luxury while the people starved. Churches were desecrated – fonts, the symbol of infant baptism, were a particular target. The death penalty was enforced for trivial offences such as swearing, complaining and gossiping. All were forced to share out their property, but the most notorious proposal was that men could take several wives in the manner of Old Testament prophets. Jan Bockelson himself took 16 wives, including the widow of Matthys. As the siege tightened, a riotous atmosphere prevailed within the town, but in June 1535 the besiegers were shown a hidden way into Münster and the town was betrayed to its enemies. The bishop's troops, supported by Catholic and Protestant forces, entered the town having been encouraged to rape, pillage and kill. The Anabaptists were executed with great cruelty.

The importance of Münster

Münster was the high point of all the millennial and messianic movements of previous centuries. The fall of Münster did not quite mark the end of the influence of the Münster experiment because a number of radical preachers still proclaimed the visions of the Second Coming. Nevertheless, the failure of Münster was a huge blow to all Anabaptists, whether peaceful or not. The lurid tales of sexual licence and orgiastic violence sent shock waves through decent public opinion. No government could trust them in their territories and authorities became very anxious about Anabaptist communities.

However, the only versions of what happened at Münster, and descriptions of Jan Bockelson, come from opponents. It could be argued that some of

Cross-reference

Philip of Hesse is profiled on page 56. He also appears frequently in the context of the spread of Lutheranism in Chapter 5.

Cross-reference

Source 1 on page 94 describes the cruel fate that befell the **Münster Anabaptists**.

his orders, such as sharing out goods, were the result of the pressures of the siege. He was clearly mentally unstable. Moreover, the Anabaptists had been elected to power in 1534 and the siege lasted 16 months. It ended only through betrayal, which perhaps indicates popular support. Its fanatical defenders gladly gave their lives for the 'New Jerusalem'.

Münster provided a reason for a new wave of persecutions between 1536 and 1543. These took place throughout Europe (in England between 1535 and 1560 there were 35 burnings) and it has been said, probably with exaggeration, that over 30,000 were killed in the Netherlands alone. Certainly many thousands were executed.

After Münster there were no more apocalyptic, millennial or messianic movements from the radical reformers. The mainstream Protestant movements had few concerns about persecuting of fellow Christians. Münster gave great urgency to the need to provide clear structures for the Protestant Church. Calvin's *Institutes* and the 1541 Ordinances were a response to Münster. Connected to this was the requirement for parishes to keep registers of births, which began in England in 1538 – it could be seen easily if a family was not going to church for infant baptism.

Anabaptism survived because the followers of Hoffman – the Melchiorites – adopted a non-violent approach while not denying their basic principles. Under the leadership of Menno Simons, a lasting community in the Netherlands – the Mennonites – was founded. The Mennonites were granted toleration in the Netherlands in 1577 and groups who sought a new life in North America gained a measure of freedom. Today, there are about 8 million Southern Baptists in the USA, although the most famous are the strict Amish Mennonites who try to preserve the principles of early Anabaptism.

The peaceful versions of Anabaptism survive in small numbers to the present day. The Moravian Brethren were scattered in 1622 by the Catholic Habsburgs, but small groups scattered worldwide. Their quiet, gentle faith and determination to live as the early Christians did in the New Testament impressed many, such as the young John and Charles Wesley, founders of Methodism in the 1730s, so it cannot be said that the Anabaptists were a complete failure.

Fig. 6 *Menno Simons, the Dutch radical reformer and founder of the Mennonites*

■ Activity

Group activity

In groups, research information on the Amish communities in the USA. Using the information in this section, give examples of how they follow the early Anabaptist ideas. (If you can, try to see the 1985 film *Witness*.)

■ Activity

Talking point

Discuss the view that Anabaptism had few of the qualities necessary to become a successful large-scale movement.

Fig. 7 *Modern-day Amish. Their way of life has some similarities with the Bruderhof tradition*

The reasons for the failure of the Radical Reformation

There were several reasons for the failure of the Radical Reformation and Anabaptism:

- The Anabaptists would not have judged success by having large numbers of converts. Most groups believed in the exclusive nature of their Church on the basis that few would be saved, not all humankind. Generally, they asked to be left alone to practise their views, although when these involved producing social disorder (as in Münster) it was hard to grant them religious freedom. They regarded their persecutions as part of the proof that the Last Days were near and that they were right in rejecting the oppressive state. Far from being a sign of failure, persecutions were a sign of the success of a suffering faith.

- The Anabaptists had few powerful supporters, except for a time in Moravia. They were a religion of the poor and artisan class.

- Anabaptism was not a single movement with a central leadership: 40 separate sects have been identified, each with a leader who claimed to be divinely inspired. This was the nature of the movement itself – everyone could interpret the meaning of the New Testament for themselves and little importance was given to formal structures or organisation. All kinds of divisions were inevitable.

- Both the religious and social beliefs of the Anabaptists were seen as a threat to the established order, and the 16th century did not like diversity, especially groups that rejected civil authority. The Peasants' War and Münster seemed proof of their danger and destroyed any arguments in favour of toleration. A contemporary commented 'at the moment they are peaceful law-abiding lambs, but soon they may be wolves, as rebellious as before'.

- Interpretations of the success of the radicals have varied. They have generally been written off as hopelessly divided groups of fanatics or peace-loving but deluded fringe members of society, but this is because their history has largely been written by their enemies. A more important criticism is that they tended to regard themselves as exclusive groups, avoiding any dealings with other Christians who had to live within the state. They were not tolerant of other Christians. They alone were the elect and their charity was inward-looking.

- Revisionist historians such as G. H. Williams have preferred to stress the fact that the radicals rejected most formal structures, did not have a theology beyond Bible study, supported the individual's right to interpret religion and rejected any interference in matters of faith and conscience, believing themselves champions of freedom of conscience and religious liberty. They tried to create communities modelled on the ethical practices of the early Church and, for them, religion was an acting out of brotherly love, supporting each member in charity. Such ideals proved to be out of keeping with the times in which they lived.

Cross-reference

To recap on the **Peasants' War**, review page 62.

Activity

Talking point

Read Chapters 6 and 7 again. In what ways was the Genevan experiment similar to, and in what ways different from, that of the Anabaptists?

Summary question

How successful were the radical reformers in influencing the European Reformation in the years 1521–40?

Learning outcomes

In this section you have learned about the reasons for the rise of the reformation radicals and why they appeared to be such a danger to both religious and secular authorities. You have examined the development of the many different Anabaptist movements and looked at significant episodes such as the Münster experiment. Finally, you have learned about the reasons for the failure of the movement and its significance.

AQA Examination-style questions

(a)   Explain why Anabaptists were persecuted in the years 1521–34.　　*(12 marks)*

In part a) you will need to explain why the Anabaptists were so disliked. The examiner is looking for reasons, not a narrative, so you will consider religious, political and social reasons as well as the intolerance of the age. For top marks, links will need to be made between reasons, e.g. religious beliefs of separation through adult baptism were linked to political beliefs of a rejection of interference from the state.

(b)   How important were the events at Münster 1534–5 in causing the failure of the Radical Reformation?　　*(24 marks)*

In part b) the main theme is the influence of Münster and the excesses of those years will easily explain how the image of radicalism was discredited by the actions of its extreme wing. The memory was fresh for many years after the event. However, balance in this question is essential and you could argue that failure was evident years before with the Swiss Brethren or the Dutch Melchiorites. The very nature of Anabaptism contained the seeds of its failure through its tendency to create schisms and its exclusive beliefs as well as its lack of leadership. Opposition from both religious and secular rulers was strong before 1534. Good answers will be aware of the European context of the success or otherwise of the radical reformers.

5 The Jesuits

9 The foundation of the Jesuit order

Key terms

Jesuits: followers of Ignatius of Loyola and members of the Society of Jesus, a Catholic religious order. This name became official in 1540.

Cross-reference

You will read more about the **Counter Reformation** and its initiatives in Chapter 11.

Cross-reference

Ignatius of Loyola is profiled on pages 114–15.

The **Spiritual Exercises** are described on page 109.

As you read Chapters 9 and 10, keep in mind that, important as the **Jesuits** were, they were one among many of the developments that emerged out of the Catholic reform programme of the mid 16th century, often known as the Catholic Reformation or Counter Reformation.

> In the hospital of the Incurabili, a leper, or one covered all over with a kind of pestilential skin condition, called one of the fathers [Jesuit brothers] and asked him to scratch his back. The father diligently performed this service, but whilst he was doing so he was suddenly struck with horror, and with the terror of contracting the contagious disease. But since he wanted to master himself and to suppress his own rebellious spirit rather than take thought for the future, he put into his mouth a finger covered with pus and sucked it. Another day, he told one of his companions about it, and said with a smile: 'I dreamed last night that the sick man's disease had stuck to my throat, and that I tried to expel it, but in vain.'

 *One of Ignatius's companions, quoted in R. Mackenney, **Sixteenth Century Europe: Expansion and Conflict**, 1993*

This story of heroic self-control was meant to inspire new members of the 'Society of Jesus' and goes a little way to explaining why the Jesuit order was feared by its enemies and perhaps even more feared by members of the Catholic Church. Its reputation over the centuries – the Jesuits have been seen as either devils or saints – has depended on the viewpoint of those doing the evaluation. The Jesuits have always created controversy.

Ignatius of Loyola and the foundation of the order in 1540

Perhaps more than any other religious leader of the time, Ignatius of Loyola was the inspiration, heart and driving force behind the organisation he created. The Society of Jesus of 1540 grew from the Company of Jesus, which Ignatius and six companions had founded in 1534. The companions soon attracted attention in Italy (which had become their base) because of their exceptional abilities and enthusiasm for serving the Church in any capacity. They undertook a wide variety of work such as serving the poor, lecturing in the universities and guiding people through Ignatius's Spiritual Exercises. They sought out the worst tasks in hospitals: as one Jesuit wrote later, the tasks were to 'make the beds, sweep the floors, wash the pots, scrub the dirt, dig the graves and bury the dead'.

■ **Cross-reference**

The support provided to Ignatius and his followers from **high-born ladies** is covered on page 127.

The **founding of other new orders**, including the Theatines, can be found on pages 32–3.

They were encouraged by Ignatius to find support from aristocratic patrons and churchmen such as Contarini and Pope Paul III, and they benefited greatly from the support of high-born ladies. By 1539 the number of companions had increased and Ignatius was reluctantly forced to create an order that could be officially recognised. This met with opposition from cardinals, who claimed there were too many orders already or suggested that the Jesuits joined the Theatines, which were superficially similar. The radical nature of Ignatius's proposed new order and the proposed exemptions from the normal rules of religious life also roused jealousy from established orders. However, the strong support of Paul III ensured Ignatius's success.

Establishment of the order

The Society of Jesus was officially founded by Paul III in the very favourable bull of 1540. The bull *Regimini militantis ecclesiae* was based on previous rules for the companions such as the Five Chapters. In 1559 the 'Constitutions' of the society, based on the 1540 bull, provided a definitive and detailed guide to their life, conduct and work.

The aims of the order were set out in the 1540 bull:

- To advance souls in Christian life and doctrine.
- To pass on and spread ('and defend' was added in 1550) the faith by public preaching, lectures and the ministry of God's word.
- To carry out spiritual exercises and works of charity.
- To hear confessions and administer other sacraments.
- To reconcile those who have quarrelled, serving those in prisons and hospitals.
- To educate in Christian doctrine children and people who could not read or write.

Fig. 1 *Ignatius of Loyola by Rubens, painted many years after his death for the Jesuit Mother Church in Rome. He is portrayed as the Christian hero*

Fig. 2 *Paul III confirms the Society of Jesus, 1540. Ignatius is kneeling*

The structure and organisation of the Jesuit order

General congregation
A meeting of the whole order. The general congregation elected
(or could depose) the General and decided on the strategy of the order.
It has met very rarely – fewer than 40 times since 1541.

↓

General provincial
'The General' of the order was elected for life (Loyola was the first
General). One of the distinctive features of the Jesuits was their
strong central direction from Rome. Only the General made
Four advisers → appointments and set policy and the General took advice from
usually four assistants. Election for life avoided the damaging
arguments over leadership that other orders experienced.
Communication to the members worldwide was made up by letters
and thousands of letters flowed back and forth from Rome. Loyola
himself wrote almost 8,000 letters in his lifetime. It was compulsory
for regular reports of Jesuit activities to be sent to Rome. This is why
historians have so much information about them.

↓

Provincials
Headed up the provinces of the order, usually a country. Unlike other
orders, provincials were not elected by the local members and had
few decision-making powers. There were six in 1555.

↓

Rectors
In charge of Jesuit 'houses' in each province. In another departure
from customs of other orders, Jesuits did not live in monasteries
but in houses or colleges. Loyola insisted that their 'best house'
was their journeys for their missions.

Fig. 3 *The structure of the Jesuit order*

Admittance into the order

The main rule about membership was that each Jesuit should work to
see that 'as many as possible of the very best' entered the society. By
the end of the training, only the best of the best would survive. One
distinctive feature of the society, however, is that they did not ask for a
'dowry' – a lump-sum payment – to join.

Most religious orders asked recruits to have a period of preparation (a
noviciate), when their fitness to join would be assessed, and the recruit
would join at the end of the year. The Jesuits had a two-year noviciate,
during which time they were expected to carry out various tests such
as working with the poor or sick or going on a pilgrimage. At the end of
two years, they were only admitted to the lowest level of the society. After
this, there would be a programme of education – called the scholasticate –
at the end of which the Jesuit was ordained (made a priest). The recruit
took the normal religious vows of poverty, chastity and obedience. Then
there was a third stage – a year-long second noviciate or third probation
when the recruit was under close observation by a senior mentor for any
signs of weakness. At last, the recruit could become a formal member
of the society, although even here there were grades of membership as
it was soon recognised that there was a role for those who were less
intellectually able. These membership grades were as follows:

- Fully professed members who formed the inner core of the society:
  they alone (and not all of them) took the 'fourth vow' of direct

personal obedience to the pope. (In 1556 only 43 out of 1,000 members had taken this vow.)

■ Spiritual co-adjutors: these undertook purely spiritual tasks such as preaching and lecture work (there were only five in 1556) and could be rectors of Jesuit 'houses'.

■ Temporal co-adjutors: these were the invention of Ignatius himself. They were not made priests. This group were usually drawn from what could be called lower-class backgrounds and were often practical craftsmen such as cooks, carpenters or gardeners who looked after the worldly (temporal) needs of the members. They did not have a formal education and were not allowed to gain one. About 25 per cent of the members were in this grade. However, they did teach the catechism, visit hospitals and prisons or do other charitable works depending on ability. This grade was popular with those who did not wish to be ordained but still wanted to work with the society.

Jesuit organisation was an important reason for their success. It was flexible and suited the needs of an organisation that was expanding rapidly. While other orders had to deal with perhaps 100 members, the Jesuits had over 1,000 by 1556. Their stress on obedience to the head of the society was a sound way of keeping control, as was the focus on the central purpose – they were not to be deflected into other roles. The key position of General ensured that consistent policies were followed.

Jesuit education and training was far more rigorous than any other order, which accounts for the high regard in which they were held and why they were in so much demand.

The nature and distinctiveness of the order

The Jesuit order undertook a large number of tasks, including:

■ missionary work

■ education

■ pastoral work – administering the sacraments; works of charity such as visiting hospitals and prisons; ministering to the dying, prostitutes and the daughters and orphans of prostitutes; preaching

■ acting as **confessors** to the rulers of Europe

■ work as theologians and diplomats. The Jesuits were particularly active at the Council of Trent, a most important general council of the Church that met in three sessions between 1545 and 1563

■ defence of the Church against the Protestant advance – Jesuit missions in Europe.

In addition to the rigorous nature of their training for membership, the Jesuit order had a number of distinctive features in comparison to other orders. They did not wear any distinctive monastic habit, nor did they hold 'chapters' – regular meetings of the membership to elect superiors and discuss common issues. They did not meet together daily to say Mass or chant the cycle of daily prayers that were the routine of monastic life. Fasting and excessive mortifications, praying and great attention to devotions were strongly discouraged. Although these privileges caused (maybe understandably) great resentment among other orders, Ignatius argued that, because their mission was worldwide, it was next to impossible to gather the membership together even at provincial level. He wished them to follow the lifestyle of the early Christian preachers, who did not wear habits or chant the office. He stressed many times that to become a Jesuit was not to retreat from the world and become a contemplative order, but to actively seek it out and deal with its problems. Finally, the Jesuits' dedication to the papacy was exceptional:

■ Cross-reference

The **Jesuits' aims** in the area of missionary work, education, pastoral work and as confessors are outlined on pages 118–123.

The Jesuits' part in the **Council of Trent** is outlined on pages 112–13.

The **general council of the Church** is covered on page 137.

The **Jesuits' contribution to the defence of Church** against the Protestant advance is discussed on pages 124–8.

■ Key terms

Confessors: priests in their role of administering the sacrament of penance (see page 24). The penitent confesses his or her sins to the priest, who offers comfort and advice as well as deciding the penance (or punishment) that the sins deserve.

This entire society and its members serve as soldiers of God in faithful obedience to Paul III and his successors. We are bound to carry out his orders instantly, as far as in us lies, without any evasion or excuses: whether he sends us to the Turks, or into the New World, or to the Lutherans, or any other realms.

2	
	*Ignatius of Loyola, **Five Chapters**, 1539*

It may be helpful to point out what the Jesuits were *not*:

- Jerome Nadal, a key shaper of the society, said: 'We are not monks, the world is our house.'
- They were not to take over the work of the parish priests (although the potential for clashes was enormous).
- They were not formed to stop the advance of Protestantism and very little work was done in this respect between 1540 and 1555. Their main activities at first were in Italy, Spain and Portugal, which were strongly Catholic and far less threatened by the Protestant advance.
- They were not a kind of religious army even though they were called 'soldiers of God' by Ignatius.
- They were not intended to be part of the established hierarchy of the Church. Even though they were sought after because of their abilities, they were banned from becoming bishops.

Fig. 4 *The triumph of Counter Reformation. A sculpture in the Jesuit Church in Rome showing Mother Church ridding herself of heretics. The little angel is tearing pages from the reformers' books*

The significance of the Spiritual Exercises

Begun in 1522, Ignatius's work on the Spiritual Exercises reached its final printed form in 1548. The Exercises were a set of prayers, reflections, mental exercises and self-disciplines that were to last between 28 and 30 days. They were the essential tool of Jesuit training, as well as a highly popular course of spiritual enlightenment for laypeople who were guided through it. They were adapted for groups and mission work, which was the intention of Ignatius himself. The aim of the Exercises was:

preparing and disposing our soul to rid itself of all its disordered affections and then, after their removal, of seeking and finding God's will in the ordering of our life for the salvation of our soul.

3	
	*From the Spiritual Exercises, quoted in J. O'Malley, **The First Jesuits**, 1993*

The Exercises were a set of materials designed for a person helping someone else through the course, a kind of teachers' manual. The best way to undertake the course was in the setting of a **retreat**, away from distractions, under the guidance of a spiritual director or supervisor. Daily instruction included various meditations and contemplation on the nature of the world, its evils and temptations, and humankind's relationship with God as revealed by Christ. The Exercises provided a focus for the mediations. Each day, the retreatant would pray with an

Exploring the detail

'Soldiers of God'

One of the strongest images of the Jesuits is that of an army or military organisation – 'the spearhead of the Catholic Church' or the 'shock-troops'. However, references in their own writings in terms of them being an 'army' are rare. 'Soldiers of God' was a common phrase for all members of religious orders and indeed could be applied to all Christians.

Activity

Talking point

Why were the Jesuits both admired and disliked in this period?

Key terms

Retreat: the time in which a person was taken through the Spiritual Exercises by his Jesuit supervisor was called a retreat. The person who undertook the Spiritual Exercises was called the retreatant.

exercise given by the director, return for discussion and then be given a further five periods of prayer – about five hours in all. At the end of the session, the director examined what the prayer experiences meant for the retreatant and their importance in daily life. The Exercises were divided into four 'weeks' of different lengths.

A closer look

The four 'weeks' of the Spiritual Exercises

In the first week, the person was invited to reflect on the sins of humanity and their personal sins. The week ended with Confession, which is a cleansing for the next stage.

In the second week, a meditation called on the person to follow Christ and then there was reflection on Christ's suffering and death. In prayer, there was the recognition of God's will and that a choice had to be made. This 'choice' is at the heart of the second week.

In the third and fourth weeks, there were reflections on the passion, death and resurrection of Christ to confirm the choice of a new life in Christ. In conclusion, the person reflected on the many gifts God had given and continued to give, and so in equal generosity surrendered himself to God.

It is impossible to show the real flavour of the Exercises in a short summary, but it is important to note that great levels of emotion were tapped by the process: fear, terror of death, shame and joy at salvation were all heavily worked on. For example, in the first week the retreatant was urged:

- to think about the pains of hell
- to see in the imagination those enormous fires and the souls as it were with bodies of fire
- to hear in the imagination the shrieks and groans
- to smell in the imagination the fumes of sulphur
- to taste in the imagination all the bitterness of tears
- to feel shame:

> I will try to be ashamed of all my sins, using illustrations: for example, I may think of a knight, standing before the king and all his court, utterly ashamed at having greatly offended one from whom he had received many gifts and acts of kindness.

The Exercises were written with a number of points in mind:

- Ignatius had in mind a person who had to make a decisive choice in their life (for example, a career or lifestyle change) and the aim was to help the person make an objective choice – this choice is at the heart of the programme at the end of the second week. However, anyone who wanted to draw nearer to Christ could benefit.
- The flexibility of the Exercises was important – many men and women were not making a life-changing decision or did not have the temperament or the time for the four 'weeks'. They could set aside an hour or so for as many weeks as they wished. The strength of the Exercises was that the Jesuits provided a spiritual director to take people through the course, which could then be matched to personal needs, but there was additional flexibility that the spiritual director was not essential.

- The assumption was that people who took the Exercises were believing Catholics. This was because there was the sacrament of penance at the end of the first week after a strict examination of past sins, which was essential – at least for Ignatius.

- The text was not meant to convey any theology – Ignatius knew little anyway when he started it – nor is it an attack on Luther, Erasmus or Calvin. It is based on personal religious experiences.

An addition to the Exercises was a short section called 'Rules for Thinking with the Church', which is perhaps the most famous part of it. This section was the last part to be written (in 1538) and the 18 rules were possibly aimed at the Lutherans. They were mostly about how the Jesuits supported all the official teachings of the Church and how the Jesuits should be cautious in their approach to their teaching and ministry. The most famous rule is Rule 13:

> To arrive at complete certainty, this is the attitude of mind we should have: I will believe that the white object I see is black if that should be the decision of the Church.

This has been often quoted to show that the Jesuits were uncritical supporters of the Church and were fanatically obedient. However, although the wording is rather dramatic, it only expressed the importance of being obedient to the Church's teaching.

Many Catholics were concerned over Rule 2, which suggested taking Communion weekly (not the practice in the 16th century) and theologians were upset about Rule 14:

> Whilst it is absolutely true that no man can be saved without being predestined and without faith and grace, great care is called for in the way we talk and argue about these matters.

The context for this is, of course, the great Reformation argument over predestination versus free will. It was given in evidence that the Jesuits glossed over difficult problems. Arguably there is no answer to this issue, so playing down the whole debate was sensible pastoral advice that shows the Jesuits' practical approach.

The Exercises could be practised without acceptance of these rules because the rules did not form part of the four-week programme. The importance of the Exercises lay in the following:

- The book helped many people to become members of the society or its strong supporters if they did not join (and could not, in the case of women). This led to a charge of brainwashing by the enemies of the Jesuits, as the spiritual director could have a powerful influence over the retreatant and the process was not public. Ignatius condemned any use of brainwashing to recruit others. Jesuits were warned that members were only to join freely. Jesuit opponents also pointed out that many who took the Exercises, especially the rich and powerful, did not seem to noticeably change their lives yet the Jesuits still did not condemn them.

- Historian Keith Randell comments that it soon became a mark of social distinction to have taken the Exercises, so the rich and powerful were demanding to take the course. As a result, kings, princes and their wives often became committed Jesuit supporters.

- Taking the Exercises bound the early followers of Ignatius together; it was (and still is) a distinctive practice of the Jesuit order and an essential part of their training. Laypeople who took the Exercises could also relate to the order itself as a common experience.

Activity

Thinking point

What is your view of the Jesuit way of thinking?

Cross-reference

The argument over **predestination versus free will** is discussed on pages 45 and 73.

Activity

Challenge your thinking

Try to find a copy of the 'Rules for Thinking with the Church'. In groups, debate the likely significance of acceptance of these rules.

Activity

Talking point

Why were the Spiritual Exercises successful?

Cross-reference

More information on the **Council of Trent** can be found on page 136.

The work and influence of the Jesuits at the Council of Trent

The Council of Trent was one of the great turning points in the Catholic Church. The aims of the Council were to arrive at clear definitions of Catholic doctrine and to reform the discipline of the Church.

The First Session of the Council met in December 1545 at Trent. The proceedings were organised by three papal legates (not Jesuits) and there were also 50 theologians. In this number were the leading Jesuit theologians Diego Lainez and Alphonsus Salmeron, and one other. As a mark of special favour, they were designated papal theologians and were among the very few that were reappointed by succeeding popes for the whole Council. However, although the Jesuits were important, they were not the guiding forces of the Council.

Fig. 5 *The Council of Trent in session*

Ignatius of Loyola was delighted that his members were so honoured, but his instructions to them according to historian J. O'Malley were surprisingly low key, advising them to be modest when giving their views, listening to both sides and weighing up arguments. There were some points about their lifestyle and advice about carrying on their works of charity. (They even managed to guide a few bishops through the Exercises – a typically Jesuit touch.) There was nothing about the mighty themes of the Council. In fact, the only point that Ignatius ever suggested to put on the agenda, in 1551, was to see if the Jesuits could be officially recognised by the Council because in some parts of the world that authority was seen as more important than that of the popes. Maybe Ignatius trusted the pair to do the right thing – there was no agenda to follow from Jesuit headquarters in Rome.

Cross-reference

More on **Diego Lainez** and **Alphonsus Salmeron** can be found on pages 116–17.

Key chronology

The Council of Trent

1545–7 First Session
1551–2 Second Session
1562–3 Third Session

Cross-reference

To recap on **Catholic doctrine** and issues such as salvation by '**faith alone**' and the **Real Presence**, revise Chapters 2 and 4.

The work of the Jesuits in supporting definitions of Catholic doctrine

Much of the work of the Council of Trent was involved with defining Catholic doctrine, especially the areas in which they were in dispute with the Protestants.

First Session

Much of the First Session was taken up with the problem of salvation and justification by 'faith alone', which were central to Protestant teaching. Some bishops and cardinals, and those who recognised the importance of the biblical studies generated by humanism, looked favourably on 'faith alone' and tried to find a compromise between earning salvation and predestination. Lainez and Salmeron represented the orthodox view and were allowed to start and sum up the session on justification – Lainez being allowed to address the assembly for three hours. Although Lainez and Salmeron summed up the majority view, their explanations impressed the assembled bishops.

Second Session

In the Second Session, both theologians commented on the doctrines of the Mass, including the Real Presence. The Emperor Charles V had wanted some compromise on the issue of whether the laity in Germany should be allowed to take Communion in Both Kinds (both the bread and wine). This had been allowed in some parts of central Europe and it would have been helpful to allow Lutherans who returned to the Catholic Church to continue to receive both the bread and wine. Salmeron argued that the true Catholic teaching was to take the bread only and denounced attempts at compromise. The Jesuits showed they were well thought-of when discussing religious problems.

Third Session

The Third Session of the Council almost fell apart over the critical issue of the nature of the authority of the bishops. The Spanish delegation of bishops argued that the presence and authority of a bishop in his diocese and indeed the office itself was commanded by divine law – that is, had its origins in Christ himself, and not in the law of the Church. Therefore, the status of bishop was not given by the pope, and indeed the pope himself was only the most important bishop (as all bishops derived from the same authority).

This might seem a trivial point, but it had great implications. If the bishop was in his diocese by divine authority, then the pope could not, for example, give permission for a bishop to leave his diocese for other work. This greatly alarmed the Italian bishops in the papal court, most of whom would have had to return to their dioceses.

The problem was that although all Catholics recognised the authority of the pope, the precise extent of this authority was the subject of bitter argument. Even the Jesuits, with their supposed total obedience to the pope, only accepted this when doing missionary work – otherwise they were quite prepared to work their way round uncongenial papal orders.

However, the Jesuits tended to raise the status of the papacy and Lainez made high profile interventions arguing this line. In October 1562 he argued strongly that the bishops' authority came not from their office but was a grant from the pope; the Council rejected this view. In June 1563 Lainez intervened in a debate about who should carry out a reform of the papal *curia* (court) – the popes themselves or the Council – to argue that the popes alone should do this. His strongly papal language apparently caused outcry among Spanish and French bishops. Lainez's motive seemed to be that he doubted if the Council could carry out reform on a practical level and he wanted to quash the dangerous view that a council was superior to a pope.

The influence of the Jesuits at Trent

The Jesuits showed themselves to be reliable supporters of Catholic orthodoxy and champions of papal authority. The Council recognised their unique organisation by exempting them from the new rule which said that a novice should be accepted into an order straight after his noviciate and their schools avoided a new tax to pay for schools to train priests. Their privileges given by the popes were confirmed.

Their close identification with the papacy was a mixed blessing. Although it gave them high status in the Church, it caused great resentment from the other orders, and some monarchs were suspicious that their loyalties were with the papacy and that they were international papal 'agents'. As the status of the papacy declined in the 18th century, demands were made for their abolition – which happened in 1773.

Summary questions

1 What were the distinctive features of the Jesuit order?

2 Why did Ignatius of Loyola insist on such a long period of training?

3 How important were the Jesuits in influencing the outcomes of the Council of Trent?

The work and influence of the Jesuits

Fig. 1 *Jesuits abroad – Francis Xavier arrives at the port of Kagoshima in Japan, 1549*

In this chapter you will learn about:

- the importance of Ignatius of Loyola

- the work and importance of other key Jesuits within the order

- the importance of the Jesuits as educators and missionaries

- the work and influence of the Jesuits as preachers and confessors

- the success of the Jesuits in reviving the Catholic Church and halting the Protestant advance.

The importance of individual members of the Jesuit order

Ignatius of Loyola

Key profile

Ignatius of Loyola

Ignatius of Loyola (1491–1556) was born the last child of a minor Spanish nobleman at the castle of Loyola in northern Spain. At the age of 15 he was sent to the castle of an official of the King of Aragon to learn courtly behaviour and military skills. He entered military service, fighting against the French, and in 1521was badly wounded at the siege of Pamplona. During a long convalescence, he read religious works and in 1522 he visited the shrine to the Virgin Mary at Monserrat and dedicated his life to the service of religion. This represented a critical turning point in his life. In 1522 he began work on the Spiritual Exercises and the following year he made a pilgrimage to Jerusalem. Between 1525 and 1527 Ignatius spent time at Spanish universities improving his education and from 1528–35 lived in Paris, where he continued his education in both the humanist and scholastic traditions.

In 1534 Ignatius and six companions vowed to remain together to go to the Holy Land or, if this was impractical, to offer their services to the pope. In effect, this was the origin of the Society of Jesus. In 1537 the companions met in Venice to take ship for the Holy Land, but war between Venice and the Turks made this impossible. The next year Ignatius and two other companions went to Rome to offer their services to the pope. Outside Rome, Ignatius had a second vision of his mission; at this point he took up residence in Rome.

In 1539 the companions' aim was still to go to Jerusalem, but Pope Paul III suggested they could save souls in Italy – 'Rome could be their Jerusalem'. Ignatius decided that the creation of an order was needed to keep the companions together, and a Constitution was drawn up. In 1540 Paul III officially founded the Society of Jesus with the bull *Regimini militantis ecclesiae*. Two years later, Ignatius elected the first General of the new order. He remained in Rome until his death, closely directing every part of the society's work.

Cross-reference

For **Ignatius's six companions**, see pages 116–17.

Ignatius as the founder of the society set the character and tone of the whole order and its early history. He struck a difficult balance between being a highly practical organiser, totally aware of the art of the possible, and a religious visionary and ascetic. His charisma hugely impressed all who met him and his prestige after his death sustained the society as they possessed an almost certain saint. His followers naturally praised him:

> His soul was invariably of an even temper. It made no difference, whether he was on his way from Mass or had had dinner or whether he had just got out of bed, whether things were quiet or the world was upside down, for he was always in a state of self-mastery.

1
By one of Ignatius's followers

Activity

Talking point

What can we learn from Source 1 about Ignatius's character and personality?

Above all, Ignatius had good sense. He did demand obedience, but only to use his members' talents to the full. He did not allow his members to fast or punish themselves through excessive physical trials. He attracted the wealthy to support the order, and taught his members to be on good terms with the highest powers in the Church and state and to use their position to benefit the society, but he did not neglect the poor. He was quite prepared to bend the strict rule of obedience to the pope if it went against the interests of the order. In the missions, he instructed his missionaries to be tolerant of the local religions if in the end many were converted to Christianity.

Above all, Ignatius instructed the society not to attack the vices of others or openly criticise their way of life. In the case of the Protestants, the Jesuits were not to heap abuse on them (compare here the printed material of the early Reformation with Luther and Calvin), but exactly the opposite: 'He who preaches with love is preaching effectively against the heretic.'

Ignatius created a unique organisation that was strongly part of the world, not separate from it. However, he did not escape criticism, even from the first companions. Bobadilla and Rodriguez did not like the way in which the early informality of the society was changing to becoming obsessed with structures, minute rules and unnecessary form-filling.

Exploring the detail

Pope Paul IV and the strict rule of obedience

Paul IV (1555–9) was hostile to the Jesuits, ruling that they say the usual prayers of a religious order – the Divine Office – and that the General was to be elected every three years. These rules would destroy their unique character. Ignatius was dismayed and worked hard not to implement these commands. On the pope's death, the Jesuits gained a decision that Paul's orders were only valid for his reign.

Ignatius himself was called a 'tyrant' in a serious conflict within the society. Other critics claimed that he was too concerned with gaining the favour of the rich and influential as he maintained a vast correspondence with Portuguese, Habsburg and Bavarian royalty as well as the leading aristocratic families of Catholic Europe.

Ignatius's companions

The six companions who joined Ignatius in 1534 were Bobadilla, Favre, Rodriguez, Lainez, Salmeron and Xavier. They came from varied backgrounds – from sons of aristocrats to a shepherd boy. Their ages varied from 19 to 43 and they ranged from brilliant scholars to men of action. Their nationalities were French, Spanish, Portuguese and Italian. All had been taken through the Spiritual Exercises. By 1537 three other Frenchmen had joined.

Key profiles

Nicolas de Bobadilla

Nicholas de Bobadilla (1518–90) was a Spanish aristocrat. He was sent to Germany in 1541 with Favre. Although he respected Ignatius, he had a fiery and restless temperament that led him to dislike publically the growing conformity and formality of the society after 1550. He found it difficult to follow orders and was involved in a great crisis after Ignatius's death in 1556, when he sided with Paul IV who wanted to reduce the privileges of the order. Later, Bobadilla was reconciled.

Pierre Favre

Pierre Favre (1506–46) was born a shepherd boy in north Italy. He was a fervent supporter of Ignatius and especially promoted the Spiritual Exercises. After 1540 he spent much time in Germany, reporting back to Rome on the spread of Lutheranism and the poor state of German Catholicism. His great achievement was to inspire Peter Canisius to undertake the Spiritual Exercises and join the Society in 1543.

Simão Rodriguez

Simão Rodriguez (d.1579) came from a Portuguese noble family. He had great academic ability and personal charm. As the Jesuit provincial in Portugal after 1540, he greatly increased Jesuit membership and expanded its work. He gained strong support from King John III (1521–57). However, Rodriguez's independent spirit and development of a highly personal ministry caused Ignatius great anxiety. Ignatius's attempts to discipline him led to his recall to Rome in 1553.

Diego Lainez

Diego Lainez (or Laynez) (1512–65) was a theologian and the second General of the Society. He attended the University of Paris and was the second to join Ignatius. From then on, he followed Ignatius through his early career and so impressed Paul III that he was asked to teach theology in Rome. His fame rests on his work at the Council of Trent. Paul IV asked him to check the details of the *Index of Prohibited Books*, which the pope produced in 1559. As a theologian and diplomat, Lainez was asked by Pius IV to be his representative at the Colloquy of Poissy in 1561, called by Catherine d'Medici, Regent of France, to find a compromise between Catholic and Calvinist. His defence of Catholic teaching, when he denounced the purpose of the colloquy, reduced Catherine to tears and doomed the colloquy.

Cross-reference

The work of **Lainez and Salmeron at the Council of Trent** is outlined on page 112.

Paul IV and the *Index of Prohibited Books* are outlined on page 138.

Alphonsus Salmeron

Alphonsus Salmeron (1515–85) is a fine example of the multi-tasking that marked out the leading Jesuits and made them so much in demand. He was one of Ignatius's first companions and followed his plan to go to the Holy Land in 1537. Waiting for the ship, he spent much time helping the poor and destitute children. Paul III sent him on a mission to Ireland and he returned to Rome through France in 1542. He spent time preaching and explaining the Scriptures there before attending the Council of Trent with Lainez. He needed extra study to take up an offer of a university post at Ingolstadt in Bavaria, but he left in 1550 to set up the first Jesuit college in Naples before returning for the Second Session of the Council. In 1555 he was sent as a diplomat to the Diet of Augsburg and afterwards to Poland and the Netherlands. Once again chosen as papal theologian, he was present at the last session of the Council. From 1564 until his death, he wrote many commentaries on the Scriptures and preached annual programmes of sermons. His life comprised virtually every aspect of the Jesuit mission.

Francis Xavier

Francis Xavier (1506–52) shared a room with Ignatius at the University of Paris and was the second of the companions. A Spanish aristocrat with an impulsive, hyperactive personality, he was given authority to carry out mission work by John III of Portugal and Pope Paul III. Ironically, he was Ignatius's second choice when another Jesuit fell sick two days before going. He arrived in Goa in 1542. For his work in the mission field, he was later made a saint. Xavier was one of the greatest Christian missionaries. In a career of about 10 years, he travelled enormous distances, encountered many dangers and devoted vast energy to his missionary work.

- Dressed virtually in rags, Xavier made his mission to the primitive Pavanas tribes of south India, then on to the Macuans, baptising 10,000 by 1544.

- He moved on to Molucca, the Malay states and the headhunters of the Molucca Islands.

- In 1548 he returned to Goa to set up a training school for priests and natives.

- Xavier had high expectations of Japan, which he felt was a sophisticated and highly moral society. In 1549 he landed at Kagashima, but found it to be a far more sophisticated society than he had realised and his poverty and rags disgusted upper-class Japanese. He failed to appreciate that real power lay not with the Emperor but with powerful local nobles. Changing his rags for rich robes and impressively clothing his retinue, and bringing gifts such as clocks, musical boxes and wine, he gained the support of an influential noble, and by 1551 some 2,000 Christians had been baptised in 5 communities. His successor de Torres continued his work. Numbers grew when a catechism was produced in Japanese in 1558. Japan was a success story at first as local nobles supported Christianity. Schools were founded for native priests and possibly 200,000 Japanese became Christians by 1600.

- In 1552 Xavier was taken ill waiting for a ship to take him to China and died two weeks later.

Cross-reference

The **Diet of Augsburg** is detailed on page 66.

Fig. 2 The Miracles of St Francis Xavier, *a painting by Rubens, who was commissioned in 1617 by the Jesuits to help the case for Xavier's canonisation. Xavier is shown here bringing an Indian child back to life, the lame to walk, and many other miracles*

Cross-reference

Xavier's dedicated missionary work is described in detail on page 121.

■ Activity

Revision exercise

Copy and complete the following table.

	Ignatius	Bobadilla	Favre	Rodriguez	Lainez	Salmeron	Xavier
Background							
When and why he joined the order							
Main activities							
Importance to the order							

■ The importance of the Jesuits as educators, missionaries, preachers and confessors

Educators

Education played a critical role in the revival of the Catholic Church. The Church needed well-trained ministers to respond to the criticisms of the Protestants and young people could be strengthened in their faith by good schools and teaching.

Ignatius was aware that he needed schools to educate future members of the society, but he did not envisage education for boys who did not wish to become Jesuits. In the late 1540s, however, he was drawn into developing a network of schools that eventually spread to all Catholic Europe and beyond. Indeed, Jesuit schools spread from Macao in south China to Lima in Peru – there were over 800 in 1773.

The first school for non-Jesuits was founded in Messina in 1547 at the request of his old friend, the Viceroy of Sicily. A second school in Sicily followed, but with the founding of the Jesuit College in Rome in 1551 (the sign over the door said 'A school of grammar, humanities and Christian doctrine – free') Ignatius signalled the expansion of the Jesuit school system. At his death there were over 30 colleges.

Although the final version of the Jesuit educational plan was not complete until 1599, its main features were laid down by Ignatius himself:

- Boys were admitted at age 10 and could expect at least five years' tuition (university education usually followed on from this). However, no beginner's level Latin was provided, which tended to exclude poorer families. The schools' clients were the noble and upper-middle classes.
- The education was free: this involved the Jesuits in massive and surprisingly modern fundraising activities (including what would today be called mailshots) to tap their wealthy supporters for funds.
- Schools were set up in large cities with universities, where people of influence could be found.
- Catholic theology was the core of each college: each classroom had a small altar with an image of the Virgin Mary, each lesson opened with prayers and attendance at weekly Mass was expected, as was a full part in the regular public worship of the Church, such as processions. There was an emphasis on the primacy of the pope.

- The curriculum was carefully structured. Boys were divided into classes (unusual at the time) and moved when the material was learned. There was great emphasis on the classical authors, the humanist skills of speaking and writing elegant Latin, and public speaking.

- There was a significant stress on extra-curricular activities such as drama (the more explicit classical texts were rewritten or new plays devised by the teachers, which could have themes from contemporary events), music and ballet. Jesuit productions became popular public events and gave witness to Catholic renewal.

Colleges soon became the main focus of the Jesuit mission, even though they stretched the manpower of the society to the limit. They were enormously successful, simply because they gave an excellent education (and, of course, it was free). They provided recruits to the society (1,000 in 1556; 3,500 in 1565) and some students were trained to be priests while others followed secular work;

> becoming princes, officials and lawyers filling the ranks of the ruling elites in the Catholic lands. Jesuit colleges became the yeast to leaven the bread of the secular society. For princes, the Jesuits schooled sons of the nobility and the bourgeoisie for service, training loyal and pious servants to the Catholic states. For city governments, Jesuit colleges provided Latin education at a bargain: in exchange for donations, the instructors came self-supported and provided free tuition for local boys, who [afterwards] entered the wider Catholic world.

2   *R. Po-Chia Hsia, **The World of Catholic Renewal 1540–1770**, 2005*

There is no doubt that Jesuit education, usually training the highest in society, contributed much to strengthen and revive the Catholic faith.

Missionaries

Ignatius expected that the main work of his society was to carry out missionary work among those who had no Christian faith. Many of those who joined were motivated by the wish to serve in the mission fields and welcomed the chance to give their lives, if need be, in the service of God and the society:

> I have great health and strength, blessed be God, and I want to spend them both in his divine service, even to the shedding of my blood and the giving of my life. I was sent with the expedition to Oran [in North Africa] and our sufferings which were heavy, have put heart in me for worse trials.

3   *By a Jesuit writing in 1560*

The dangers were spelt out to the novices. Their dining room at St Stephano Church in Rome was painted with scenes of the most appalling tortures to show future missionaries what could be their fate. Such attitudes gave the Jesuits enormous missionary enthusiasm.

While the conflicts of the Reformation were dominating Europe, the Catholic Church was winning new converts in the New World. In the same year as the Diet of Worms, Hernando Cortés conquered the Aztec Empire in the name of Charles V. Francisco Pizarro had conquered the Inca Empire in 1532. It has been estimated that 10 million new converts were made in the Americas alone.

Did you know?

Ignatius banned the cane and beatings in his schools, but objections were raised by the teachers. In a typically Jesuit compromise, someone was hired to do the beatings – no Jesuit was allowed to do them himself.

Cross-reference

More detail on the **founding of schools and colleges in Germany, Poland and the south Netherlands** is provided on pages 125–6.

Fig. 3 *A Jesuit church in Cusco, Peru*

Activity

Source analysis

How useful is Source 3 as evidence of the attitude of the Jesuits to mission work?

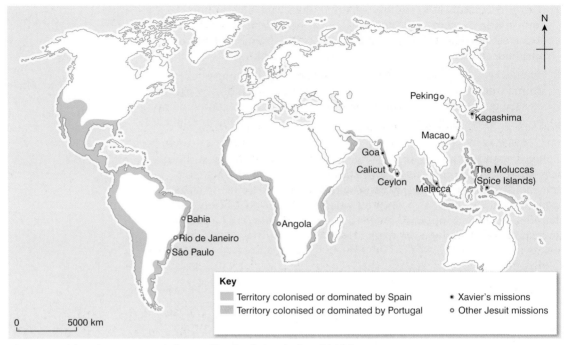

Fig. 4 *Spanish and Portuguese empires, and Jesuit missions in the mid-16th century*

We have now some of the Society in all parts of India where there are Christians. Four are in the Moluccas, two at Molacca, six in south India. The distances between these places are immense; for instance the Moluccas are more than 3,000 miles [4,800 km] from Goa. I have learned from good authorities that there is a country near China called Japan.

*Extract from a letter by Francis Xavier to Ignatius of Loyola,
15 April 1549*

However, the Jesuits were late to mission work. Since 1500 the orders of mendicant friars (first Franciscans, then Dominicans and Augustinians) had been at work in the Christian missions. The Jesuits did not work in the Spanish Americas until the late 1560s.

Brazil

The Jesuits concentrated on working with the rulers of Portugal, with whom they had a better political relationship. Unlike Spain, Portugal lacked the resources for colonisation and concentrated on building a series of trading ports stretching round west Africa through to Sri Lanka, India and the Spice Islands of the so-called East Indies. Even in Brazil, there was a limited settlement – no university or printing presses were opened.

The Jesuits arrived in Brazil in 1549 and they became the dominant religious order. They were appalled by the treatment of the local Indian populations who were exploited for their labour and made slaves; women were used as sexual company. An outstanding Jesuit, Manuel de Nóbrega, began a policy of bringing **'Indians'** together in communities under Jesuit protection, mostly against the slave traders – such 'reductions', as they were called, supported perhaps 40,000 'Indians' by 1564.

The Jesuits were amazingly active:

- Within two weeks, Portuguese and native children were organised into catechism classes, taught to sing hymns and read and write.
- They started to develop settlements and Nóbrega founded the city of São Paulo. Hospitals and churches were built.

Exploring the detail

Exploration and colonisation

Western world exploration and colonisation was dominated by the Catholic powers of Spain and Portugal. To try to avoid rivalry, in 1493 Alexander VI acted as arbitrator to define the limits of expansion by drawing a north–south line on the world map. Spain received whatever was to be discovered west of the line and Portugal whatever was to be discovered to the east. A condition of this grant was that any new peoples conquered should be converted to Christianity.

Key terms

'Indians': missionary groups made little attempt at first to distinguish local populations. Because the early explorers were searching for a way to India by going westwards, they called the first peoples they met 'Indians'.

- José de Anchieta stayed in Brazil for 44 years, writing the first grammar in the local language, training in basic skills and setting Christian doctrine to local native tunes (a typical piece of Jesuit adaptation).

- They took a stand against the slave trade (the morality of which was being debated at the highest levels in the Church) and opposed the mass baptisms given without proper preparation.

However, they faced opposition from local bishops who felt they were too tolerant of the natives (for example, the Jesuits were ordered to stop the natives going around naked. The Jesuits said they were too poor to buy clothes and the Jesuits had no money to help them.) After the first excitement, the Jesuits were faced with major problems. The local natives, the Tupis, had no concept of God and the drunkenness and cannibalism of some appalled the Jesuits. Similarly, the Tupis had no concept of stable relationships and changed partners frequently. The Jesuits failed to change sexual practices, but complex debates were created about whether such behaviour made it impossible to offer baptism.

Goa and India

The most famous missionary work was concentrated in the Far East, based on the Portuguese trading station at Goa. Xavier made it the base for all Jesuit activities in the Far East. The Franciscans had arrived in 1518 and Goa already possessed a bishop, cathedral and school buildings. It was known as the Rome of the East. The arrival of the Jesuit mission under Francis Xavier in 1542 kickstarted a new advance; he made it the base for all Jesuit activities in the Far East, setting up schools for children and developing the College of Holy Faith to train native priests and catechists. Jesuit missionaries were tempted by the vast size of the sub-continent and Xavier himself ventured more than 6,400 km beyond India to the Moluccas. Work began on the Malabar coast and Xavier concentrated on the Tamil-speaking pearl fishers of the Gulf of Mannar. His successor in 1549, Henrique Henriques composed a grammar and services in Tamil. The Jesuits created the basis for a long-lasting Catholic community.

The example of Xavier and his letters home describing his travels electrified Catholic Europe. They inspired many others to follow him. However, objectively he is open to criticism. Historian Keith Randell comments that he was an extremist who took unreasonable risks with his own health and had no thought to how practical his journeys were. He had no knowledge of local languages or any financial support. 'It was not surprising that he was judged by most of those he met to be a madman.' He did gain some converts, but not among the higher classes.

 Cross-reference

To recap on the importance of **Francis Xavier**, look back to page 117.

Cross-reference

The Jesuits also sent **missions to Europe** and these are discussed on pages 124–6.

Question

Why was Francis Xavier important to the success of the Jesuit movement?

Activity

Revision exercise

Copy and complete the following table to help you consider the question: How successful were the Jesuit missions overseas?

	Jesuit work in Brazil	Jesuit work in Goa and India	Jesuit work in the Far East (including Japan)
Successes			
Failures			
Problems encountered			

Preachers

The revival of preaching in the Catholic Church had started well before 1517 as the evidence of the popularity of printed guidance for preachers shows. The Jesuits, with other orders, were part of this revival and they developed the practice in Rome of preaching sermons on Sundays outside the seasons of Christmas and Easter, which was the general custom of the time.

Although the Jesuits produced no outstanding preachers, they had some effective ones such as Diego Lainez, Alphonsus Salmeron and Peter Canisius. Preaching was a core activity and the first section of the Jesuit Constitutions – the definitive rule book of the order. Its importance in spreading the Word of God and strengthening faith was highly valued. Jesuits were expected to preach two to three sermons a day if this was their skill, often for two hours at a time. The themes of their sermons were typical of other orders: vices and virtues, the pains of hell and the joys of heaven. Often sermons were given in the open air to huge crowds. They were told not to enter into theological debates, but to make their sermons dramatic both visually and verbally. The effectiveness of a sermon was judged by its ability to move people's emotions – they were expected to laugh, weep plentifully and break down as they felt their sinfulness.

Cross-reference

For the importance of **preaching in the 16th-century Catholic Church**, look back to page 60.

Lainez and Salmeron are profiled on pages 116–17.

Key profile

Peter Canisius

Peter Canisius (1521–97) was the most influential Jesuit in Germany – the Jesuits owed their success there almost entirely to his work. His aim was to prevent the whole of Germany becoming Protestant and he stayed in the country from 1549–80. He founded the first Jesuit college in Germany at Ingolstadt and helped to found 18 other Jesuit colleges. Over time, thousands of students were educated.

He targeted Catholic rulers to ensure they did not change their faith. He was successful in gaining the support of Ferdinand I (the Holy Roman Emperor), his son Maximillian and Albert V (Duke of Bavaria). Canisius also worked hard to try to make the decrees of the Council of Trent accepted by the rulers of Germany.

He was an exceptional example of holiness and an inspirational character. He had huge energy and determination, travelling nearly 10,000 km to visit the colleges he had started. His preaching was said to influence many to become Catholics. In 1555 he wrote a clear statement of Catholic belief – the Summary of Christian Doctrine – and a catechism for young people. These were very successful and adopted throughout Catholic Europe.

Confessors

The Jesuits were well respected and popular as confessors. They were unusual in that they supported frequent confessions (the official requirement being once a year) and that they did not charge for their services. They also supported confession as a general review of one's life (rather than the period since the last confession) and became skilful in offering guidance. The question of deciding a 'punishment' gained the Jesuits a reputation for a lax approach, as they fitted cases to individual circumstances and were adept at explaining away cases of conscience (for example, the killing of someone would depend on motive, circumstances, etc). They were accused of hypocrisy and of having relative standards, not fixed ones.

Their ability and supposed moral flexibility made them confessors to the aristocracy and rulers of Europe, including the kings of France, Poland and Portugal and the German emperors. The problem is what use did they make of this access to so many royal hearts and consciences? To their deeply suspicious enemies (both Catholic and Protestant), they advised them to put the interests of the Catholic Church first whatever the moral problems involved. Most notoriously, the assassination of opponents, including rulers, was justified by some Jesuit theorists if it led to the greater good of the triumph of the Church.

There is no definite conclusion on whether the Jesuits directed the consciences of kings into ways they would not have followed without their confessors' advice. King John III of Portugal (1521–57) highly valued Simão Rodriguez as his confessor. Indeed, Rodriguez had a room in the royal palace itself, much to the annoyance of Ignatius. Even so, this did not prevent the king from ordering Rodriguez to obey Ignatius's command to go to Rome in 1553.

As confessions are secret, we do not know what was said. Kings did use other confessors (especially Capuchins), including some very Catholic kings, notably Charles V and Philip II. What was good for the Church was usually good for the state. The sacrament of penance has always attracted the blackest suspicions and the legend of Jesuit influence over their penitents has been hard to dispel.

A closer look

The pastoral work of the Jesuits

Work in hospitals and prisons was an essential Jesuit activity. At first, a month in a hospital was part of the novices' training. Carrying out the most menial activities was expected, but they were highly dangerous places because the Jesuits tended to throw themselves into the worst situations of contagion. As a result, significant numbers died (17 in one plague outbreak in 1579). The need for manpower elsewhere led to a scaling back of this work.

Work in prisons was more successful. Jesuits taught the faith, tried to get prisoners to give up gambling and swearing, and begged for food for them, as well as caring for them. In one prison, a fund was set up to pay off debts. In another, efforts were made to care for prisoners' families.

In both hospitals and prisons there was a need to comfort the dying. In the 16th century there was a great interest in 'dying well' (Erasmus had written a best-seller on the theme). The society produced its own manual for its members, although it was stressed that advice must fit the person. The Jesuits offered consolation and much more: dealing with problems, ensuring families were looked after. Their abilities made them sought after to offer a ministry to condemned men, often because some priests were superstitious about doing this task.

Officials became more aware of prostitution in the early 16th century because of the growth of cities and the spread of syphilis, which created a major public heath problem. Thousands of wretched prostitutes worked the streets out of sheer desperation. The Jesuits, as other new orders, believed that preaching was the best way to reform prostitutes and this was supported by city

Did you know?

Juan de Mariana (1536–1624), a Spanish Jesuit, wrote in his work *De rege et regis institutione* (1598) that murder of a tyrant was right if the state was badly governed.

Cross-reference

Simão Rodriguez is profiled on page 116.

Did you know?

In the 16th century people were imprisoned for debt or on remand, and the delays and corruption of city governments were a constant Jesuit criticism. Therefore, they were welcomed in prisons.

Cross-reference

For more on the spread of syphilis, look back to page 26.

Did you know?

It was noted at the time that prostitutes seemed very interested in religion, though it was also noted that Churches were good places to find clients.

authorities who insisted on brothels closing on the Sabbath or, as in Florence, an annual service for all prostitutes at which the advice to repent was preached.

The Jesuits supported the solutions common at the time – marriage, service in a respectable household or entering a strict convent – indeed, wealthy supporters were urged to take girls and dowries were provided. However, Ignatius proposed a new solution, a kind of halfway house in which girls could stay until they had made decisions about their lives. In 1543 the Casa Santa Marta opened and became a model for houses in a dozen Italian cities often lasting for centuries.

Linked to prostitution were the many young children, orphaned or abandoned, who lived on the streets of great cities. Ignatius set up the Company of Orphans in 1541, a group of laypeople who set up two homes for boys and girls in Rome. More creatively, he wished to break the cycle in which daughters followed mothers into prostitution by setting up the Company of the Virgin in 1546, the idea of which was to take girls aged 10–12, give them basic skills such as reading and writing and later provide a dowry for marriage. By 1585 the Company (run by laypeople) was helping 150 girls. Other Italian cities followed suit, often under direct Jesuit pressure.

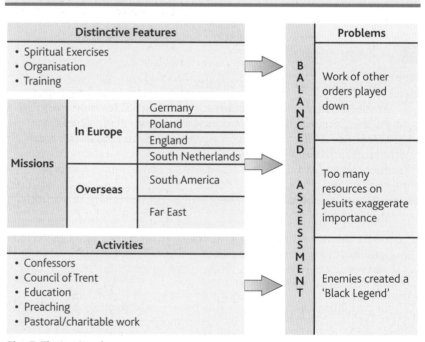

Fig. 5 *The Jesuit order*

The extent to which the Jesuits revitalised the Catholic Church and halted the Protestant advance in Europe

The Jesuits in Germany, Poland and the south Netherlands

The Jesuits were not founded to combat the advance of Protestantism. Ignatius himself was inspired by his personal religious conversion, not a desire to 'halt the Protestant advance'. However, a sense of urgency began

Cross-reference

For more details on the **Counter Reformation**, look ahead to page 130.

to develop about the advance of Protestantism in the 1540s, which could be called a Counter Reformation.

Germany

In 1543 Pope Paul III ordered three Jesuits – Favre, Jay and Bobadilla – to check out the situation in Germany. All were appalled by the weakness of the German Church. Paul III indicated that the defence of the Church was now a vital role.

Many serious-minded people thought that Germany was a lost cause, with Protestantism spreading in Catholic areas such as Bohemia, Bavaria and Austria itself. Germany was to become the central focus for the Jesuit mission. The Jesuits, and many other orders, appreciated that a much higher quality of education was needed to raise the standards of the parish clergy and develop an educated laity. When Ignatius was asked what was needed for Germany, he said 'colleges' and the instructions he gave for an earlier mission also apply to the 'German' one:

> If you could start up grammar schools in some places and find efficient masters for them, it would be a great remedy for the great ignorance of that country ... and it would be a good thing, too, to provide cheap loan banks, for the assistance of the poor, and hospitals and other pious institutions.

5   *Ignatius's instructions to a mission, 1541*

Peter Canisius provided the energy and inspiration for Jesuit success. A programme of setting up Jesuit schools in Germany began, which helped to create a new generation of priests and laypeople who were given a confident, positive attitude to their Catholic faith. Important also was the German College set up in Rome in 1552 to train German boys for the priesthood since they had the language skills. Over the next 200 years, almost 4,000 students were sent out into the German lands. The German College was the model for other colleges in Rome that concentrated on training priests, such as the Greek College (1577) and the English College (1578).

The first Jesuit college for laypeople was set up at Cologne in 1544. There were six Jesuits. By 1630 there were 3,000 working in 5 provinces, and over 40 colleges. When you add up the number educated in the German colleges as well as those from the German College in Rome, you have a great force for reviving Catholic central Europe. By 1630 Germany had over 2,200 Jesuit educational institutions.

The Jesuits did not only concentrate on secondary education; they were also able to dominate university education. Their main interests were in the arts, theology and philosophy. In some universities they were reserved

Activity

Source analysis

What does Source 5 tell us about the ways in which the Jesuits tried to strengthen support for the Church?

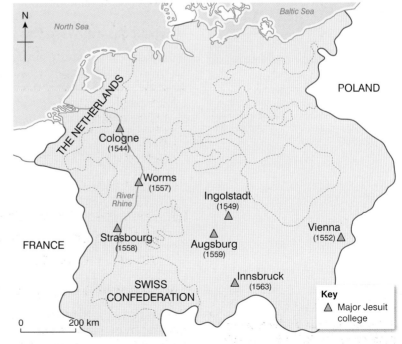

Fig. 7 *The Holy Roman Empire and Jesuit colleges*

Activity

Source analysis

Study Figure 7 on page 125 showing the distribution of major Jesuit colleges. Does a pattern emerge?

Fig. 8 *The Archduke Albert and Archduchess Isabella, rulers of the southern Netherlands from 1598, by Rubens. Isabella joined a religious order after Albert's death in 1621*

special posts; in others they controlled departments; in five or six, they controlled the whole university.

Jesuit work in Germany and elsewhere was more than education. There were powerful attempts to take the Christian message to an audience which needed to be strengthened in the faith. A Jesuit mission would find a town with plenty of surrounding villages and encourage people to come into the town by staging preaching sessions using every dramatic method to fix people's attention – often they involved elaborate processions carrying statues of the Virgin Mary. Their charitable work was also an example of a renewed Catholic spirit.

Poland and the south Netherlands

Poland is often claimed as a Jesuit success. In 1564 it was a complex mixture of faiths: Catholic, Lutheran, Calvinist, Russian Orthodox and Anabaptists. About 15 per cent of the nobles were not Catholics. Cardinal Stanislaus Hosius (d.1579) was a dynamic counter-reformation bishop who asked for the Society of Jesus to come to Poland. By 1586, 44 Jesuit colleges had been started and these played a strong part in educating a Catholic nobility. Catholic success was aided by the Polish kings, who became strong supporters of the society. Stefan Bathory (1576–80) turned the Jesuit college at Vilnus into a university; Sigismund III (1587–1632) was known as the 'Jesuit King' or 'the Polish Philip II' because of his support for the reconversion of Protestants. His son John Casimir (1648–68) was a Jesuit novice before becoming king. Jesuit success also was built on gradually gaining the support of the Polish nobility.

As a result of a long struggle with Spain, the Low Countries had divided into a Calvinist north and a Catholic south (roughly modern Belgium). In the 1590s the Catholic rulers, Albert and Isabella, were enthusiastic supporters of a Catholic revival. They encouraged many new orders including the Jesuits, who built up a large presence in Belgium – over 1,500 members by 1630. There was a great push for more education (Sunday schools were particularly successful) and expressions of Catholic devotion were popular. The south Netherlands became a model Counter Reformation state.

How successful were the Jesuits?

Judgements about Jesuit success would ideally need much more detail about what happened after 1564. The older histories make huge claims for Jesuit success, arguing, for example, that Peter Canisius virtually alone turned back the forces of Protestantism in Germany or that the Jesuits were the leading craftsmen of the Counter Reformation, the shock troops of the papacy or the 'spearhead' of the Counter Reformation.

If success means the rolling back of Protestantism, their success was mixed. There were possible dangers that parts of eastern Europe would have mixed religions. There did seem to be a Protestant threat to Austria and Bavaria. South Germany and the Rhineland, on the 'frontier' with the Protestant north, was more uncertain, as were some of the states of the Church such as Cologne. A good case can be made that Jesuit colleges and the Jesuit example revived the Catholic faith in these parts.

However, existing Protestant states were not reconverted, and there were important failures. Ninety-eight Jesuits died in an attempt to revive the Catholic Church in England after 1580, but this was based on poor knowledge of English conditions and the numbers of English Catholics. Missions to Ireland, Scotland and Scandinavia also failed. In north Germany, Protestants extended their gains after 1560. France seemed to be in greatest danger because there was a serious Calvinist threat to the state after 1562. There was a real danger that Calvinism would at least be given toleration with the official Catholic Church. However, because there was a long hostility in the French Catholic Church to papal authority, the Jesuits had little influence in France until the 17th century.

The success of the Church very much depended on the support of Catholic rulers and it could be claimed as a success of the Jesuits that their abilities were recognised by Catholic rulers in the Habsburg lands, Poland, Portugal and Bavaria who gave them great support. However, such support came at a price. The dukes of Bavaria, who raised their Catholic credentials to almost cult status, extracted concessions from the popes which gave them total control of their Church.

It is hard to establish cause and effect in the case of religious change. In the case of the Jesuits, the evidence is one-sided and has created perhaps an exaggerated picture of the Jesuits' success. They generated a mass of written sources: Canisius's printed letters alone cover 7,500 pages and no other order has as much evidence. Yet we know, for example, that new orders such as the Capuchins – significantly known as 'the poor men's Jesuits' – also helped the poor, nursed the sick, went on preaching missions to Protestant areas, gained the favour of princes, popes and aristocrats and created great respect for themselves and the Church. Similarly, the older orders, so much under criticism from the Protestant reformers, also revived. The Dominicans, for example, doubled in number from 1500 to 1700. The Franciscans were much involved in international missions.

The Jesuits created feelings of both admiration and dislike. Their multi-talented abilities and zeal were envied or feared by other religious groups; their privileges and special relationship with the papacy (which they did little to play down) made them feared by those who disliked papal interference with the affairs of states; their presence in some universities was strongly resisted (for example, Paris and Prague). Their methods, especially over confession, were mistrusted, as was their seeking out the rich and influential for their supporters. It was easy for Protestants to create a 'black legend' of the Jesuit order.

It could be argued that the Jesuits had so many aims that their resources were spread too thinly, some of their schools failed for lack of funding and they provoked clashes with other orders. However, their successes could be:

- their role in international and European missions, especially in Brazil, south Germany and Poland
- the schools network they created, which influenced generations of young Catholics as well as training priests
- their setting of the highest standards for a revived Catholic Church
- their wide range of charitable work
- the fact that the 'Jesuit way' particularly the Spiritual Exercises, greatly influenced Catholic leaders, both in the Church and European states.

The society was successful because:

- the Spiritual Exercises proved popular and effective
- it stressed the highest standards of training and education for its members
- its members had great flexibility and could work in any sphere; preaching, teaching, caring for the poor, as spiritual advisors or foreign missionaries

Exploring the detail

The Jesuits and important women

Ignatius's pastoral care for Margaret of Austria, the illegitimate daughter of Charles V who was married to the grandson of Paul III, saved her marriage but also earned the gratitude of the pope.

A Portuguese noblewoman, Leonor de Mascarenhas, the governess of Charles V's legitimate daughters, helped to allay the suspicions of the Emperor about the early Jesuits and supported the beginning of the order in Spain. Her kinswoman helped to introduce the Jesuits into Portugal, as well as ensuring they had a church in central Lisbon to be near her house.

The wife of the Viceroy of Naples was another active supporter, as was one of Leonor's charges, the Archduchess Juana, sister of Philip II of Spain. Later female supporters provided the funding for many Jesuit schools.

- the structure of the order was clear and focused on control from the centre

- its members had great religious zeal and determination, inspired by the charisma of Ignatius

- the abilities of the members of the society were quickly recognised by the Church when there was a task to be done. Lainez and Salmeron built up international reputations as theologians and the Jesuits became useful as able defenders of Catholic orthodoxy, for example at the Council of Trent

- it was lucky to win the admiration and support of the popes, especially Paul III (1534–49) and Julius III (1550–5). It helped that the society was the leading supporter of the primacy of papal authority

- it had the ability to attract support from the rich and influential: its members could move easily in the highest circles. Ignatius stressed that it was essential to win over persons of rank and power. He gave advice on how to do this, wisely suggesting that Jesuits should be tolerant of their faults and not adopt a critical tone

- in particular, the extraordinary devotion of high-born female supporters was crucial, both in securing support from critical figures of influence and in attracting funding.

Historian H. O. Evennett supports the importance of the Jesuits in the Counter Reformation:

> It was the spearhead of the pastoral, active spirit of the Counter Reformation, international, confident, determined; yet at the same time flexible, adaptable, ingratiating, modern. It was determined that nothing should be allowed to stand against its will to serve the Church.

6	
	*H. O. Evennett, **NCMH**, vol. 2, 1962*

However, this view needs to be balanced with the contribution of other orders and the limitations of the Jesuits' work. An alternative interpretation is that, though important, they were one of the many developments that emerged from the Catholic reform movement after 1540, rather than being the dynamic force. It is impossible to evaluate accurately the extent of their influence.

Learning outcomes

In this section you have studied the foundation of the Jesuit order and the importance of Ignatius of Loyola. You have explored in detail the aims, organisation and training methods of the society and should be able to understand the importance of the Spiritual Exercises. You have gained an understanding of the work of the Jesuits at the Council of Trent as well as their role as educators, missionaries and confessors. You have considered the activities of the society in the defence of the Catholic Church against the advance of Protestantism and have been invited to reflect on why the society was successful by 1564.

Did you know?

Archduchess Juana insisted on being admitted to the Jesuit order, even though it was a society for men only. Ignatius allowed this, although he insisted on secrecy. She was the only female Jesuit. It was hard to refuse the sister of the King of Spain!

Activity

Talking point

1. In groups, discuss the following statement: How can success be defined for a religious organisation?

2. How do the Jesuits fit the definition of success your group decides?

AQA Examination-style questions

(a)   Explain why the Spiritual Exercises were popular among laypeople.   *(12 marks)*

AQA Examiner's tip Part a) questions require you to focus on explaining, not describing, so you will need to think of various reasons why the Spiritual Exercises were popular, reflecting on what they offered to laypeople at the time,. You should try to link those reasons and perhaps show how one reason was more important than any others.

(b)   How successful were the Jesuits in defending the Catholic Church against the Protestant advance?   *(24 marks)*

AQA Examiner's tip All part b) questions require a balanced response. The definition of 'success' is essential, although it is hard in the case of a religious movement. You could also discuss the nature of the evidence about the Jesuits. Elements of their success will include such themes as their schools, preaching and charity work, as well as an explanation of the limitations of their work, which is important for balance. You could point out that to make a judgement of Jesuit success needs more knowledge of their work in the later 16th and 17th centuries.

11 The revival of papal authority

In this chapter you will learn about:

■ the Renaissance popes and their weaknesses, and in particular Julius II, the 'warrior pope'

■ the work of Paul III in the years 1540–9

■ the importance of the Council of Trent

■ how much the Catholic Church was reformed in the period.

Exploring the detail

Counter Reformation or Catholic Reformation?

The changes that took place in the Catholic Church in the 16th century are sometimes known as the Counter Reformation. This implies a counter-attack, an aggressive process inspired by the shocks of the successful Protestant assault on the unity of the Church. The dates for its start vary from as early as 1517 to as late as the accession of Paul III in 1534. Its ending is given as sometime in the mid-17th century. However, the term Catholic Reformation is in some ways more appropriate; using this terminology, the movement could be seen to start with the reforms of the 15th century that continued until 1700. The desire for reform was not just caused by Lutheranism and Calvinism. Catholic historians in particular have argued strongly that a Catholic Reformation would have occurred without any Protestant Reformation.

Key terms

Nepotism: promoting one's own family to positions within the Church.

An anonymous pamphlet of 1501 declared:

> There is no sort of outrage or vice that is not openly practised in the palace of the pope. He is the deepest depth of vice, a subverter of all justice, human and divine.

This comment on Pope Alexander VI shows contemporary attitudes towards the papacy in the early 16th century. It was condemned for its lack of spiritual example, for perpetuating abuses and for its love of extravagant display. However, throughout the 16th century, the popes began to re-assert their authority and raise their prestige. This process much depended on the personality of the incumbent and progress was not consistent. Even so, by 1564 the popes were the acknowledged leaders of Catholic reform.

Renaissance popes

During the early 16th century, the papacy was the target of considerable criticism. Visitors to Rome, such as Erasmus and Martin Luther, were shocked by the splendour and ceremony of the papal *curia* (court) and the cardinals in Rome seemed to set a poor example of holy living. One problem was that between 1492 and 1503, 86 new cardinals were appointed. Many were young noblemen who had little interest in the Church and had no knowledge of what duties were required of them. They could not inspire respect but their luxury, display and vices contrasted with the poverty of the ordinary parish priest. It was bad luck that the three popes spanning a critical period of great crisis in the Church's history did nothing to improve its image.

Alexander VI

Alexander VI has been painted as thoroughly evil. As well as the fairly routine accusation of having bought the papacy by bribing the cardinals to vote for him, Alexander VI was accused of incest with his son and daughter and of poisoning possible opponents. His daughter Lucrezia supposedly poisoned her three husbands. It was true that Alexander had eight children by three different women before he became pope and it was a scandal that he openly kept a 20-year-old mistress while he was pope. He was excessively fond of his own family and was accused of **nepotism** by giving them offices within the Church – eight of his relations were made cardinals. To some extent, this is understandable. As his family was Spanish, they had no group of Italian cardinals to give them loyal support. It was almost inevitable that family connections should be strongly developed.

Recent historians such as Michael Mullett have corrected the lurid picture of the family as guilty of incest and expert poisoners, but at best Alexander was not a holy figure. On the other hand, he made an excellent ruler of the papal states. Given the political problems of the popes, trying to control their

Fig. 1 *Pope Alexander VI. An able administrator and diplomat, his enemies and his own actions blackened his character*

territories and balancing between France and the Habsburgs, it required a cunning man of the world rather than a saintly but politically innocent figure to be in charge.

During his reign Alexander managed to keep the papal states independent of foreign powers. At the same time, his son Cesare waged successful campaigns against the cities in the Romagna that refused to accept his father's authority. Alexander hoped that Cesare would keep the title of Duke of Romagna after his death. In Rome itself, successful actions against the two great Roman noble families of the Orsini and Colonna meant the popes were at last masters of Rome.

By 1503 Alexander was at the height of his power, but in the stifling summer heat of malaria-prone Rome both the pope and Cesare became ill and Alexander died of the fever. His greatest enemy Cardinal della Rovere was elected Pope Julius II.

Julius II, the 'warrior pope'

Christine Shaw, the recent biographer of Julius II, uses the phrase 'warrior pope' in her book – a title that was used of Julius II by his contemporaries, as was *papa terrible* – the 'fearsome pope'. Although not guilty of the supposed vices of Alexander VI, he was, according to Shaw, a 'plain-spoken, short-tempered, act first, think later, dynamic man of action'. He put himself at the head of his troops fighting in northern Italy and this man of peace could be seen, sword in hand and in full armour, directing the fighting and storming city walls. In an anonymous pamphlet of the time, *Julius Exclusus* ('shut out') which was possibly written by Erasmus, the pope is portrayed having a shouting match with St Peter, who refuses to let him in to heaven in his armour, full of pride and anger. Julius threatens to bring up his cannon to batter down the gates. To the humanist writers, the contrast between the Christ of the Gospels and the pope was plain to see.

However, if he had not been pope, Julius II would have been an excellent ruler. His campaigns finally gave the popes control over their territories in the Romagna and so he gave them control over central Italy. He took a full part in the shifting alliances of the Italian wars and even hoped to drive the foreign invaders out of Italy. He introduced administrative and financial changes in the running of papal government. As he had promised at his election, he called a Lateran Council to discuss reforms in the Church that many were demanding.

Cross-reference
For the **criticisms levelled at the papacy**, look back to page 15.

Key chronology
Popes who earned a poor reputation
1492–1503 Alexander VI
1503–1513 Julius II
1513–1521 Leo X

Cross-reference
To revise the **political problems of the popes**, look back to page 16.

Fig. 2 *Julius II by Raphael, c.1511. The artist conveys the energy and latent power of the old pope – note his grip on the arm of the chair*

Cross-reference
The **Lateran Council** is outlined on page 29.

Key terms

Old St Peter's Basilica: a huge church in Rome, begun in the 4th century. It was built over the tomb of St Peter and therefore a great place of pilgrimage. By 1500 it was falling down and in need of costly repairs.

Julius II will be remembered if only for employing Michelangelo to decorate the Sistine Chapel and Raphael to adorn the Vatican Palace. He also ordered Michelangelo to build a massive tomb for him.

The **Old St Peter's Basilica** in Rome was demolished and foundations of the new St Peter's were laid (April 1506). His successors were committed to building a massive church as the ultimate statement of the power of the popes. It took 120 years to complete. The cost was paid for by faithful Catholics, indirectly the cause of Martin Luther's protest in 1517.

A closer look

The popes and patronage of the arts

The popes and the papal court played an important role as patrons (supporters) of the arts. When the popes finally returned to Rome in 1417, they aimed to increase their image by creating a splendid city from the shabby, neglected capital that had fallen into decay. Spending lavish sums on artists and architects was also part of this process. Pope Nicholas V planned a new city with churches, monasteries, palaces and pleasure grounds. Sixtus IV continued the process, bringing the best talents from Italy to redesign and decorate the city. Later popes commissioned works from the greatest artists of the Renaissance and supported humanist writers.

Activity

Preparing a presentation

In groups, research the work and lives of Michelangelo and Raphael to establish why they were paid to produce their paintings and sculpture as well as the significance of the content. Prepare a short presentation to the rest of the class.

Key profiles

Raphael

Raphael (1483–1520) was a leading artist of the Italian Renaissance. In 1508 he was summoned to Rome to decorate some official rooms in the Vatican called the Stanze. His major work was *The School of Athens*, in which the most important thinkers of the classical world were represented; he also designed tapestries for the Sistine Chapel. His portraits of Julius II and Leo X with two cardinals are brilliant insights into their characters, although he is perhaps most famous for his paintings of Madonnas (the Virgin Mary with the child Jesus).

Fig. 3 The School of Athens *by Raphael, c.1511. This huge work (7.72 m wide) contains thinkers of the classical world such as Plato and Aristotle (centre) – humanist heroes placed at the heart of the Catholic Church*

Michelangelo

Michelangelo (1475–1564) was acknowledged as a great genius in his own lifetime. He was an artist, sculptor and poet. His most famous sculpture is perhaps a huge figure of the young David (standing 4.34 metres tall) for the Republic of Florence. His decoration of the ceiling of the Sistine Chapel is regarded as his greatest achievement. This vast painting, extending to 40.5 metres long and 14 metres wide and finished in 1512, depicts the story of the creation in a highly complex fashion, including figures from the classical past as well as Jewish prophets from the Old Testament. Between 1536 and 1541 Michelangelo completed the west wall of the Sistine Chapel with a tremendous and terrifying vision of the Last Judgement.

Leo X

Leo X was 37 years old when he was elected pope. He had been educated by humanist teachers and was a skilful judge of art. He loved lavish display, hunting, games and songs, and his good temper and pleasant manners made him popular. Leo was reputedly a pleasure-loving, superficial character – spineless in a crisis. He was pope at the time of the start of the German Reformation.

Fig. 4 *Part of the ceiling and end wall of the Sistine Chapel in the Vatican, Rome, by Michelangelo*

The new pope was nothing like Julius II. Of a most refined and cultured mind, a protector of humanists, artists and scholars, he seemed to begin an era of tolerance and generosity, just as his round plump face and idle look contrasted with the savage features of Julius II.

1   *H. O. Evennett, NCMH, vol. 2, 1962*

Leo was a diplomat rather than a warrior and his skilful policy of alliance with the Habsburg ruler Charles V resulted in the French being expelled from Italy in 1521. The Lateran Council continued to meet until 1517 and passed some useful reforms. Attempts were made to limit the numbers in the cardinals' households and their extravagant lifestyles, but the pope set the worst example so there was little chance of success.

The impact of reforming popes

Of the popes who reigned between 1493 and 1534, few had great faith and sanctity. They could be criticised for not giving a spiritual example or perpetuating abuses such as nepotism and pluralism. Their vices, however, were not as gross as painted by hostile propagandists. Some were efficient rulers of the papal states. Clement VII disappointed the reformers by his lack of purpose and decisive action. By contrast, Pope Adrian VI (1522–3) – who came directly after a number of 'bad' popes – came into office with a huge determination to cut out the luxury of the papal court and he lived a simple, austere life.

Despite the clamour for the popes to take a lead and carry out reform, for example by Savonarola and above all Erasmus as well as by liberal-minded cardinals such as Contarini, the popes before Paul III would not or could not begin reforms. Possibly it was the Sack of Rome

Activity
Thinking point

Write a practice essay on the theme: How successful were the popes of the period c.1500–21 in fulfilling their role as head of the Church?

Cross-reference

See page 30 for the **development of the papacy** from Adrian VI (1522–3) to Clement VII (1523–34) and the early years of Paul III until 1540.

Savonarola is introduced on page 29.

Erasmus is discussed in detail on page 11.

Cardinal Contarini is profiled on page 33.

The **Sack of Rome** is described on page 30.

in 1527 that altered the climate to favour change. Paul III (1534–49) became the great motivator, giving force and urgency to the internal reform of the Church.

The impact of Paul III from 1540

Paul III was willing to support attempts to reach a reconciliation with the Lutherans. On both sides there were many who were dismayed that the Church had been split by the Protestant Reformation and they longed for reconciliation. The demand for compromise was strongly supported by the Emperor Charles V, who saw it as a way to reunite the German Church and strengthen his political position in his conflicts with France and the Ottoman Turks.

Charles V therefore set up a colloquy (meeting) between leading moderates on both sides at Regensburg in 1541. Paul III gave his support for Contarini to attend. Moderate Lutherans led by Philip Melanchthon and Martin Bucer spoke for the Protestants. These were all men of goodwill, believing in the need for reconciliation. The delegates quickly agreed on the first five points of the draft document, the *Book of Regensburg*. Great excitement was created when it was announced that agreement had been reached to find in favour of Luther's main doctrine that 'faith alone' saves rather than the Catholic view of 'faith and works'.

This early success soon evaporated because there was no real discussion of other points of disagreement such as transubstantiation or the Real Presence. The key question of the authority of the pope was not mentioned. Both Luther and Paul III refused to agree to anything that gave away essential doctrines, and Francis I opposed further progress because he feared agreement would strengthen Charles V's power in Germany. The colloquy was abandoned in 1542.

Its failure was important because Paul III turned to give his support to the more backward-looking, conservative wing of the Church as the attempt at reconciliation had not worked. Paul now made more urgent efforts to call a general council. The year 1541 is arguably when 'Catholic Reform' merged into the 'Counter Reformation'.

However, the search for reunion was not given up. There were further attempts in 1546 and in 1552 a Protestant delegation attended the Council of Trent. In practice, compromise was doomed because from the 1520s Protestants had refused to accept the position of the papacy.

The Roman Inquisition

Strong evidence of the change of emphasis was when Paul III accepted Carafa's recommendation to found a Roman **Inquisition**, which was effected by the bull *Licet ab initio* in July 1542. The bull created the Sacred Congregation of the Holy Office (also known as the Holy Office or Roman Inquisition) under the leadership of Carafa.

Fig. 5 *A procession of heretics sentenced by the Inquisition in Portugal, from an 18th-century engraving*

■ Cross-reference

Emperor Charles V is profiled on page 56.

Philip Melanchthon is profiled on page 54.

For more on **Martin Bucer**, look at page 77.

The doctrines of **'faith alone'**, **transubstantiation** and the **Real Presence** are explained on pages 45–6.

■ Cross-reference

The **Council of Trent** is introduced in Chapter 3 and is discussed in more detail on pages 136–40.

■ Key terms

Inquisition: a Church court whose purpose was to discover and prosecute heretics – that is, those who had been baptised Christians but who refused to accept (or had rejected) the Catholic faith. The aim was to recover heretics for the Church and therefore save their souls from eternal damnation. Linked with this, heretics needed to be discovered to stop them influencing others.

■ Cross-reference

Cardinal Carafa is profiled on page 33.

Action was needed because in 1541–2 there was evidence that Italy itself was in danger. The cities of Modena and Lucca seemed about to turn Lutheran, suspect groups met openly in Venice and Naples and there were two sensational high-profile defections when Bernardino Ochino (the Capuchin General) and Peter Martyr Vermigli (a leading preacher) fled to Protestant Switzerland.

The plan was to create a network of courts throughout Europe and these courts would be superior to all others. They could investigate any cases without reference to local courts and had sweeping powers to arrest people under suspicion, to act on the assumption that they were guilty, to seize property and order executions. Carafa relished his role:

> Carafa would not wait for the papal treasury, but bought a house which he fitted out with offices, dungeons and shackles. He issued a set of rules for the Inquisition, the fourth of which was 'No man is to lower himself by showing toleration to any sort of heretic. Least of all a Calvinist.'

2   O. Chadwick, *The Reformation*, 1972

The plan for a Europe-wide Inquisition was never implemented. Portugal had its own Inquisition and the Spanish Inquisition had been operational for over 60 years. Both were under the control of the state and did not welcome papal interference. France refused to allow it and some Italian states, especially Venice, carefully restricted its work. Essentially it was effective in most parts of Italy.

The Roman Inquisition was active in the 1540–60 period, summoning before it suspect groups and people in many Italian cities – key figures preferred exile to any judgements against them. It made a practice of attacking leading public figures such as Cardinals Carranza and Morone on the grounds that they were too sympathetic to the Lutherans. This indicated that lesser persons were even less safe. It was particularly hard on the new orders of women such as the Barnabites, insisting that they accepted enclosure and a male superior.

Carafa used his authority to undermine the liberal reformers who were so prominent before 1540. Any cardinals and bishops who showed sympathy for Protestant ideas were at the very least warned about their conduct. The liberal wing of the Church was in slow but inevitable decline.

Although claims of devastating success are perhaps exaggerated, by 1580 there was no evidence of Protestantism in Italy. The Inquisition was an effective deterrent because it had extensive but ill-defined powers. It created fears because its proceedings were secret and informers were encouraged to come forward to denounce suspects. Occasional spectacular executions added to the fears. Although it cannot be compared to a modern secret police, it generated similar fears by similar methods. The fact that, according to recent research, the Roman Inquisition followed legal procedures, used torture perhaps less than the secular courts and mostly administered light penances does not mitigate its influence.

There were possible costs. Restrictions placed on trade with heretical areas reduced commerce and censorship of books reduced access to new literature and ideas. However, claims that the Inquisition stifled intellectual life are now disputed. Making a firm judgement on the

Exploring the detail
The Spanish Inquisition

The Spanish Inquisition is much more well-known than the Roman version. It was founded in 1478 to deal with specifically Spanish problems such as converted Jews and Muslims. In the 1520s it investigated the influence of the ideas of Erasmus and in the 1540s turned on the small number of Protestants. It played a large part in eliminating any danger of heresy in Spain.

Activity
Group activity

There is plenty of material on the Spanish Inquisition, especially on its legendary cruelty, use of torture and unfair procedures. Protestant writers hugely inflated the numbers of its victims and its power. In groups, try to find a balanced view. (Edgar Allan Poe's short story 'The Pit and the Pendulum' is a fictional episode about its work.)

Did you know?

There were about 100 executions in Rome between 1542 and 1721, and after 1580 the Roman Inquisition was concerned more with cases of immorality and supposed witchcraft.

success of the Inquisition is difficult because the records have not yet been fully opened.

Paul III and the Council of Trent

The Council of Trent was Paul III's greatest achievement. It was the result of years of patient diplomacy. In 1534 Paul's knowledge of the German situation was minimal, but he soon appreciated that the spread of Lutheranism into Scandinavia and Germany, and the formation of Protestant military leagues, meant that a general council had to be called to deal with the two problems of the spread of heresy and demands for reform from both Protestants and liberal Catholics.

Paul called a council to meet at Mantua in 1536, which failed. It was not until December 1545 that a council actually began its work at Trent. Paul had managed to overcome considerable obstacles to make this happen:

- The Emperor Charles V needed a general council to solve the religious division of Germany. He was faced with a conflict with Francis I and pressure from the Ottoman Turks to the east. He needed soldiers and resources from his German lands to sustain these conflicts. Religious compromise and reforms which met Lutheran criticisms would reunite the empire and thus increase his political and military authority. He therefore demanded that any council must meet within the empire. Reform of discipline was his priority. However, the price of his support for a council was complete support for Habsburg policy, which the pope could not agree to.

- Francis I of France took the opposite view. He opposed the calling of a general council because if it reunited Germany it would increase Charles's power. He could wreck the Council by refusing to allow French bishops to attend.

- A council held considerable dangers for the papacy. The Conciliar Movement of the 15th century had undermined papal authority and since 1460 the popes had been strengthening their control over the Church. Now, only a pope could call a council, but the Lutherans rejected any council called by the pope. Popes were afraid that reform would begin with the pope and the papal *curia* itself. Paul III had to create a delicate balance – confronting the Lutheran heresy was the first priority; any reform must not challenge the powers of the pope. Any council must take place in Italy, where the pope could monitor its work. On the other hand, if a council was seen merely as a papal rubber stamp, it would have little attraction for many bishops. Free speech had to be allowed.

- There was political instability – dangers of war and actual wars between Francis I and Charles V; between the German Protestant princes supported by Francis I against the Emperor; and between the Emperor and the Turks.

Paul used his diplomatic skills to reduce the obstacles:

- The issue of a venue was decided when Charles V suggested Trent in 1542. It was technically inside the Holy Roman Empire, but south of the Alps. The only problems were that it was bitterly cold in winter and had a fly-blown, frontier town atmosphere with poor accommodation.

- Paul III succeeded in establishing the method of voting. In previous councils each nation (English, French, etc.) had had one vote. Paul insisted that voting should be by individuals actually present and only by those with pastoral authority in the Church (when Trent met, there

Cross-reference

The formation of **Protestant military leagues** is discussed on page 66.

Cross-reference

To recap on the **threat to the papal states**, look back to page 30.

The **Conciliar Movement** of the 15th century and its effect on papal authority is covered on page 2.

were hundreds of theologians, experts and representatives of states also present).

- Papal control was also secured by other decisions. The call for a council must come from the pope; the sessions would be chaired by three papal legates (representatives), who decided the agenda and ruled on procedure; and the Council's decisions would be advisory only, making recommendations for the pope to accept (or not).

Attempts to call a council were stalled by outbreaks of war between Charles V and Francis I in 1538 and 1542. The year 1544 was an ideal window for the Council because Francis I had been defeated and peace had been made at Crépy.

The Council of Trent: First Session, December 1545 – June 1548

When the Council opened in December 1545, there were 29 voting delegates, mostly Italian bishops with one English, one French and one German bishop, and two from Spain. A debate at once started on which should be discussed first – discussing reform or doctrine. Although a majority wanted reform first, the papal legates secured a compromise by which both should be discussed in parallel.

The members of the Council decided to discuss only doctrinal differences between Catholics and Protestants and not any differences within the Catholic Church. Discussions on doctrinal decrees were the most important success of the First Session. By contrast, the decrees on discipline tended to repeat the commands of many previous councils.

In March 1547 an outbreak of plague at Trent was used as a reason to move the Council to Bologna in the papal states. Even without this, Paul III feared the rising power of the Emperor after the Battle of Mühlberg and when the Duchy of Piacenza, ruled by the pope's son Pierluigi, was occupied by imperial troops and Pierluigi was murdered, a breakdown of relations was virtually complete. The pope suspended the Council in June 1548. However, neither side wanted a complete end to the Council and it remained suspended when the pope died in November 1549.

> ### Cross-reference
>
> For the **Battle of Mühlberg**, see page 67.

> ### Activity
>
> **Revision exercise**
>
> Write an assessment of Paul III's pontificate. You could include the following comments:
>
> - He made little attempt to reform the papal court.
> - He was guilty of nepotism and political intrigue in favour of his sons.
> - He spent lavishly on entertainments and high living.
> - His pontificate gave the Catholic reform movement drive.
> - Because of his work, the Counter Reformation gained in momentum and was virtually unstoppable.

Further reform to 1559 and the Second Session of the Council of Trent

Julius III (1550–5)

The reign of Julius III shows that there was not a smooth transition to a reformed papacy. Julius III was an effective legate at the Council of Trent, but he enjoyed good living and promoted his family to key

> ### Did you know?
>
> Julius III revolted the Romans with his passion for onions, which he consumed by the cartload. He promoted his teenaged monkey-keeper, Innocenzo, to a cardinal.

positions. Although not against reform, he had too much timidity and too little drive. He possessed none of the greatness of Paul III, but he did commission another report on reform of the papal *curia* and ordered the Council to return to Trent for its second session.

The Second Session achieved little. An important doctrinal definition was the decree on the Communion. Once again, no compromise was given to Protestant views. The Second Session also witnessed the last important example of Charles V trying to reach a compromise. Protestant representatives, including some from Brandenburg and Saxony, were persuaded to attend. However, as major doctrinal decrees had already been passed in the First Session, there was no hope of a reunion. Although some work was done on disciplinary reforms such as the duties required of bishops, it was not conclusive.

Julius III was succeeded by Marcellus II, a recognised reformer who had been a papal legate at Trent. However, he died three weeks later. The cardinals reluctantly chose Gian Pietro Carafa, who became Paul IV.

Paul IV (1555–9)

The reign of Paul IV showed that the personality of the pope was a critical factor in driving on reform. He was a zealous reformer with little time left to him (he was 79 in 1555), but his methods, violent hatreds and vitriolic temper set back the progress of reform. His rule has been described as a reign of terror:

- Jews in the papal states were put into ghettoes.
- He tried to alter the Jesuits into a more conventional religious order.
- He persecuted liberal cardinals such as Pole and Morone, who was imprisoned as a suspected heretic.
- He had a strong Puritan streak and hated the nudity that he felt defiled Renaissance art; artists were employed to paint fig leaves and wisps of cloth in appropriate places. Sculptures were altered with hammer and chisel. A determined attempt was made to whip prostitutes out of Rome.
- He hated everything to do with the Habsburgs (Spain occupied his homeland, Naples), so he managed to offend sincere Catholic supporters such as the Emperor Ferdinand who had signed the Peace of Augsburg, and Philip II of Spain with whom he senselessly went to war in 1556–9. Mary I of England's wish to return England to the Catholic fold was obstructed because she was married to Philip II and her chief adviser was Cardinal Pole, whom the pope demanded should return to Rome to stand trial for heresy.
- As the founder of the Roman Inquisition, he stepped up its work with enthusiasm, attending most of its sessions.

The creation of the Roman Inquisition's *Index of Prohibited Books* in 1559 was a response to the vast quantities of potentially suspect literature available to influence the religious beliefs of Catholics – the success of the printing industry and its distribution methods was inevitably followed by censorship. The *Index* was divided into three parts: authors whose work was completely banned, individual books that were banned, and books that contained dangerous teachings.

The pope was not the first to do this (there were precedents in Spain, Paris, some Italian cities and Henry VIII's England), but the *Index* was full of sweeping condemnations. J. O'Malley calls it one of the most fanatical documents of even that fanatical pontificate. It included all the work of Erasmus, much to the dismay of the Jesuits. One Jesuit school

Fig. 6 *Pope Paul IV*

Cross-reference

For the **Peace of Augsburg**, see page 68.

Cross-reference

The **growth in the printing industry** and the **distribution of printed books** are described on pages 35–6.

head commented, 'We have no books for certain classes except those of Erasmus!' The *Index* certainly encouraged intolerance – the Inquisition in Venice burned 10,000 books in 1558 – but how effective it was is debatable. Like the Inquisition, it created an atmosphere of fear and the impression that the Church opposed open debate.

Paul was essentially a tragic figure, next door to madness. His death in August 1559 led to an explosion of joy in Rome – the offices of the Inquisition in Rome were wrecked and set on fire and his statues were smashed. Historian Eamon Duffy comments that he was the most hated pope of the century.

Pius IV and the Third Session of the Council of Trent

Pius IV was chosen as a total contrast to Paul IV. He released those whom Paul had imprisoned, including Cardinal Morone, and drove out Paul's relatives. Two were executed. His greatest achievement was to recall the Council of Trent.

Fig. 7 *The* Index Librorum Prohibitorum, *the list of books forbidden to Catholics. The* Index *was not offically abolished until the 20th century. This version was issued by Philip II*

Activity

Talking point

How effective would a list of prohibited books be in preventing dangerous ideas?

Key profile

Pope Pius IV

Pius IV (1559–65) was a lawyer and father of three children. His brother had married into Paul III's family. He enriched his family in office. He had left the papal *curia* in 1558 in protest at Paul IV's policies. He was an able administrator, civilised and diplomatic. He was tolerant and showed no great zeal for reform.

Cross-reference

To recap on **indulgencies** and the controversy they aroused, return to page 42.

The Third Session brought together the work on discipline. There was a redefinition of the role of bishops: they had to stay in their diocese and visit each parish at least once a year; preaching and pastoral work was their chief role; they had to be legitimate, of a mature age and well-educated. Attempts were made to raise the standards of the parish priests by insisting on celibacy (no partners, and housekeepers had to be respectable older women); higher levels of education – priests had to be aged at least 23 and show evidence of a pure life before ordination; wearing distinct clerical dress. Duties were clearly defined. Indulgence sellers and relic merchants were banned (but not indulgences or relics themselves).

The bishops would now have the chance to manage their dioceses, as exemptions from their authority were greatly reduced (at a cost to the papal *curia*, which sold the exemptions) and they were given responsibility for ordinations. If they paid a substitute, that substitute would receive the bishop's income. Education of the clergy was seen as vitally important and a practical result was to order each diocese to set up a **seminary** or training college to ensure a good supply of priests.

Other decrees defined standards of monastic life and the status of the sacrament of marriage. There was concern over **secret marriages** or ones that did not have the consent of both parties. For a marriage to be valid, vows now had to be made before a priest, with two witnesses present. The marriage had to be announced on three successive Sundays.

Key terms

Seminary: boys would attend from about age 12 and be educated for 10 years. There was a fierce debate about what should be taught. The liberal Catholics' demand that biblical studies and modern humanist methods should be taught was defeated in favour of a traditionalist approach.

Secret marriages: Church law on marriage was unclear. Two people could agree to make a contract to be married and, if the marriage was consummated, that was a Christian marriage. A secret marriage could be carried out with a priest, but without parental consent or witnesses – as in Shakespeare's *Romeo and Juliet*. Luther had said the clergy should not be involved in marriage at all.

Priests had to keep a register of marriages as well as baptisms. This was the only original decree of the Council, but it had a great impact on parish life.

The decrees on doctrine showed that all thoughts of compromise were over. Each decision started with a Protestant doctrine and went on to affirm the Catholic view. Anyone who held the Protestant view was solemnly cursed. Therefore, it was affirmed that:

- there were seven sacraments
- belief in purgatory, the veneration of saints and images, pilgrimages and every traditional practice of popular Catholicism was correct
- good works were essential to salvation, not 'faith alone'
- the only acceptable version of the Bible was the Vulgate, although its errors would be corrected. Other translations, or reading in the **vernacular** were not banned
- the traditions and teaching authority of the Church were on an equal footing to personal interpretations of the Scripture
- laypeople should only have the bread at Communion
- the only orthodox explanation for the Real Presence of Christ on the altar was transubstantiation.

The Third Session of the Council had been attended by 255 bishops, representing all areas of Catholic Europe. All the decrees from the three sessions were read and affirmed. The bishops proclaimed their determination to carry them forward.

The extent to which the Catholic Church was reformed

The success of the Council of Trent

The success of the Council of Trent is difficult to evaluate. One view is that the Jesuits and the Roman Inquisition had more importance in terms of slowing the advance of Protestantism.

The definition of Catholic doctrine was important. Although it did not make Christian reunion impossible (in practice, that was the case long before 1545) the establishment of a clear statement of Catholic belief was a great achievement. At last ordinary Catholics knew what the beliefs of the Church were and it was clear what a Catholic had to believe. The Church was certainly strengthened, but the effect stifled different opinions that had been tolerated before 1545 and liberal Catholic churchmen became an isolated minority.

The decrees on discipline were much less successful. Their implementation was patchy and success would have to be measured in decades or even centuries.

- In the longer term, the Council of Trent strengthened the authority of the bishops who were now clearly responsible for managing their dioceses. Very much depended on the quality of the bishops and, although there were examples of outstanding bishops such as Carlo Borromeo, there were still plenty of examples of lacklustre ones. The main problem was clerical wealth – richer bishops enjoyed the display of it (one legate arrived at Trent with over 100 servants). It is an interesting contrast that whereas Protestantism either downplayed the role of bishops or did not have them at all (for example, Calvinism), the Catholic Church chose to raise their status. Perhaps what Trent did

Key terms

Vernacular: the everyday language of the people.

Cross-reference

The **Roman Inquisition** is covered on page 138.

Did you know?

If a clear doctrinal statement on justification by 'faith alone' had existed in 1517, there would have been no hesitation in condemning Luther. One of the reasons for his success was that he could argue that he did reflect the teaching of the Church. Liberal Catholics tended to agree with him.

was to change attitudes – it was no longer acceptable to have bishops treating their pastoral mission casually. A new standard had been set.

Key profile

Carlo Borromeo

Carlo Borromeo (1538–85) was a pattern for a Counter Reformation bishop. He was the nephew of Pope Pius IV, and was appointed Archbishop of Milan (covering a huge area of north Italy) in 1565. He was the first archbishop to live there for 80 years. He spent his last years implementing the Council of Trent and carrying out the new duties of a bishop. A major diocesan seminary was set up and he regularly visited all parishes.

- The stress on an educated clergy and seminaries produced great benefits in the long term. However, this took time. In 1600 there were 20 in Spain, 11 in Italy and none in France. Even in 1630, only half of all Italian dioceses had a seminary.

- The success of the decrees on discipline depended on the support of the secular rulers, but many of the changes cut across their own interests (such as control of clerical appointments). Bishops could not use their new powers without their support. Pius IV accepted them at once for the papal states, and Portugal and Poland almost at once. Philip II accepted the decrees in a limited way, and France and the Imperial Diet not at all, although a few individual rulers did. Most important were the dukes of Bavaria. Albert V greatly reduced the freedoms of the nobility in 1564 and began a programme that made accepting orthodox Catholicism the only way to social advancement. The Jesuits were welcomed and encouraged. The Bavarian dukes were model Catholic rulers, but accepting Trent also supported their policy of political centralisation.

- The Council was silent on a number of important issues such as the role of the new orders; the role of the Inquisition; the great missionary work worldwide; the exact relationship between Church and state; and the role of women in the Church.

- Above all, the Council did not define the exact position of the pope within the Church, although the debate of 1562 had strengthened the papal position. It also said little about reforming the papal *curia* (court), which had been the butt of criticism for centuries.

The papacy was the real winner after Trent because the Council entrusted it to carry out its decrees. Pius IV moved quickly to build on this by ruling that the pope would have the sole right of interpreting what the decrees meant; no one could comment on them without papal permission; and a Congregation (committee) was set up to carry out the conciliar decrees. He also issued a Confession of Faith including a vow of obedience to the pope, which all church officials and degree course candidates had to accept.

Pius V carried out the requests of the Council to publish an authoritative Roman Catechism in 1566, which was for pastoral workers rather than students (Canisius had published a popular but unofficial catechism for young people in 1558). In 1568 a new version of the Breviary (the book containing the daily service of the Church) was published, which had (and has) to be said daily by every Catholic priest, and finally in 1570 a new Roman missal was issued that contained the order of the Mass for each part of the year. It allowed little freedom to adapt and virtually eliminated regional variations.

Exploring the detail

The role of women in the Church

In the 1530s the new orders for women had been allowed to work freely, and without specific religious habits, to help the poor and sick. Trent curtailed this freedom by insisting on enclosure. For example, an Englishwoman, Mary Ward, tried to establish a female order having Jesuit freedom of action in 1609, but it was officially suppressed by the Pope a few years later.

Cross-reference

For the **debate of 1562**, see page 113.

Activity

Group activity

The popes after Pius IV are, strictly speaking, beyond the date of the specification. However, group research into their work would give much better evidence of the long-term importance of the popes in the work of Catholic reform.

Background
• Conciliar Theory v. supremacy of the pope
• Habsburg v. Valois conflict
• Success of Lutheranism
• Choice of venue
• Paul III's preparations

Session 1 1545–7	Doctrine defined	
Session 2 1551–2		
Session 3 1562–3	Discipline reforms	

Importance	Short term	• Supremacy of reform popes • Clear doctrine • Focus on resisting Protestant advance
	Long term	• Slow improvements in standards • Enhanced attempts to win back or consolidate Catholic lands • Change in the nature of the Church

Fig. 8 *The Council of Trent*

Cross-reference

For the **criticisms of religious orders**, look back to page 17.

The papacy was now of central importance. Its authority was raised above any possible alternative. Pressure to carry out the reforms of Trent had to come from the papacy. Fewer unsuitable bishops were appointed; local initiatives for reform would be supported rather than undermined. Rome was the headquarters of every agency of Catholic reform. The magnificent redevelopment of the city and the near completion of St Peter's Basilica at the end of the century was intended to create a setting worthy of revived papal authority. By 1600 the moral authority of the papacy had greatly increased from the low point of 1517.

On the other hand, although standards improved, there was a real failure to improve the papal court, despite the reforms of Sixtus V. Popes saw nothing wrong with putting their relatives into key Church positions and selling offices in the Church. Nepotism was not ended until 1692. Although the worst excesses vanished, there was still tension between the 'Renaissance-style' pope and the spiritual Counter Reformation reformer. For example, Paul IV was followed by the worldly Pius IV.

Other reforms

There was greater clarity of doctrine, but this was at the expense of a broad range of beliefs (for example, Erasmus would not have survived in the 1550s).

The new orders, especially the Jesuits, had created a new sense of urgency through their work as educators, preachers and pastoral workers in the poorest parts of the cities, reaching out to where they were most needed. The criticisms that were made of religious orders in 1500 would have been impossible in 1564. More work was done with the poor, sick and outcasts of society. Laypeople came forward to support charitable activities. Much more stress was placed on education, both through Jesuit colleges and through teaching the catechism.

Catholic reforms (many beginning before 1517)		Counter Reformation (a definite attempt to resist and turn back the Protestant advance after about 1540–50)		Revived and renewed Catholic Church 1550–1648

• Demands for change from Christian humanists and lay people
• Improvements in existing religious orders
• Catholic monarchs (as in Spain) supported
• New orders before 1540
• Lateran Council 1512–17
• The Consilium 1537
• Reforming bishops
• Attempts at reconciliation
	...merges into the...	• New aim for the Jesuit order
		• Other new orders (e.g. Capuchins)
		• Council of Trent
		• Inquisition and Index
		• Reform popes:
		  – Paul III
		  – Paul IV
		  – Pius V
		• New model bishops after Trent
		• No further attempts at reconciliation after 1561
			The Catholic offensive	Revived and renewed Catholic Church 1550–1648

Fig. 9 *Catholic and Counter Reformation*

Bishops were a vital agent in the reform process and their work in their individual dioceses, though patchy, forwarded the reform process. The quality of bishops slowly improved and there is evidence of more diocesan meetings and inspections of parishes.

There is plenty of evidence for a growing insistence on high moral standards in the Church. Paul IV sent over 100 disreputable monks to row in the galleys, and both he and Pius V tried to eradicate prostitution and homosexuality in Rome. Nudity in art was condemned by the Council of Trent.

It is difficult to assess if the quality of popular religion began to improve. The Council of Trent did encourage more preaching and education and better qualified Catholic priests. However, it is impossible to quantify if ordinary Catholics understood the beliefs of the Church any more accurately and Trent did confirm all the popular religion that the Protestants had condemned as superstitious. The centuries-old religious practices, which were a part of the fabric of rural life, continued.

Learning outcomes

In this section you have studied the developing role of the Renaissance papacy, especially in the period after 1540. The work of Paul III has been evaluated, especially the creation of the Roman Inquisition and the calling of the Council of Trent. You have explored the problems created by Paul IV and analysed the importance of the Council of Trent. You have considered the success of the Council of Trent and the reform of the Catholic Church in this period.

AQA Examination-style questions

    (a)   Explain why Pope Paul III had difficulty in calling a general council.   *(12 marks)*

Examiner's tip This question asks you for detailed reasons why a general council, which was demanded by so many, did not meet until 1546. This is a good example of using long- and short-term reasons. You could focus on long-term reasons such as the fear of the popes about what would happen to them if a council was called. They had the bad experience of the Conciliar Movement in the 15th century. Politically, the rivalry of Francis I and Charles V and the different reasons for wanting a council held things up. In the short term, after 1536, wars, the issue of where to hold a Council and plagues got in the way.

    (b)   How important was the Council of Trent to the reform of the Catholic Church?   *(24 marks)*

AQA Examiner's tip This question requires analysis of the significance of the Council of Trent in the wider movement for the Catholic and Counter Reformation. You will need to stress the importance of the decrees on doctrine, which gave clarity and certainty to what Catholics had to believe. Heresy was now obvious. On the other hand, the work of reform was patchy; the papal *curia* especially took years to change; seminary colleges were significant, but slow to develop; improvements in the standards of bishops were slow, but gained importance. Arguably, the Jesuits and other orders were more significant in raising educational standards and the popes drove reform on. You could argue that reform could have happened without a council.

7 Conclusion

Studying a map of Europe of religious changes by the end of the 16th century shows that much had changed. In 1500 western and northern Europe and much of eastern Europe was Catholic; by the end of the century there had been a radical transformation. Much of northern Germany and Scandinavia had become Lutheran; there were strong Lutheran minorities in Poland, Austria and Bohemia. There were small pockets of Anabaptism. Zwingli and Calvin hold their place in the Swiss cantons and Geneva, while Calvinism was spreading through France.

However, although a map has its uses, it is a source to be evaluated like any other. Christendom seemed united in 1500, but there were pockets of unorthodoxy with the Hussites and Lollards. The pressure of the Ottoman Turks in eastern Europe was creating a fluid situation with the real danger of much of eastern Europe falling under Muslim rule. On the other hand, in 1564 much religious change was yet to happen. Calvinism became a major force for religious change in the second half of the 16th century, converting a number of states in Germany, spreading into eastern Europe and becoming the dominant force in Scotland and the northern Netherlands. The Ottoman Turks had at least been held at bay, consolidating their gains in eastern Europe. The Catholic Church had at least contained the spread of Protestantism in Germany (although much was to change within that religious divide) and it would consolidate its hold on Germany, Austria and Bohemia. The Church also managed to keep control of the 'ecclesiastical lands' of Cologne, Mainz and Trier.

Key

Principal divisions:
- Lutheran
- Calvinist
- Anglican
- Roman Catholic
- Greek Orthodox

Minorities:
- × Roman Catholic
- ▲ Calvinist
- ■ Lutheran
- □ Anabaptists
- ✳ Islamic

Fig. 1 *Religious divisions c.1600*

This gave it greater strength in western Germany. Much more significantly, it had gained a worldwide influence in Latin America, India, parts of Africa and the Far East. A map may help to show the *quantity* of religious change, but it cannot show its *quality*.

In 1500, although there were some concerns about heresy and heretics were burned at the stake, in general the Catholic Church was tolerant of diversity – for example, the Brethren of the Common Life, the humanist critique of its failings, and the early 'new orders' – and it did not have a clear Confession (statement) of Belief or even standard services. By 1564 the Church had produced a Confession in response to those produced by Lutherans, Calvinists and the Swiss reformers. The belief in the 1520s of a new freedom from the control of the Catholic Church had been replaced by a new age of religious division, with the Protestants deeply divided within themselves, disliking each other and initiating persecutions as much as the Catholics. The easy tolerance of 1500 had been replaced by a world of Inquisitions, censorship of books, persecutions – the Anabaptists, Jews and witches, for example – and obedience to defined beliefs for Protestants and Catholics.

Arguably, religious change was notable for its destructive effects. Monasteries and convents were closed down and their occupants pensioned off or turned out to the streets, although some found employment in the new religious framework of their states. Priests and other workers for the Church found their futures uncertain as they had to decide between the old and the new. Catholic churches were stripped of their ornaments and interiors whitewashed over. A wave of Puritanism encouraged by zealous popes challenged and ended the exuberance of the Renaissance; Calvinists were determined that religious belief would be reflected in high, and enforced, moral standards. On the Catholic side, those who enjoyed the comforts of pluralism or an easy benefice or diocese found their comfort challenged by the new standards of the Counter Reformation.

The debate on the effects of religious change on the quality of the clergy and the spiritual condition of the laity is still going on today. There were far more demands made of the clergy during the period. They had to preach effectively, do pastoral work and educate their parishes. Especially on the Protestant side, there was stress on teaching the Scriptures. These demands required a far more highly educated workforce and there is evidence of shortages of suitable priests and ministers – not enough to carry out their new duties. Furthermore, Catholics and Protestants placed great stress on education for the laity, from Jesuit schools to Calvin's classes for young people. All produced catechisms to be learned by heart, but this did not necessarily mean that people were more committed Christians or understood their faith more confidently.

Ordinary Catholics, it appears, did not wish to give up their old customs and ceremonies and all the aids to salvation condemned so roundly as superstitious and unscriptural by Luther and Calvin. Surveys showed they had little understanding of what theology lay behind them. The lavish decoration and emphasis on visual imagery ('scripture for the illiterate' in the words of the Council of Trent) in churches, as well as the theatre of the Mass with its music and complex ceremonies, was a conscious attempt to engage the rural and urban populations with the concepts of 'awe and wonder'. The Protestants tended to create more records and detailed criticisms were plentiful. People did not know the basic prayers and few attended many services. It was hard for Protestantism to convert in rural areas where people clung to the old faith; the stress on reading and hearing the Word was more abstract than Catholic services and churches, and tended to appeal to the educated. In all denominations, the drive to learn catechisms was a turn-off for many whose literacy was poor.

Fig. 2 *The Jesuit church in Vienna. Although at first Jesuit churches were quite plain, they later became famous for their elaborately decorated style*

By 1564 the Catholic Church was in a much stronger position than 1500; the Protestants had created permanent institutions, built an educating mission and pushed on with their evangelisation of rural populations. However, winning hearts and minds to the Christian message would make slow progress in populations who understood little of the theology behind their beliefs and probably were apathetic about knowing. Nevertheless, for those who could value such things, the Reformation was a liberating experience – freedom from the influence of clerics and their control over the means of salvation, the ability to study the Scriptures and form opinions, the stress on personal faith and developing an individual relationship with God.

Glossary

A

altar: the table in the sanctuary of a Catholic Church, used to carry out the Mass or Communion service.

alum: a crystalline mineral used to fix dye in cloth.

Annates: payments made by bishops to the pope when they succeeded to their dioceses – about one-third of a year's income.

anti-clericalism: opposition to the power of priests, especially their political power or power to raise money by taxes.

Apostles: the first twelve chosen followers of Jesus Christ.

archbishop: the man in charge of a number of bishops and their dioceses.

Augustinians: a Catholic order of friars founded in 1256 following the teachings of St Augustine.

B

bigamy: marriage to more than one person at the same time.

bishop: a priest in charge of a diocese.

blasphemy: speaking or writing in a profane or contemptuous way about God or sacred things.

Both Kinds: both bread and wine given to the communicant at Communion (One Kind was the bread only).

Byzantine Empire: another name for the Eastern Roman Empire, with its capital of Constantinople (or Byzantium).

C

canon law: laws drawn up by the Catholic Church.

canton: the name given to each of the self-governing units that made up the Swiss Confederation.

cardinal: a leading official of the Catholic Church. As the College of Cardinals, they elected the pope.

Carthusians: an order of monks and nuns founded in 1084, well known for its strictness.

catechism: a book giving the basic beliefs and practices of a Church, usually in question and answer form.

congregation: people gathered together for worship in a church.

crucifix: a cross with the image of the crucified Christ on it.

D

devotion: a special affection for a saint, the Virgin Mary, or a religious practice.

diocese: an area ruled by a bishop, also called a see.

Divine Office: the daily religious services set out in the Catholic book of services (or Breviary). All orders have to say this.

Dominicans: an order of mendicant friars (Blackfriars) founded by St Dominic in 1221.

E

early Church: the first centuries of the Christian Church, seen as a model for Protestant Churches.

enclosure: being enclosed with walls in a religious community.

Evangelicals: Protestants who believed that salvation comes from 'faith alone', accepting the Bible as the only authority. They wished to preach to spread the good news of Jesus Christ.

F

faction: a small group that disagrees with the views of the larger group.

First Fruits: payment to the pope of one-tenth of the year's income from every benefice.

Franciscans: an order of mendicant friars founded by St Francis of Assisi in around 1220 (the Grey Friars).

friars (mendicant): originally members of a Catholic order who depended on mendicancy (begging for alms) for support.

G

gargoyle: a hideously carved figure acting as a downspout from a church roof.

ghetto: an area of a town set apart for a particular racial or religious group, especially Jews.

H

habit: the clothing worn by members of Catholic religious orders.

heresy: an opinion in opposition to the orthodox doctrine of the Catholic Church.

heretic: someone who holds opinions that oppose the doctrine of the Catholic Church.

I

iconoclasm: the violent destruction of holy images, ornaments and pictures (usually in a Catholic church).

Imperial Diet: the assembly of the Holy Roman Empire, resembling a parliament.

Inquisition: a church court generally responsible for eliminating heresy, as well as unacceptable opinions on many issues of moral standards.

L

laity, laypeople: members of the Christian community apart from the official hierarchy or religious orders.

Last Judgement: the time at which the living and the dead will be finally judged by God.

legate: an official representative of the pope, appointed for a specific task (or commission).

M

manuscript: a document written by hand.

Mass: Catholic term for the celebration of the Eucharist.

mendicant orders: religious orders that depended for support on people giving them alms.

minister: in the Protestant Church, the man in charge of a congregation or attached to a Church to preach and support.

missionary: someone who is sent out on a mission to preach to and convert others, especially in foreign countries overseas.

N

nepotism: appointing one's own relations to posts in the Church or any similar institution.

O

order: a religious community living under a rule.

P

pacifist: someone who is opposed to all wars and thinks that they are wrong.

Paul's letters: in the New Testament, a series of letters giving advice concerning matters of faith and behaviour sent to the early Christian communities.

pluralism: holding more than one office, especially in the Church.

priest: an ordained minister in the Catholic Church.

prophet: someone who is inspired to proclaim messages from God or claims to be the voice of God.

purgatory: a place where souls after death are purified for their sins before going to heaven.

R

radical: a supporter of fundamental and drastic changes in a religious or political system.

Real Presence: the belief that Christ is actually present at the moment of consecration during the Mass.

rector: the head of a college or university, especially a Jesuit school.

S

secular: literally, 'in the world'; belonging to the world, the part of society that is not connected to religious organisation.

simony: buying and selling of offices within the Church. Declared canonically illegal.

St Peter: the leader (or 'prince') of the Apostles. His shrine is in Rome.

superior: usually the head of a convent or female religious community.

Synod: an assembly of the clergy to discuss and decide Church matters.

T

tithe: the tenth part of the annual production of a person's land or work, usually given as a monetary payment for the upkeep of the priest and church.

V

Virgin Mary: the mother of Jesus Christ, believed by Catholics and Protestants to have been born without sin.

Bibliography

Students

Armstrong, A. (2002) *The European Reformation*, Heinemann.

Armstrong, A. (2008) *The German Reformation*, Heinemann.

Johnston, A. (1992) *The Protestant Reformation in Europe*, Longman.

Mullett, M. (1984) *The Counter-Reformation (Lancaster Pamphlets)*, Routledge.

Mullett, M. (1989) *Calvin (Lancaster Pamphlets)*, Routledge.

Scribner, R. (1986) *The German Reformation*, Macmillan.

Tarr, R. (2008) *Luther and the German Reformation*, Hodder Murray.

Articles

Mullett, M. (1996) *Counter-Reformation and Catholic Reformation*, History Review.

Pettegree, A. (1996) *The Execution of Martin Luther*, History Review.

Teachers and extension

Bireley, R. (1999) *The Refashioning of Catholicism*, Macmillan.

Cameron, E. (1991) *The European Reformation*, Clarendon.

Collinson, P. (2005) *The Reformation*, Phoenix.

MacCulloch, D. (2004) *Reformation: Europe's Divided House 1490–1700*, Penguin.

O'Malley, J. (1993) *The First Jesuits*, Harvard University Press.

Pettegree, A. (2001) *The Reformation World*, Routledge.

Pettegree, A. (2005) *Reformation and the Culture of Persuasion*, Cambridge University Press.

Pettegree, A., Duke, A. and Lewis, G. (1996) *Calvinism in Europe 1540–1620*, Cambridge University Press.

Po-Chia Hsia, R. (2005) *The World of Catholic Renewal 1540–1710*, Cambridge University Press.

Rublack, U. (2005) *Reformation Europe*, Cambridge University Press.

Scribner, R. (1994) *For the Sake of Simple Folk: Popular Propaganda for the German Reformation*, Clarendon.

General reference

Cook, C. (2001) *Longman Handbook of Early Modern Europe 1453–1763*, Longman.

Duffy, E. (2006) *Saints and Sinners: A History of the Popes*, Yale University Press.

Greengrass, M. (1998) *The Longman Companion to the European Reformation 1500–1618*, Longman.

Hillerbrand, H. J. (1996) *The Oxford Encyclopaedia of the Reformation*, Oxford University Press.

Lotherington, J. (ed.) (1999) *Years of Renewal 1470–1600*, Hodder and Stoughton.

Mackenney, R. (1993) *Sixteenth Century Europe*, Macmillan.

Murphy, D., Walsh-Atkins, P. and Tillbrook, M. (2000) *Europe: 1450–1661*, Collins Educational.

Musgrave, P. (1999) *The Early Modern European Economy*, Macmillan.

Biographies

Bouwsma, W. (1989) *John Calvin: A Sixteenth Century Portrait*, Oxford University Press.

Mullett, M. (2000) *Martin Luther*, Routledge.

Websites

www.activehistory.co.uk Subscription site that contains much helpful material, including suggestions for classroom activities.

www.fordham.edu/halsall/mod/modsbook.html Comprehensive range of primary sources on all parts of the unit.

www.historylearningsite.co.uk Useful introductory material on each section of the unit. Particularly helpful on Luther.

www.projectwittenberg.org Comprehensive collection of primary sources about Luther.

Acknowledgements

The author and publisher are grateful to the following for permission to reproduce copyright material:

Text acknowledgements

p3 Short extract from R. Hole *Renaissance Italy*, 1998, Hodder and Stoughton; p9 Short extract from D. MacCulloch *Reformation: Europe's House Divided 1490–1700*, 2004, Penguin; p12 Short extract from Erasmus 'Handbook of a Christian Soldier' as cited in J. McConica *Erasmus*, 1991, OUP; p25 Koenigsberger, Mosse and Bowler *Europe in the Sixteenth Century*, 1989, Longman; p26 Short extract from R. Bainton *Here I stand*, 1978, Abingdon Press; p26 Short extract from A. Johnston *The Protestant Reformation in Europe*, 1998, Longman; p32 Short extracts from K. Randall *The Catholic and Counter Reformations*, 1990, Hodder and Stoughton; p35 Short extract from K. Randall *The Catholic and Counter Reformations*, 1990, Hodder and Stoughton; p37 Short extract from EJ Rice *The Foundations of Early Modern Europe*, 1971, Wiedenfeld and Nicolson; p41 Short extract from D. MacCulloch *Reformation: Europe's House Divided 1490–1700*, 2004, Penguin; p70 Short extract from O. Chadwick *The Reformation*, 1972, Penguin; p72 Short extracts from K. Randall *Calvin and the Later Reformation*, 1988, Hodder and Stoughton; p73 Short extract from John Calvin 'Institutes of Christian Religion' as cited in J.P. Jones *Europe 1500–1600*, Nelson; p86 Short extract from D. MacCulloch *Reformation: Europe's House Divided 1490–1700*, 2004, Penguin; p91 J. Lotherington *Years of Renewal 1470–1600*, 1988, Hodder and Stoughton; p94 N. Cohn *The Pursuit of the Millennium*, 1970, OUP; p97 Koenigsberger, Mosse and Bowler *Europe in the Sixteenth Century*, 1989, Longman; p97 Short extract from D. MacCulloch *Reformation: Europe's House Divided 1490–1700*, 2004, Penguin; p99 N. Cohn *The Pursuit of the Millennium*, 1970, OUP; p105 Short extract from R. MacKenney *Sixteenth Century Europe: Expansion and Conflict*, 1993, Macmillan; p119 R. Po-Chia Hsia *The World of Catholic Renewal 1540–1770*, 2005, CUP; p121 Short extracts from K. Randall *The Catholic and Counter Reformations*, 1990, Hodder and Stoughton; p135 Short extract from O. Chadwick *The Reformation*, 1972, Penguin

Photo acknowledgements

Alamy 11.3, 11.4; **Ann Ronan** 1.5, 2.5, 2.6, 5.2, 6.1; **British Library/HIP/Topfoto** 5.4; **Edimedia Archive** 0.1, 1.1, 1.2, 1.3, 1.6, 1.7, 2.1, 3.3, 3.4, 4.4, 4.7, 4.8, 5.1, 6.3, 7.3, 7.5, 9.1, 10.2, 10.8, 11.2; **Photo 12** 2.4, 6.7, 7.2, 9.5, 11.1; **Photo 12/Oronoz** 3.1; **Print Collector/HIP/Topfoto** 8.6; **Public Domain** 0.2, 3.2, 4.3, 6.4, 7.1, 8.1, 8.5, 8.7, 9.4, 12.2; **Topfoto** 2.3, 4.1, 5.6, 5.8, 9.2, 10.1, 10.3, 11.6; **Topfoto Art and Architecture** 4.5; **WHA** 3.6, 5.5, 6.2, 8.2, 11.5, 11.7

Every effort has been made to contact the copyright holders, and we apologise if any have been overlooked. Should copyright have been unwittingly infringed in this book, the owners should contact the publishers, who will make corrections at reprint.

Index